Praise for *Queen of All W*

"An outstanding book about the history and transformation of the Mother Goddess. A literary journey to take you through the myths—and books—historically used to build and shape the face of the goddess cult, but it does not end there. Jack Chanek takes the assignment of analyzing and deconstructing the sources of these cults, leading the reader to understand their origin and the deep connection between them. Jack gives you everything you need to know in a very well-researched book filled with stories, folklore, and marvelous rituals."

—Elhoim Leafar, author of *The Magical Art of Crafting Charm Bags*

"Jack Chanek offers a brand-new understanding of a goddess we all thought we knew. Both historical and modern, both scholarly and intimate, *Queen of All Witcheries* takes the reader on a journey that encompasses the past, present, and future of goddess worship. Replete with exercises and rituals to make it all personal and real, this book will open your eyes and deepen your knowledge. An impressive feat and an instant must-have in any witch's library."

—Deborah Lipp, author of *Bending the Binary*

"Jack Chanek gives readers a simple, clear, and spiritually informed biography of the Goddess. As he reviews the works of key innovators in the modern Goddess movement—people like Margaret Murray, Robert Graves, and Gerald Gardner—Chanek sorts the wheat from the chaff, finding interesting and useful religious themes while discarding problematic scholarly and/or ethical materials. Anyone curious about how the history of the Goddess in the modern West can interact with contemporary devotion to her will find this book a rich resource."

—Cynthia Eller, author of *Living in the Lap of the Goddess* and *The Myth of Matriarchal Prehistory*

"An important exploration of the modern historical roots of Goddess tradition in the West. Tracing the first early mention of the Goddess in the 1860s through to feminist Goddess worship in the 1990s, Chanek's book skillfully weaves three threads of wisdom: his own personal experiences with the Goddess, his thorough scholarship of the transformation of Goddess traditions, and Goddess rituals for both group and solitary practitioners. A wonderful guide for those seeking to know the ever-changing path of the Goddess in modern times."

—HeatherAsh Amara, author of *Goddess Warrior Training*

QUEEN
— OF ALL —
WITCHERIES

About the Author

Jack Chanek is a Gardnerian Wiccan priest and the author of *Qabalah for Wiccans* and *Tarot for Real Life*. He has been reading tarot since he was eleven years old and has taught workshops on tarot, Qabalah, and Wicca around the country. Jack has appeared on podcasts including *Seeking Witchcraft, The Magic Monday Podcast,* and *The Witching Hour with Patti Negri,* as well as teaching at festivals such as Free Spirit Gathering and LlewellynCon. He lives in New Jersey, where he works as an academic philosopher specializing in Immanuel Kant's philosophy of science. He can be found online at www.JackOfWandsTarot .wordpress.com.

© Jen Davis

To Write to the Author

If you wish to contact the author or would like more information about this book, please write to the author in care of Llewellyn Worldwide Ltd. and we will forward your request. Both the author and publisher appreciate hearing from you and learning of your enjoyment of this book and how it has helped you. Llewellyn Worldwide Ltd. cannot guarantee that every letter written to the author can be answered, but all will be forwarded. Please write to:

Jack Chanek
℅ Llewellyn Worldwide
2143 Wooddale Drive
Woodbury, MN 55125-2989

Please enclose a self-addressed stamped envelope for reply,
or $1.00 to cover costs. If outside the U.S.A., enclose
an international postal reply coupon.

Many of Llewellyn's authors have websites with additional information and resources. For more information, please visit our website at http://www.llewellyn.com.

QUEEN

— OF ALL —

WITCHERIES

A BIOGRAPHY
OF THE GODDESS

JACK CHANEK

LLEWELLYN PUBLICATIONS | WOODBURY, MINNESOTA

FIRST EDITION
First Printing, 2023

Book design by Samantha Peterson
Cover design by Shannon McKuhen
Interior art by Llewellyn Art Department

Llewellyn Publications is a registered trademark of Llewellyn Worldwide Ltd.

Library of Congress Cataloging-in-Publication Data (Pending)
ISBN: 978-0-7387-7342-1

Llewellyn Worldwide Ltd. does not participate in, endorse, or have any authority or responsibility concerning private business transactions between our authors and the public.

All mail addressed to the author is forwarded but the publisher cannot, unless specifically instructed by the author, give out an address or phone number.

Any internet references contained in this work are current at publication time, but the publisher cannot guarantee that a specific location will continue to be maintained. Please refer to the publisher's website for links to authors' websites and other sources.

Llewellyn Publications
A Division of Llewellyn Worldwide Ltd.
2143 Wooddale Drive
Woodbury, MN 55125-2989
www.llewellyn.com

Printed in the United States of America

Other Books by Jack Chanek

Qabalah for Wiccans
Tarot for Real Life

Featured In

Aries Witch

For the source of all life, the great Mother Earth;
For the one who went down to the underworld's dust;
For the mother of witches who conquered the light;
For the queen of the sabbat, eternal in mirth;
For the arch of the stars and the deep cup of lust;
For the moon on the waves of the ocean at night;
For the mistress of death, of beauty and birth;
For the holiest name that must not be discussed;
For the champion of justice, the good and the right;
For the Goddess without whom we could never be:
My Lady, I offer this book to thee.

CONTENTS

DISCLAIMER

SOME OF THE EXERCISES provided in this book involve working with herbs, some of which are potentially poisonous. Always exercise extreme caution when using toxic herbs. The recipes provided here are tested for safety, but please do not experiment on your own unless you have significant experience with herbalism. You can kill yourself if you don't know what you're doing. Likewise, if you have medical conditions such as epilepsy or pregnancy that are contraindicated with the use of some herbs, please consult with a doctor before proceeding with any foray into herbalism.

You will also find mentions of essential oils. Essential oils are potent; use care when handling them. Always dilute essential oils before placing them on your skin, and make sure to do a patch test on your skin before use. Perform your own research before using an essential oil.

ACKNOWLEDGMENTS

I STILL CAN'T BELIEVE this book exists. The whole time I was writing it, up until well after the manuscript was written and accepted, I referred to it as "the book I'm never going to write," because the project of it just seemed too monumental to accomplish. I am indebted to so many people who helped make *Queen of All Witcheries* a reality. First, as always, thanks to the incredible team at Llewellyn: Heather Greene, Terry Lohmann, Nicole Borneman, Markus Ironwood, and everyone I haven't had the chance to interact with directly. Without your work, this book would never have been possible.

I would like to thank Katherine Palakovich and William Breeze at the Ordo Templi Orientis for granting permission to use the Gnostic Mass and for insightful commentary about Thelema and the goddess Babalon. I also owe thanks to Julia Belham-Payne and the other trustees of the Doreen Valiente Foundation, who granted me permission to reproduce "The Charge of the Goddess" in full. Angela Z. is a perpetual source of wisdom and inspiration, but I am especially grateful for her expertise on Thelema and historical baking techniques. Silver Daniels shared invaluable knowledge about the chemistry of flying ointments. Deborah Lipp initiated me into the mysteries of the Goddess, and Mab Borden taught me to drink deeply from the Goddess's cup.

I am blessed to have a religious community that has been willing to join me in exploring many of the topics and texts discussed in this book. Maggi Rohde and the members of my Gardnerian book club have shown incredible patience with me as we dived into the history of the modern Goddess movement, and this book would not be what it is without the work we've done together. Finally, thanks to every priestess, ritual facilitator, friend, lover, coven sibling, and stranger who has shown me a new face of the Goddess and deepened my relationship with her. I am grateful beyond words for all of you.

FOREWORD

THE PRACTICE OF WITCHCRAFT, Wicca, and Goddess worship has grown in recent years, which is wonderful. Unfortunately, the spread of misinformation and blurred lines between historical fact and modern fictional ideas has also exploded.

Whilst I always encourage those new to the path to read everything they can get their hands on, it also comes with a warning that not everything found in books or on the internet is, for want of a better word, gospel. Reading books on Witchcraft, Wicca, and deity from the birth of the modern Wiccan inception up to and including today is a very useful endeavour. But we need to remember that some of the information is perhaps a little sketchy, maybe not researched properly, or even just plucked from the air.

My own style of the Craft is miscellaneous, a pick and mix from many traditions and practices fused together to make my own unique pathway, and I believe that is how it should be, if it works for you.

The problem lies in people promoting Goddess worship practices or Witchcraft ways as the old, original, or only way—without doing their homework. Social media doesn't help, with sometimes-ridiculous memes full of misinformation being shared hundreds of times. We need people to check, to research, to investigate, and to fact-check before passing ideas, workings, or practices off as original or ancient. Actually, I don't think it matters if ways of working with the Craft or Goddess worship are ancient or modern, as long as they work for you. But I do believe it is important to know the source and history of them.

I also believe it helps to know why you are doing something. Why does a ritual work that way? Why do we call upon the Goddess for this or that? Why do we work with magical tools for such a purpose? Lots of whys, and it is important to have at least some sort of explanation. Why? Because it helps with our understanding of how magic works and what the reasons are for certain things.

Whilst I do always trust my intuition, particularly in relation to working magic, it helps immensely to understand the foundations of the "why." A lot of my own practice has come from reading about folk magic and historical documents. As a newcomer to the Craft over thirty years ago now, I read a lot of the texts Jack references in this book. And I took them all as fact; they were textbooks to be taken as historically and factually correct. It took me a while before I realised that some of the information was a little bit "off." *Queen of All Witcheries* has shown me even more "off" areas than I realised! You never stop learning, that's for sure.

We also find a lot of misunderstanding within areas of the Craft and Goddess worship. The Wiccan Rede is a good example. Where did it originate from, and what was its original meaning and intent? I see so many people quoting it and using it as a disclaimer or excuse in ways far removed from the original use and meaning. If you use something such as the Rede, does it not make sense to understand and know its origins?

The "old ways" are not necessarily the right ways for everyone, and as with all things, time moves forward and changes happen. It is fascinating to research and read how things were done originally or historically, but not everything translates easily to modern times. Sometimes things need to be tweaked, and that's a good thing, but we need to recognise that information has been brought up-to-date and not misrepresent it as "ancient." *Queen of All Witcheries* includes some wonderful updated, modern rituals.

We seem so focused on which Goddess we work with and how many items we can fit on an altar to her that we forget to just *be*—to really feel her energy and presence in all things. You can have the biggest altar, the most candles, and every incense blend and crystal, but unless you open up and feel her energy, it is all pointless decoration. Perhaps we all need a reminder on occasion to make those connections, to just open ourselves to the energy of the day, the place, and the Goddess. She does not judge; she does not discriminate; she just is.

Jack Chanek has researched, discussed, and covered in great detail all the above subjects and a great deal more, and he's given answers to the questions that needed to be answered. This book is a much-needed tome of knowledge and a resource for everyone on a Witchcraft, Wiccan, or Goddess-worship pathway. It makes for fascinating (and more importantly, enlightening!) reading.

Knowledge is power.

—Rachel Patterson
High Priestess, Witch, and author of many books on the Craft, such as *Curative Magic*, *The Triple Goddess*, and *Witchcraft into the Wilds*

PREFACE

IN 2016, THERE WAS a full moon on the night of the summer solstice. This is a relatively rare astronomical phenomenon; the last time it happened was in 1948, and it won't happen again until 2062. At the time, I was a fledgling witch living in New York City. I had already begun training with the group that was later to initiate me into the Gardnerian tradition of Wicca, but I hadn't yet fully committed to the initiatory path. Nonetheless, I wanted to mark the occasion, so I did a short ritual prior to sunset: I filled a cup with fruit juice, wreathed it in flowers, and left it on my windowsill to take in the light of the full moon. The plan was for me to leave the cup out overnight, then drink it the following morning, symbolically taking the power of the moon and the solstice into myself.

That night, I had an experience that changed my life forever.

There was a public screening of *Ferris Bueller's Day Off* happening in Bryant Park. I was in college at the time, working a summer job at the Bronx Zoo, and most of my friends had left New York for the summer, so I decided to go to the movie on my own. After I finished my little ritual, I took the subway down to Midtown Manhattan, found an unoccupied spot of grass, and settled in to watch the show.

As the night wore on, the moon rose above the Manhattan skyline. As it crested over the top of the buildings behind me, the whole park was bathed in a gentle silver glow. I looked up to catch a glimpse of the moon above me—

And there she was.

A figure of a nude woman stretched across the night sky. Her skin was the color of freshly tilled soil. Her hair was braided through with white flowers, and she smelled of jasmine and copal. Her hands, raised high above her head, cradled the full moon between them, and her eyes shone silver. I was filled with an indescribable sense of awe.

Seeing her, that night in Bryant Park, I knew with absolute certainty that Wicca was the right religion for me. She didn't say anything. She didn't look at me. She was just there, regal and powerful, the queen of the heavens in all her glory. As Ben Stein droned out "Bueller…Bueller…" on the big screen, I was seized by a religious ecstasy that I had never experienced before. The rest of the world faded away. There was only her. In that moment, I committed myself to the Goddess, and I have never looked back since.

INTRODUCTION

IF YOU SPEND MUCH time around Pagans and witches, regardless of your personal beliefs and practices, you will sooner or later hear people talking about "the" Goddess. The use of the definite article can be confusing, and even jarring—don't Pagans worship multiple goddesses?—but more often than not, people are using the term to refer to one particular deity. Some people refer to her as "the" Goddess because they think her true name is unknowable. Others know her privately by a secret name but use the title to describe her in public. Still others believe that all the goddesses of world mythology are just different names and faces of one Great Goddess who transcends them all, so the name by which she's called doesn't matter.

Who is this Goddess? What do people say about her? Often, she's described as a mother. She is variously described as the Great Mother, the mother of the universe, Mother Earth, or the mother of us all. She is associated with the cycles of life: birth, youth, adolescence, adulthood, old age, death, and—for those who believe in it—reincarnation. She is understood to watch over, protect, and nurture humanity, and to offer a boundless, unconditional love. One author in the twentieth-century Goddess feminism movement, Carol P. Christ, describes the Goddess as "the intelligent embodied love that is the ground of all being."[1]

In this vein, the Goddess is associated with love of all kinds. She is a deity not only of maternal love, but also of romantic, sexual, filial, fraternal, collegial, and friendly forms of love. All love is sacred to her, and, as early Wiccan author Doreen Valiente notes, "all acts of love and pleasure" are rituals of the Goddess.[2] Sex and sexuality are honored and celebrated by the Goddess, rather than being seen as sinful or shameful—but the choice not to have sex is just as sacred as the

---

1. Christ, *Rebirth of the Goddess*, 107.
2. Valiente, *The Charge of the Goddess*, 13.

choice to have it. The human body is often described as sacred to the Goddess, and everything people do joyfully with their bodies can be viewed as an act of celebration and worship in her honor.

This connection extends beyond the realm of interpersonal love, and it applies to all forms of joy and beauty. The Goddess rules over art, music, and poetry. She is a guide and inspiration for those seeking connection to something higher, in all its forms. Any expression of human creativity, be it through dance or through blacksmithing, is sacred to her. She is a patron of storytellers and craftspeople, of creativity and creation in all their forms.

In the world, the Goddess is seen as the immanent power of nature. People describe her as a goddess of the earth, the sea, or the stars. Wild animals and wild places are sacred to her, and her worshippers often choose to conduct rituals outdoors. These things are not merely symbols of the Goddess; in many ways, they are the Goddess herself. The earth is the body of the Goddess, and by honoring the earth, Pagans honor her directly. Because of the Goddess's association with nature, many of her worshippers are vocal environmentalists, or they will seek to connect to her through gardening, hunting, herbalism, or similar activities.

The Goddess embodies a cyclical, nonlinear understanding of time. Rather than progressing from a strict starting point to an end point, time is seen to ebb and flow in cycles of increase and decrease. This is seen in the stages of human life, but also in the life cycles of plants and animals, the flow of the tides, and the changing seasons of the year. All things rise and fall, come and go, without beginning or end—simply participating in a great cosmic dance. The quintessential symbol of the Goddess's cyclical nature is the moon, which waxes and wanes every month. The moon begins as a crescent, grows until it is full, and then darkens again until it is renewed, representing the eternal cycle of life, death, and rebirth. As such, it is associated with the cyclical Goddess, who is often depicted wearing a lunar crown on her brow.

Through her associations with transformation and change, the Goddess is also a patroness of magic. Not all Pagans or Goddess-worshippers practice magic, but many do. For these, the Goddess is a source of inspiration and power, enabling them to change themselves and the world around them. Many who worship the Goddess call themselves witches, and a sizable portion of these practice the religion of Wicca in one form or another. The Goddess, then, is not only a deity of nature and embodied love; she is a divine sorceress and queen of the witches.

Finally, the Goddess is not always depicted in isolation. Some—particularly members of the twentieth-century Goddess feminism movement—worship the Goddess exclusively, but others depict her as having a divine consort. Often, this consort is imagined as a sun God to complement the moon Goddess; he may variously be associated with hunting, agriculture, sex, death, and kingship. In Wicca and traditions influenced thereby, this consort is frequently depicted with horns or antlers.

Some people draw on a seasonal myth of the Goddess and God. In this myth, the Goddess gives birth to the sun God at the winter solstice. He grows through the spring and reaches maturity in the summer, when he becomes her consort; the two of them are married, and she conceives a child. Then, as autumn sets in, the God dies and is banished to the underworld—only to be reborn again when the Goddess gives birth at the solstice. Not everyone likes or uses this myth, but it's widespread enough that you will likely encounter some version of it in the broader Pagan community, so it's worth mentioning here. In addition to all of her own qualities, the Goddess may sometimes also be understood through her relationship to a divine son and/or lover.

Goddesses and the Goddess

In just a few pages, I have painted what I hope is a vivid picture of who the Goddess is. However, there is a puzzle here. The worship of this Goddess is a fairly modern phenomenon. She springs up with the rise of modern Paganism in the twentieth century, but prior to that, it is difficult to identify any one deity who is exactly like the figure I have just described, and who is associated with all of the following:

+ Motherhood
+ Love, not limited to romantic love
+ The sacred body
+ Art and creativity
+ Immanence in nature
+ Cyclicality

- The moon
- Transformation and magic
- A horned or solar consort

This is not to say that she doesn't relate to ancient goddesses at all; quite the contrary. There are an abundance of deities in the ancient world who have traits in common with her. Demeter is the Corn Mother, Freyja is a goddess of magic, Brigid watches over artists and craftsmen, and so on. Nonetheless, none of these deities is quite the same as the Goddess I've described. Demeter has little to do with witchcraft or magic, Freyja is not much interested in the cycles of the seasons, and Brigid is not a mother. If you go to an open Pagan circle and someone invokes "the" Goddess, they're probably not thinking of any of these deities, or any other specific goddess from world mythology. Conversely, if you were to invite a devotee of Demeter, Freyja, Brigid, Hecate, Amaterasu, or any other goddess to a ritual honoring that particular deity, and brought them instead to a rite for "the" Goddess, you'd be likely to ruffle some feathers.

For this reason, I employ a capitalization convention to distinguish "the" Goddess from goddesses in general. When I am talking about the Great Goddess, whose particular nature and associations I have detailed here, I capitalize the word. When, however, I am speaking about goddesses of pagan antiquity, I leave the word decapitalized. In a book about the Goddess, the G-word gets used quite a lot, and I think that making this typographical distinction helps keep clear when I am talking about her versus the various pagan deities who helped inspire the modern conception of her. I employ a similar convention with the word *god*: I will capitalize it if I am speaking of "the" God who is the Goddess's consort, but otherwise I leave it lowercase. Finally, the word *pagan* is capitalized when referring to contemporary religion, but decapitalized when talking about ancient paganism.

I mentioned earlier that some people see all goddesses as different faces or aspects of one singular Goddess. For these people, the distinction I am trying to draw here may feel arbitrary, incorrect, or forced. After all, if all these goddesses are different manifestations of the same Goddess energy, then Demeter just is Freyja, and Freyja just is Brigid, and so on down the line. She may be known by different names in different circumstances, the same way someone might go by

Katherine at work and Kate at home, but the same Goddess underlies all those names and all the different myths and rituals with which she is honored.

This is a question of theology, and each person is going to have their own views on the matter. Some people believe that all goddesses are one Goddess, and others believe that each goddess in world mythology is a unique individual who is metaphysically distinct from every other. These positions are known as "soft" polytheism and "hard" polytheism, respectively. Still other people will take a stance somewhere in the middle, viewing deities as distinct beings that sometimes share a similar divine essence; I suppose one could call this stance "semifirm" polytheism, if one wanted to categorize it.

On the question of hard versus soft polytheism, I'll remain agnostic for the purposes of this book. My own views about deity are somewhere in the semifirm camp, but one of the hallmarks of Goddess worship and of Paganism more broadly is that it is intimate, personal, and subjective. Everyone brings their own experience to the table, and no one has the authority to dictate anyone else's experience. I'm not in the business of telling people what they should or shouldn't believe about the nature of the Gods.

What I hope we can all agree on, regardless of theological perspective, is that the way people talk about the Goddess today is unique. There are similarities with ancient paganism, but the Goddess as she is known today is not quite identical to any figure from the ancient world. The worship of the Goddess in the twentieth and twenty-first centuries is not merely the continuation of any one goddess cult from pre-Christian times. It is a particular, new, special thing. The language used to describe the Goddess, the features attributed to her and the symbols associated with her, did not exist in quite this way at any point in the past—though there are similar elements scattered through world mythology. The Goddess herself may be ancient and beyond time, but the modern cult of the Goddess is just that: modern.

The Goddess in Modern History

In this book, I am going to explore the modern mythology of the Goddess. I'll look at the development of modern ideas about the Goddess in order to better understand how the world ended up with the form of Goddess worship found in Paganism today. Along the way, I discuss famous witches, Pagans, and ceremonial magicians who shaped the ritual and mythology of the Goddess in the twentieth century: figures like Aleister Crowley, Dion Fortune, Gerald Gardner, Doreen

Valiente, and Starhawk. However, my investigation will not be limited to practitioners. I will also introduce historians, folklorists, and anthropologists from the nineteenth and twentieth centuries, whose ideas changed the way people today think about Paganism, the Goddess, and the ancient world.

Throughout this book, I'll explore the relationship between the present and pagan antiquity. What I aim to show is that this relationship is not static and fixed. It is eternally evolving, changing as we change. Modern-day practitioners see history through a glass darkly. Our view of the past is neither authoritative nor impartial; much of the time, we look at history and see what we want to see or what we expect to see. Consequently, when thinking about the history of Goddess worship, modern practitioners have to ask ourselves what people in the early days of the movement wanted and expected to see. This book will look at nineteenth- and twentieth-century narratives about ancient paganism, witchcraft, and goddesses, because these narratives affected the movers and shakers of the modern Goddess revival. My question has to be not only "What was ancient goddess worship really like?" but "What did people *think* ancient goddess worship was like?"

This is a hard question, and it can lead to some uncomfortable places. Many of the influential figures who shaped ideas in contemporary Goddess worship were men, and that can be an awkward thing to reckon with in a religious tradition that focuses so much on women's voices and women's power. Moreover, I will claim that many commonly held ideas about the Goddess—from her association with nature to the myth of her dying-and-resurrecting consort—are less ancient than they are sometimes imagined to be. Much of who the Goddess is and how people today talk about her is rooted in postindustrial narratives about ancient paganism, more so than in ancient paganism itself.

When I say that, it may feel threatening. In discussing the Goddess, I am talking about a sacred and profound topic. It may sound like sacrilege, then, for me to say that many of the ideas associated with this timeless figure are modern in their origin. Situating the Goddess at a particular moment in history may give the impression that I am trying to profane her—that I am trying to reduce her to some modern literary trope. If you've read this far and your hackles are starting to rise, that's a completely understandable and human reaction to have. However, I promise, that is *not* what I'm seeking to do.

This is something I should be clear about before proceeding any further: *examining the history of the Goddess in the modern world does not mean she's just made up.* It doesn't make her any less real, or any less of a goddess. Rather, it means that I am searching for a deeper understanding of how this Goddess came to be known and worshipped in this way, at this time, by these people. It means I am looking at how the Goddess relates to modern society, which turns out to be quite different from how other goddesses related to other societies. This should come as no surprise, because our world today is definitely not the same as the Mediterranean in 1500 BCE or the Baltic in 600 CE; why, then, would the Gods look the same way now as they did then, when our civilization is so strikingly different?

This book is subtitled *A Biography of the Goddess*, and that's exactly the project that I see myself undertaking here: a biography. This book is not *How the Goddess Was Invented by a Bunch of Victorian Colonialists*, nor *Nine Reasons the Goddess Is Fake and You Should Stop Believing in Her*. It is, rather, the Goddess's own personal history, the story of how she came to be where she is today.

My purpose is the farthest thing from sacrilege. I am seeking a deeper, richer connection with the divine. I deeply believe that the way to know the Goddess is to tell her story—not just in myth, but the story of how contemporary worshippers came to know her and how our relationship to her has changed alongside our society up to the present day. Our understanding of the Goddess, and of what we are doing as Goddess worshippers, can only be made stronger by knowing the roots of what we do.

I invite you to join me on this exploration. In this book, I will discuss the development of the Goddess's modern mythology through nine major texts, starting in the 1800s and working my way up to the early 1970s. I'll also look at several related thinkers, practitioners, and books that influenced or were influenced by these nine core texts. These books are:

- *Mother Right* by Johann Jakob Bachofen
- *The Golden Bough* by Sir James George Frazer
- *Aradia: The Gospel of the Witches* by Charles Godfrey Leland
- *The Witch-Cult in Western Europe* by Margaret Alice Murray
- *Liber AL: The Book of the Law* by Aleister Crowley

- *The Sea Priestess* by Dion Fortune
- *The White Goddess* by Robert Graves
- *Witchcraft Today* by Gerald B. Gardner
- *The First Sex* by Elizabeth Gould Davis

It should be noted that the history of the Goddess movement is complex and layered; by focusing on the modern world, I am not denying that the worship of the Goddess is rooted in ancient paganism. There can be no question that it is. Goddess worshippers today look to the pagan past for a deeper understanding of divinity, and there is an undeniable resonance between what Pagans do now and what pagans did in their temples thousands of years ago. However, history is not a static thing, and modern Pagans' understanding of it is inescapably situated in a modern context. By understanding that context, and the way Paganism's relationship to pagan antiquity has developed since the nineteenth century, you can gain an insight into Goddess worship that would not be available to you if you only looked to ancient mythology.

Likewise, the modern context of Goddess worship is complex. In choosing to focus on these nine texts, I am not saying that they are the only influences on Goddess worship, or even the only ones that matter. They are important, but that does not mean that other thinkers, authors, books, or ideas are not. There are many things I will not discuss in this book—ranging from the Church of All Worlds to the Tantric writings of Sir John Woodroffe—that shaped the development of Goddess religion as it is known now. The ideas discussed in this book are not the only ones that matter, but they're the ones I choose to bring to the fore because they have been the most helpful to me in understanding who the Goddess is. It is my hope that discussing these ideas will prove equally helpful to you.

Each chapter of this book will include a ritual inspired by the material discussed in that chapter, as well as a practical, hands-on exercise to help you connect to the ideas I discuss; remember, the project of this book is not just to talk about the Goddess, but to actively engage in worshipping her. Each ritual includes two versions: a group variation and a solitary variation. The group variations can all be performed by any group ranging from four to a dozen people, while the solitary variations are designed for a lone practitioner. I encourage you to perform all of these rituals in order as you work your way through the book, using either the solitary or group versions of the rites. They are designed to help you connect to the Goddess in her various guises throughout history, building a ritual understanding of her alongside your analytic and historical understanding.

Many of the rituals provided include apparently gendered roles, such as a priestess or someone acting out the role of the Goddess. These roles are flexible, and a person of any gender may play any part in all of the rituals I've provided here. Where I include gendered language, it is to help the rituals fit with the historical period and ideas discussed in the accompanying chapters, but you should not feel bound to follow rigid gender norms in performing these rites.

In this book, I'll look at evolving views of the Goddess throughout modern history, how those views relate to the way people talk about the Goddess today, and how they can be leveraged to provide you with a richer, more powerful experience of ritual and devotion. By the end of the book, you'll come out with a stronger connection to her, a mastery of the history of the modern Goddess movement, and hopefully a little more besides.

1

AN IMAGINED
MATRIARCHY (1861)

WHEN I WAS EIGHT years old, I was baptized into the Serbian Orthodox Church. My parents were never particularly religious, and in fact my father was a vocal atheist, but my great-grandmother—my mother's grandmother, whom we called Baba—was devout. She was the child of immigrants from the city of Bosanska Gradiška in the Austro-Hungarian Empire, in modern-day Bosnia. Fleeing political turmoil, her parents had settled in Wisconsin in 1910. There, they found themselves part of a Serbian Orthodox enclave, building a community based on their shared language, religion, and culture with other immigrants. Baba grew up in a world where the church was everything. It was her source of community and identity: the place where she made her friends, learned traditional Serbian customs and recipes, and eventually met her husband. The church was her life.

By the time I turned eight, Baba was in her nineties and her health was declining. She laid down the law: "He must be baptized before I die." It was of the utmost importance to her that she would live to see me join the church. There was no arguing with her on this point, and so after a great deal of discussion, we flew out to Milwaukee for a weekend and I was baptized in the St. Sava Serbian Orthodox Cathedral.

The space was grandiose, with vaulted ceilings, gold chandeliers, and mosaics depicting the life and works of Christ. A brass censer on a swinging chain perfumed the cathedral with frankincense, and the smoke was so thick that I could barely see the priest in front of me. After a series of prayers and exhortations,

I was prompted to renounce the devil, blessed with holy water, and anointed with oil. The priest then taught me the proper Orthodox way to cross myself, and I was presented with a set of gifts, including a gold cross on a chain that I still have to this day. After the service, there was a feast of traditional Serbian foods and a parade of Baba's friends excitedly welcoming me to the church.

It may seem strange to include the story of a Christian baptism in a book about Goddess spirituality, but this service was one of my first encounters with the Goddess. As I stood in that cathedral, dwarfed by the lapis arch above me and half-choked on incense smoke, I was struck by a feeling of overwhelming awe. I knew that this moment was holy, not because of Christ or the devil, but because of Baba herself.

That baptism forged a deep connection between me and my ancestors. It was the same rite that Baba had undergone, and her mother, and her grandmother before her. It connected me to a line of ancestors stretching back hundreds of years. More than that, it connected me to Baba, specifically: it made me a part of her world, of the community that had defined her life for almost a century. For the first time in my life, I felt aware of a connection to something that transcended my individual identity. That night, as I looked at Baba across a table laden with grilled meats, I saw that she was not just my great-grandmother. She was the archetypal matriarch, the head of the family and the keeper of traditions that connected me to those who had gone before me. She was the embodiment of something ancient and powerful, greater than any one person.

She was the Goddess.

It Begins with the Mother

The story of the Goddess begins long, long ago…in the mid-nineteenth century. It starts with a Swiss anthropologist named Johann Jakob Bachofen, who in 1861 published a book called *Das Mutterrecht*. In English, the title of this book translates to *Mother Right*. In the book, Bachofen proposed that all early human societies had been matriarchal in their structure; that is to say, that social and political power had been vested primarily in women. He looked at ancient pagan societies throughout the Mediterranean, including in Athens, Crete, and Egypt, and he concluded that they had originally been matriarchal, only to be taken over by male rule as a later development in their history. A key feature of these matriarchal societies, in Bachofen's view, was Goddess-centered religion.

It is crucial to state from the outset that Bachofen was wrong about the existence of ancient matriarchy. Some scattered societies around the world do exhibit certain features that Bachofen ascribed to matriarchy, but there is no conclusive evidence to suggest that there was a universal matriarchal stage in civilization. The vision of antiquity conjured in *Mother Right* was a fantasy, an imagined history rooted in his conception of how human society *ought* to have developed. Bachofen's historical claims have been thoroughly debunked by modern historians and archaeologists.[3]

However, Bachofen's idea of an ancient matriarchy was an appealing one. It took root and grew, and it had wide-reaching effects for the way people thought about the role of women, paganism, and goddesses in the ancient world. Nearly every historical figure or movement I'll discuss throughout this book was working under the belief that at one point in time, human civilization had been matriarchal—and, moreover, that an essential feature of this matriarchal society had been the worship of a great Mother Goddess. If you open any book on the Goddess from the twentieth century, and even many books that have been published more recently, you will run into Bachofen's imagined matriarchal past. In order to understand modern Goddess worship, then, you must understand Bachofen and his matriarchy.

What did these matriarchal societies supposedly look like? Bachofen's view of matriarchy and of the role women would have played in it was strongly influenced by mid-nineteenth-century gender norms and stereotypes about the respective natures of men and women. He theorized that in ancient times, child-bearing women were seen as the source of all life. Children were born from the womb of their mother, just as plants came from the womb of the earth, and so the mother and the earth were identified with each other and considered sacred. Bachofen suggested that in the matriarchal mindset, "this mother is always the same: ultimately she is the earth, represented by earthly woman throughout the succession of mothers and daughters."[4] As such, women were seen as primordial life-givers. Life was sacred and powerful, and therefore women were sacred and powerful. They would have occupied the primary roles both in statecraft and in religion, as embodiments of the life-giving principle.

---

3. Eller, *Gentlemen and Amazons*, 13.
4. Bachofen, *Myth, Religion, and Mother Right*, 128.

Equally, Bachofen thought that matriarchy placed great emphasis on the mysteries of death, and on the idea of rebirth: "Death itself is the precondition of life, and life dissolves into death in order that the race may remain imperishable in the eternal alternation of the two poles."[5] Bachofen had an idea that matriarchal culture would reconcile itself to the impermanence of individual human lives by emphasizing the permanence of motherhood as an overarching principle; individual people die and are born, but the original mother from which they all come is eternal. She is the source of death as well as of life, and by honoring death and the dead, matriarchal peoples would be honoring her.

Bachofen associated war, industry, and intellect with masculinity, and as such, he imagined that these things would have been absent from matriarchal society. Matriarchy was envisioned as a sort of primitive utopia, where peaceful, gentle women maintained harmony with each other and with the land. He thought of women as sensitive, emotional, and sensuous—in contrast with the aggressive, rational, inventive nature he ascribed to men: "To man's superior physical strength woman opposes the mighty influence of her religious consecration; she counters violence with peace, enmity with conciliation, hate with love."[6] Matriarchal society was imagined to be a seat for agriculture and basic domestic crafts, but also undeveloped in key ways. Intellectual pursuits, science, and philosophy were, Bachofen suggested, the hallmarks of a patriarchal society. A civilization run by women might be in harmony with the land, but it would also lack what Bachofen saw as the fundamentally masculine drive to move beyond the physical realm.

Consequently, he envisioned matriarchal societies as fundamentally materialistic, concerned with the body rather than with the immortal soul. He suggested that "no era has attached so much importance to outward form, to the sanctity of the body, and so little to the inner spiritual factor...In a word, matriarchal existence is regulated naturalism, its thinking material, its development predominantly physical."[7] Matriarchal cultures were defined by a close connection to the natural world, but Bachofen saw this connection as something limiting and det-

---

5. Bachofen, *Myth, Religion, and Mother Right*, 126.

6. Bachofen, *Myth, Religion, and Mother Right*, 86.

7. Bachofen, *Myth, Religion, and Mother Right*, 92.

rimental. He viewed matriarchies as being mastered by the natural world, not masters of it. To his mind, this was a grievous flaw.

The society Bachofen envisioned was not only matriarchal in the sense that positions of power were held by women in society at large. It was also matrifocal, in that the mother would be the head of the household rather than the father, as was ubiquitous in the modern Europe that Bachofen knew. Likewise, it would be matrilineal, in that family lineage would be traced through the maternal line. Rather than organizing family structures around fatherhood by having a woman move to her husband's house upon marriage, or having children take their father's surname, this society would organize the family around motherhood in a parallel way.[8]

Matriarchy and the Goddess

All of these ideas worked their way into Bachofen's conception of matriarchal religion. A matriarchal society would naturally worship a Goddess rather than a God, and this Goddess would feature the same "feminine" traits ascribed to society as a whole. As such, she was, first and foremost, a deity of motherhood. Bachofen imagined that the worship of motherhood, the elevation of birth as the most sacred mystery, would be central to a matriarchal culture.

The Goddess would also be associated with the earth, and with the wildness of nature. She would be celebrated not only as the giver of human life, but of plant and animal life as well. On the whole, the Goddess would be a peaceful, loving figure, a bringer of harmony and balance, because aggression and conflict were alien to the society that worshipped her. The leaders of her cult would be women, who may even be venerated as the Goddess incarnate.[9]

Bachofen identified a few other key themes, which he considered essential to a matriarchal worldview: "The religious preference given to the moon over the sun, of the conceiving earth over the fecundating sea, of the dark aspect of death over the luminous aspect of growth, of the dead over the living, of mourning over rejoicing."[10] Matriarchal religion according to Bachofen focused on the veneration of the moon, the earth, the night, and the chthonic spirits of the dead. This,

---

8. Bachofen, *Myth, Religion, and Mother Right*, 109.

9. Bachofen, *Myth, Religion, and Mother Right*, 123.

10. Bachofen, *Myth, Religion, and Mother Right*, 77.

in turn, was contrasted with Bachofen's vision of the eventual rise of patriarchal society and religion. He saw the latter as focused on the sun that gives the moon its light, the sea that fertilizes the land, the day born out of the night, and the promise of eternal life rather than ministration to the dead.

All of these ideas about an imagined historical culture laid the foundation for the way the Goddess would come to be worshipped in the modern world. Some of these ideas have genuine parallels in ancient paganism; there certainly were mother goddesses, or earth goddesses, or goddesses of the moon. However, Bachofen's story about ancient matriarchy was the first to synthesize these various strands and bring them together into one cohesive, overarching narrative. For the first time, the pagan past was not populated with goddesses; it was populated with the Goddess. Not only that, but the Goddess had a very particular sort of being. She had a clear, definite personality, things that she was and was not associated with, and these traits would carry on into later forms of her worship in the twentieth and twenty-first centuries.

The Elephant in the Room

Bachofen's ideas about gender were reductive in the extreme, and pinned to a particular view about the relationship between gender and biology. He saw women as innately pliant, peaceful, emotional, and above all else, as fertile bodies that could serve as incubators for human reproduction. The year 1861 was, needless to say, not progressive by today's standards of thought about sex and gender.

I will have more room to problematize this essentialist view of gender later in the book. For now, I just want to call out that I'm aware of the essentialist language used in Bachofen's vision of matriarchal society, and I'm not trying to uncritically rehash it. Throughout this book, I will do my best to avoid leaning on essentialist, reductive, or outdated stereotypes about gender, but the fact of the matter is that many of the most influential figures in the development of modern Goddess worship were buying in to those exact stereotypes.

As such, a particular outdated view of gender is the elephant in the room with any discussion of modern Pagan Goddess worship. Reading through many texts that shaped the movement, it can sometimes feel like the Goddess is seen as a parody of womanhood: it's almost like she's nothing more than a cosmic vagina, a nubile nymph who menstruates in sync with the phases of the moon and who exists for no purpose other than to be beautiful and pop out babies. If

I may speak from the heart for a moment, this is emphatically not the Goddess as I know and worship her. Yes, the Goddess has associations with motherhood and with a certain constructed notion of femininity, but she is also so much more than that. To reduce her to a stereotype, to make her into a Barbie doll wearing a flower crown, is entirely to miss the point.

As I continue the exploration of the Goddess in later chapters, keep this in mind. There will always be a view of gender in the foreground of any discussion of the Goddess, and through much of modern history, that view has been largely regressive by today's standards. I have to confess, the phrase "divine feminine" makes my ears burn, because it's so tangled up in the idea that the Goddess is womb power and nothing else. However, as you will see, some of the gendered ideas associated with Goddess worship were actually quite radical and inclusive for their time. When you look at the gendered attitudes that shaped modern Goddess religions, you'd do well to consider them in a historical light. Even if these ideas no longer fit with current views about gender, they were often put forward by people who were reaching for a deeper, more nuanced understanding of gender, and who were doing their best with the language and concepts available to them.

Moreover, it's worth keeping in mind that while gender is in the foreground of discussions about the Goddess, there is also a great deal in the background. Ideas about gender shaped the modern understanding of the Goddess, yes, but so did ideas about paganism in general, nature, magic, witchcraft, the moon, the arts, and much more besides. It's important to talk about gender, and to critically engage with the unstated assumptions about gender made by figures like Bachofen, but I also want to be careful not to let that discussion preclude talking about other things as well.

Social Darwinism

In order to better understand Bachofen's theory of ancient matriarchy, it's helpful to discuss a theory of social evolution that defined mid-nineteenth-century thinking about the development of human civilization. In 1859, Charles Darwin published *On the Origin of Species*, and the radical theory of evolution seized the popular imagination. All of a sudden, the diversity of the natural world could be explained in an orderly, consistent way. The features of different plants and animals were illuminated in a way they never had been before. It was now possible to explain how two animals could look widely different from each other and still be the same species, while two other animals could look nearly identical and yet be completely unrelated. Biologists no longer needed to refer to an inscrutable divine plan in order to account for the structure of nature; suddenly, all life was connected and had emerged as part of a consistent and observable natural process.

It cannot be overstated how revolutionary this idea was. And as it worked its way into society and people began to fully grasp its implications, a question emerged: Might the theory of evolution apply to things other than mere biology? Might it describe the course of civilizations too?

Evolution, as Darwin originally introduced the concept and as it is still used by scientists today, is a nonlinear process. It's not a progression from less sophisticated organisms to more sophisticated ones, and there is no final purpose or goal to it. It is, rather, the process by which certain biological traits are passed on across generations, becoming more common in a species if they are well adapted to survival in their environment. As organisms compete for resources—nutrition, shelter, protection from predators—some traits prove particularly helpful. Individuals with those traits are more likely to survive in a harsh environment, and are therefore more likely to reproduce and pass their genes on to the next generation. Over time, those useful traits become more and more common in the population, and as organisms develop more adaptive traits, they eventually form into entirely new species. Evolution as Darwin introduced it was not about the development of *individuals*, but of *traits*, which would survive across generations as species became more and more adapted to their particular environments.[11]

As a simple example of this, I'd like to introduce the peppered moth. This species of moth used to be predominantly white, prior to the industrial revolution. Its coloration allowed it to camouflage easily on light-colored tree bark, lichens, and the like, keeping it safe from birds and other predators. However, once coal-powered factories became popular, the resulting soot and air pollution began to turn trees black. Suddenly, white-bodied moths stood out starkly against tree trunks, and they were easy pickings for predators. Having white coloration was no longer an evolutionary advantage, and the moths that were more likely to survive in this new environment were the darker ones. Over time, individual moths with dark colors survived and reproduced, and the common color-

---

11. Darwin, *On the Origin of Species*, 61.

ation of this species became darker and darker, until they were predominantly black! Then, when air pollution was curbed and tree trunks were no longer sooty and black, the coloration of the peppered moth population gradually shifted back once more from black to white, as the lighter color became better adapted to the change in environment.[12]

Neither of these colorations, the dark or the light, is better, more sophisticated, or more "evolved" than the other. They are simply traits that emerged in the population and became more or less common depending on how well they were suited to the moth's environment. Darwinian evolution is, at bottom, a fairly simple and mechanistic process.

What does all this have to do with Bachofen's theory of matriarchy? I promise, it's relevant. As the idea of evolution took root in common parlance, people began to interpret it in a different way than the theory Darwin had originally intended. People began to see evolution as a linear, teleological process, whereby "primitive" organisms evolved into "advanced" ones. Moreover, they tended to think of evolution as something that happened at the individual level: the survival not of the fittest traits, but of the fittest individuals, which were in some fundamental way superior to others and more deserving of survival. As the public turned its attention to subjects other than biology, it brought this myopic view of evolution with it.

This led to a view known as *social Darwinism*, the idea that human society had evolved in a linear process through a series of stages, beginning with "primitive" tribal hunter-gatherer societies and culminating with the apex of "advanced" civilization: the Victorian period.[13] This, in turn, opened the door to the view that societies outside of western Europe were backward, behind, and insufficiently evolved—that they were stuck in an earlier phase of the evolutionary process, and that they needed to catch up to the Victorians by advancing themselves. This became the ideological basis of much of colonial exploitation in the late nineteenth century, as Europeans patted themselves on the back for civilizing these other societies and helping them evolve. It was a racist, exploitative, and self-congratulatory doctrine that led to immeasurable harm for the members of those societies.

---

12. Zimmer, "Evolution in Color."
13. Spencer, *The Man Versus the State*, 110.

Bachofen's theory of a prehistoric matriarchy aligned neatly with this paradigm of social Darwinism.[14] He viewed matriarchy as an early, primitive stage of human society. Matriarchal society was romanticized as part of an idyllic imagined past, but it was also seen as something backward and uncivilized; in Bachofen's view, it was a good thing that humanity had moved beyond matriarchy, and patriarchy was a more evolved stage of human development.

This raises an important point, which you will continue to see throughout this book: the relationship between the present and the real or imagined pagan past is complicated, and often contradictory. In one sense, Bachofen romanticized matriarchy and presented it as an idyllic state of grace for human civilization; in another, he sneered at it and dismissed it as primitive. The construction of an imagined past that is at once admired and derided is a weird, complex phenomenon, but it's one that's found over and over again throughout the nineteenth and twentieth centuries—and particularly with regard to narratives about the Goddess.

——— EXERCISE ———
YOUR MATERNAL LINEAGE

For modern worshippers of the Goddess, Bachofen's description of a matrifocal and matrilineal society may be of particular note. Even though this description is not historically accurate—at least, not with the universality that Bachofen ascribed to it—there is something radical and powerful in it. Particularly for worshippers of the Mother Goddess, there is something quite beautiful in the idea of tracing family lineage through the mother line.

For this exercise, do some research into your own family tree. Try to trace your maternal lineage as far back as it can go: your mother, your maternal grandmother, your maternal great-grandmother, and so on. This doesn't need to be restricted to biological family; if you or a family member were adopted, you may choose to trace the lineage of your adoptive family rather than your genetic ancestors. Depending on where your family came from and what kind of records survive, you may not get very far; one branch of my own family tree were immigrants to America from the Balkans, and there are no surviving records of the family prior to their arrival at Ellis Island. However much or little you find, that's okay; the purpose of this exercise is just to see what you can learn.

---

14. Bachofen, *Myth, Religion, and Mother Right*, xxxvii.

Don't just look for names. If there's biographical information available about who these people were and how they spent their lives, try to dig that up as well. This part of things will not just involve digging through records; you'll also want to talk to your living relatives and find out what they can remember about the people who have passed on. You'll learn lots of things that won't be written down in newspaper clippings or census results.

When you've amassed all your information, take some time to sit and meditate on your lineage. Who were these people? What were they like? Do you feel connected to them? Distant from them? Are there some who feel closer to you than others? From what you've learned about them, what do you have in common with some or all of them? Personality traits, physical characteristics, hobbies, employment, even your name? What are the ways that you're unique and separate from them?

You can set up a small ancestor shrine in your home dedicated to these figures. It can be a temporary or permanent installation, depending on what feels more appropriate to you. This shrine might include photographs of your more recent ancestors, particular items that belonged to them or that they liked, or even just slips of paper with names written on them. This is a place to sit and meditate, to feel communion with your ancestors, or to make offerings of flowers, alcohol, tobacco, or anything personal that you know your ancestors would like. As a note from personal experience, I have found that I have an easier time connecting to ancestral spirits when I make hearty offerings such as alcohol, pastries, or meat—as opposed to something like water or rice.

There is an important caveat that I should discuss with regard to this exercise. Not everyone knows who their mother is—and of the people who do know, not everyone has a relationship with their mother that's worth venerating. Some people have been horrifically mistreated, abused, or disowned by their parents and may not wish to engage in any kind of ancestor veneration. If that's you, *that's okay*. Skip this exercise altogether if doing it would negatively affect you.

Alternatively, I invite you to think about someone who has acted as a maternal figure in your life, and to explore tracing lineage of a sort through them. Lineage is not just about your parents. It is about the people who made you who you are, and that can manifest in all sorts of ways. Another family member, a mentor, a High Priestess or similar religious leader, or a valued teacher or guide may have had a significant impact on your life, and that may be worth honoring in a similar way. If you are unable to perform this exercise tracing lineage through your mother, or even if you just don't want to, try tracing lineage through other kinds of family instead. This may be literal—in the form of an aunt—or it may be more abstract, as with an intellectual or religious lineage. Don't feel too confined by the idea of "motherhood," and instead allow this exercise to be about honoring where you came from in one form or another.

The Power of the Matriarchal Myth

Although *Mother Right* does not hold water as a work of academic history, it is nonetheless incredibly valuable as a work of mythopoesis. The story that Bachofen told and the picture he painted have power to them, and they would continue to inspire people for more than a century to come. Bachofen looked down on matriarchy, but at the same time, he envisioned a world in which women were genuine equals to men: a world in which they had rights, power, and the ability to speak for themselves and navigate their society with full autonomy. In Europe in 1861, this was a radical and transformative idea. It allowed people to imagine a different world, and it opened the door to a completely new model for religious experience. For advocates of women's rights, Bachofen gave them a platform. They could demand the greater inclusion of women in public spaces, religious communities, or political organizations—and rather than presenting it as something new and unprecedented, they could argue that they were trying to reconnect with an idyllic past. The equality of women could be presented in a new light, as the return to a mythic golden age rather than a controversial push forward into modernity.

The idea of the golden age is, of course, a double-edged sword. It could provide an ideological underpinning for progress, but it could just as easily be the opposite; across history, the image of a utopian past has often been conjured to justify clinging to outdated prejudices or practices. After all, if the "good old days" were really so good, why would anyone need to try for anything different or better in the future? The romanticization of the past is a complicated, messy thing, and it was used by people of all persuasions for their various and often contradictory agendas. For that reason, it's not easy to say whether this kind of romanticism was a good thing or a bad thing. It was complicated. Regardless of how complicated it was, though, it was *powerful*, and it had a dramatic effect on the world.

Its effect on modern Paganism and modern Goddess worship cannot be overstated. The idea that the Goddess is the original source of authority and religious power, and that she is the seat of the sacred, was revolutionary. For those who were seeking a different kind of religious experience, it promised that what they were looking for was real, and possible. If it had existed once in the past, it could exist again now. The new religious movements inspired by the idea of matriarchy modeled themselves off of Bachofen's imagined past, not only in their theology but in their social structure as well. Many religious and occult movements were designed to be run chiefly by women, including Wicca and the women's spirituality movement of the late twentieth century. Some strains of Wicca trace religious lineage primarily through a priestess, mimicking the matrilineal family structure of Bachofen's historical matriarchies. Other groups, including British secret societies like the Hermetic Order of the Golden Dawn, were not explicitly matrifocal but placed a heavy emphasis on gender equality, allowing women to occupy positions of authority and to serve as officers within the structure of the organizations themselves.

The greatest effect Bachofen had on Goddess worship, however, was on the way the Goddess herself was perceived. By 1861, the world had well and truly met the Earth Mother as she is known even up to the present day. Inspired by Bachofen, people came to call her by countless names, connecting her to myths from ancient mythology like the stories of Demeter, Isis, or Danu. Some would invent new names and new mythologies for her. But for the first time in modern history, people gave expression to the idea of a Great Goddess who encompassed all others, who had been at the beginning of human civilization and was the mother of us all.

This Goddess was the Earth Mother, the Lady of the Moon, the keeper of the mysteries of death. She was associated with agriculture and the turning of the seasons, the eternal death and rebirth of the land as well as of humankind. She did not always have a consort, but when she did, he was the power of the fertilizing sea and the light-giving sun. She was the Goddess of peace, harmony, and love.

This is the Goddess of the modern world. This is the Lady as she is invoked in Wiccan circles across every continent, at women's retreats, and in ceremonial temples. By the year 1861, she had made herself known to the world in more or less the form she would have up until the present day. The rest of her modern history will be a matter of deepening and strengthening the connections her worshippers have to her, building a mythology and ritual practice, and allowing robust religion to grow up around her. But the Goddess herself is already here. The rest of the time spent between Bachofen and the present day is just a matter of the world trying to figure out how to worship her.

Key Takeaways: Bachofen

+ Motherhood as the original divine principle
+ Identification of motherhood with the earth
+ Association of the Goddess with the moon and nighttime
+ The Goddess as a queen of the underworld offering the promise of rebirth
+ Woman as the Goddess incarnate

——— RITUAL ———
MY MOTHER'S CHILD

This ritual explores the idea of matrilineal family and mythic matriarchy for a religious context. It draws on your maternal lineage to forge a connection to the Goddess through the people who have gone before you. Remember that you do not have to trace your lineage through blood relatives; your bond of familial love with these ancestors matters more than biology.

Group Variation

This ritual is designed with one person directing most of the rite and the other participants following their lead. It is structured as a call-and-response, where each individual line is repeated back by the group as a whole.

You Will Need

- A small table
- A cup full of milk or a nondairy substitute
- Percussive instruments for all ritual participants
- Research on the family trees of all participants

Preparation

Place the table in the center of the ritual space, and put the cup full of milk on top of it. Everyone in the circle should have a tambourine, sistrum, drum, rattle, or similar instrument; in a pinch, simply clapping hands will do. Prior to the rite, all participants should have researched their matrilineal family lineage going back three generations: they'll need the names of their mother, maternal grandmother, and maternal great-grandmother. If for some reason this information is inaccessible, any name may be substituted with "a nameless one" during the ritual itself.

Performance

Everyone stands in a circle. The group takes a moment of silence all together, and then the leader raises their hands and says:

LEADER: Mommy, Mother, Mama, Mum!

ALL: Mommy, Mother, Mama, Mum!

LEADER: We invoke thee in thy ancient names.

ALL: We invoke thee in thy ancient names.

LEADER: Be now with us. Be here for us.

ALL: Be now with us. Be here for us.

LEADER: Be in our circle, mother of us all.

ALL: Be in our circle, mother of us all.

The leader then takes a step forward into the circle. All participants begin to drum or rattle as the leader chants:

LEADER: I am [name], child of [mother's name], child of [grandmother's name], child of [great-grandmother's name], child of the Mother.

ALL: We are [name], child of [mother's name], child of [grandmother's name], child of [great-grandmother's name], child of the Mother.

The leader steps back to the edge of the circle. The next person to the leader's left takes a step forward and recites their own family lineage, and the group echoes it back in the same way. This is done, one by one, for every person in the circle. When everyone has had their turn, the group does one final round of the chant. This time, each person chants their own lineage, with everyone else doing the same, allowing all the different names to overlap and blend together simultaneously:

ALL: I am [name], child of [mother's name], child of [grandmother's name], child of [great-grandmother's name], child of the Mother.

At the end of this chant, everyone stops drumming. The leader walks to the center of the circle and lifts the cup of milk, saying:

LEADER: Mother, we praise you.

ALL: Mother, we praise you.

LEADER: Mother, we honor you.

ALL: Mother, we honor you.

LEADER: Mother, we thank you.

ALL: Mother, we thank you.

The leader then takes a sip from the cup. After drinking, they lift the cup and say:

LEADER: The blessings of the Mother.

ALL: The blessings of the Mother.

The cup is passed around the circle so that everyone may drink from it. After each person drinks, the refrain "The blessings of the Mother" is repeated. When all have drunk, the leader replaces the cup on the altar and returns to the edge of the circle. All participants join hands, and the leader closes the ritual:

LEADER: Mother, you have been with us.

ALL: Mother, you have been with us.

LEADER: Mother, you are with us still.

ALL: Mother, you are with us still.

LEADER: Mother, you will always be.

ALL: Mother, you will always be.

LEADER: And now we say farewell!

ALL: And now we say farewell!

Solitary Variation

This ritual is designed for a more private, personal exploration of maternal lineage. In it, you trace your family back and identify yourself successively with each member of your maternal line before arriving at the altar as a nameless child of the Goddess.

You Will Need

- A small table
- A cup full of milk or a nondairy substitute

- A hand drum, tambourine, or other percussive instrument
- Research on your family tree

Preparation

Place the table at one end of the ritual space, with room for you to stand about eight paces away. Put the cup full of milk on top of it. Put your drum or tambourine in the ritual space where you'll have easy access to it. Prior to the rite, research your matrilineal family lineage going back six generations: you'll need the names of your mother, maternal grandmother, great-grandmother, great-great-grandmother, thrice-great-grandmother, and four-times-great-grandmother. If for some reason this information is inaccessible, any name may be substituted with "a nameless one" during the ritual itself.

Performance

Stand holding your drum or tambourine at the edge of your ritual space, eight paces back from your altar. Close your eyes and take a minute to center yourself, then raise your hands and say:

> *Mommy, Mother, Mama, Mum! I invoke thee in thy ancient names. Be now with me. Be here for me. Be in my presence, mother of us all.*

Take a step toward the altar. Begin to beat your drum as you say:

> *I am* [your name], *child of* [mother's name], *child of* [grandmother's name], *child of the Mother.*

Take another step toward the altar. Say:

> *I am* [mother's name], *child of* [grandmother's name], *child of* [great-grandmother's name], *child of the Mother.*

Step forward again. Say:

> *I am* [grandmother's name], *child of* [great-grandmother's name], *child of* [great-great-grandmother's name], *child of the Mother.*

Step forward again. Say:

> *I am* [great-grandmother's name], *child of* [great-great-grand-mother's name], *child of* [thrice-great-grandmother's name], *child of the Mother.*

Step forward again. Say:

> *I am* [great-great-grandmother's name], *child of* [thrice-great-grandmother's name], *child of* [four-times-great-grandmother's name], *child of the Mother.*

Step forward again. Say:

> *I am* [thrice-great-grandmother's name], *child of* [four-times-great-grandmother's name], *child of the Mother.*

Step forward again. Say:

> *I am* [four-times-great-grandmother's name], *child of the Mother.*

Step forward a final time so that you are standing at the altar. Continue to chant:

> *I am a child of the Mother! I am a child of the Mother! I am a child of the Mother!*

Keep chanting this until you have built to a crescendo. Then, stop chanting and drumming. Set the drum or tambourine down on the ground next to the altar. Lift the cup of milk, saying:

> *Mother, I praise you. Mother, I honor you. Mother, I thank you.*

Take a sip from the cup, then lift it again and say:

> *The blessings of the Mother.*

Set the cup back down, then kneel at the altar. Now is a time for medita-tion, prayer, and personal reflection in the presence of the Goddess. When you are done, stand and back away from the altar until you are once more at the edge of your ritual space where you began the rite. Lift your arms and close the ritual by saying:

> *Mother, you have been with me. Mother, you are with me still.*
> *Mother, you will always be. And now I say farewell!*

2

A UNIVERSAL MYTH (1890)

I WAS BORN AND raised in the rain shadow of the Sierra Nevada mountain range. The mountains block most weather blowing in off the Pacific Ocean, so the area just east of them gets very little precipitation; it's what's known as a "high desert" climate. At that altitude, and with that little moisture, there's not much vegetation. The area around my hometown mostly has desert scrub and ever-green trees like the Jeffrey pine or the white fir. Most of the deciduous trees we have are non-native plants that people put in their yards, but these trees require constant watering and are expensive to maintain.

As a result of this climate, I grew up without the cycle of four seasons as most of us know it. We had hot, dry summers and cold, snowy winters, but there wasn't much of anything in between. Autumn lasted about a week, as strong winds blow-ing down from the mountains would quickly strip the few changing trees of any colorful leaves. Spring was similarly fleeting without flowering trees native to the region.

I never understood why popular culture made such a big deal out of spring-time. Sure, it was nice when winter ended and the days started to get longer and warmer, but the land itself didn't change much. The earth was mostly barren and brown, and most of the trees we did have were green all year round. Many of the wild animals in the region hibernated in the winter, but even in the summer they kept away from people and interactions with them were rare, so it wasn't noticeable when they woke in the spring. The landscape in Nevada doesn't have the same ebb and flow of life and death that we see in much of the US; the living things are always living, and the dead things are always dead, but the land doesn't die and come back to life.

It was only when I moved to New Jersey for graduate school that I met with a seasonal cycle of death and rebirth. Winters in New Jersey are bleak and dismal in a way they're not in the mountains; vegetation disappeared, the whole earth turned brown and hard, the sky was a flat shade of gray, and the cold settled deep in my bones where nothing I did could banish it. By the end of my first February in New Jersey, I felt like winter had gone on forever. Everything was dead and depressing. I had never before lived somewhere that life could disappear so completely from the earth.

But then the spring came.

I woke up one day in April to sunshine and birdsong. There wasn't a cloud in the sky, and it was warm enough for me to go out in shorts and a T-shirt. As I stepped outside, I caught the sweet fragrance of flowers, and I saw that the cherry and magnolia trees outside my home had started to bloom. After months of gray, dead ugliness, the world was suddenly washed in pastel pinks, blues, and greens. Life had returned.

The cycle of natural death and rebirth is a key feature of the Goddess's mythology. Everything that lives will die, but equally, everything that dies will be reborn. The Goddess governs a constant rhythm of growth and decay, and Goddess worshippers are invited to see her presence in the passing of the seasons. Until I moved to New Jersey, though, that cycle was purely abstract for me. It was something theoretical, an imagined story about the seasons with little connection to the actual land I lived on.

That day in April, something changed. I was flooded with relief as I stepped into springtime, and I realized that on some level, a part of me had worried that winter would never end. For the first time in my life, the earth had been truly dead—and for the first time in my life, I saw it reborn. I sank to my knees, kissed the ground in front of me, and thanked the Goddess for her gifts.

The Origins of Myth

The late Victorian period saw a continuation of the obsession with categorizing society into linear stages of development. By the end of the nineteenth century, this obsession had taken on a particular flavor: Victorian anthropologists, and Victorian society at large, wanted to find a unifying theory to explain all of world mythology. The Victorians didn't only want a story about the linear development of politics and general culture. They wanted to understand *people*, and as a part of that project, they needed to understand the stories people told. How was mythology shaped by culture, and how was culture shaped by mythology? Why did so many myths from unrelated cultures around the world seem so similar? And could the development of world mythology fit into a neat linear narrative, just as the development of patriarchal society supposedly did?

George Eliot's 1871 novel *Middlemarch* features the character of Casaubon, a pedantic scholar consumed by writing a *Key to All Mythologies*. He is a sort of archetypal figure of anthropology at the end of the nineteenth century, as many real figures were actually engaged in this exact project. The most famous of them— the one who is remembered for having succeeded—is a man named James George Frazer.

In 1890, Frazer published a book called *The Golden Bough: A Study in Magic and Religion*. He claimed to have written the book in order to understand one puzzling passage from Ovid's *Fasti*.[15] In this passage, Ovid describes a sanctuary of the goddess Diana in a region of Italy called Aricia. This sanctuary was guarded by a priest known as the "king of the wood." The king gained his position by murdering the man who had held it before him, and he would reign as king until someone murdered him in turn: "The strong of hand and fleet of foot do there reign kings, and each is slain thereafter even as himself had slain."[16] The new king would seal his victory by plucking a golden branch from a tree consecrated to Diana, thus becoming her new priest. In *The Golden Bough*, Frazer attempted to offer an explanation for why the priests of Diana at this grove should engage in such a violent custom.

In fact, however, the book turned out to be anything but a humble interpretation of a few lines of poetry. Frazer laid out a theory of all world mythology, from Japan to Kenya to Mexico—and even including modern European Christianity. In subsequent editions, Frazer revised and expanded his work; by the third edition, completed in 1915, *The Golden Bough* comprised a whopping twelve volumes and nearly five thousand pages. It was a monumental work, wherein Frazer outlined his theory of the origins and development of all religion and myth.

---

15. Frazer, *The Golden Bough*, 10–11.
16. Ovid, *Fasti*, 271–72.

Like Bachofen, Frazer was a flawed scholar. Contemporary anthropologists neither accept his methods nor his conclusions. Frazer had never interacted directly with the cultures he wrote about, and he had to rely on secondhand accounts; consequently, his information was filtered through other people's eyes, and he never knew about many of the relevant details of other cultures' customs and beliefs. In reaching for the universal, he often missed out on the particular, erasing many of the things that make each culture unique. Reading *The Golden Bough*, it is easy to believe that societies around the world all have the same mythology with the serial numbers buffed off, but if you take the care to study those societies more carefully, you'll find a wide range of beliefs, myths, and rituals that look nothing alike.

But like Bachofen, Frazer was incredibly influential, and his ideas overtook modern discourse about folklore and mythology. One hundred and forty years later, he is still taught in universities, if only for his historical significance and with a severely critical eye. The universal myth that Frazer invented has a deep appeal, and can easily be superimposed on stories from around the world. It also became the central structuring myth of modern Pagan Goddess worship.

Now, of course, I turn my attention to that myth.

Aphrodite, Ishtar, Cybele, Isis

Although Frazer drew examples from all over the world, he was particularly interested in the ancient Mystery cults of the Mediterranean and western Asia. It is no accident that this is the same geographic region Bachofen had examined in *Mother Right*; Frazer took Bachofen's theory of a Great Mother and expanded on it. In Frazer's version, the Great Mother was everywhere accompanied by a male consort, who was the embodiment of vegetation. The God was born annually during the planting season, grew until he reached maturity, and then died during the harvest when the crops were cut down. Thus, Frazer hypothesized, all of world mythology was a variation on a single core myth: the eternal Mother Goddess and her consort, the dying-and-resurrecting God.

As evidence for this universal myth, Frazer drew extensively on four historical myths, all from the Mediterranean. He claimed that "Under the names of Osiris, Tammuz, Adonis, and Attis, the peoples of Egypt and Western Asia represented the yearly decay and revival of life, especially of vegetable life, which they personified as a god who annually died and rose again from the dead."[17] Thus, to understand Frazer's new myth of the Mother Goddess, I want to look at four ancient myths: Aphrodite and Adonis, Ishtar and Tammuz, Cybele and Attis, and Isis and Osiris.

Aphrodite and Adonis

This myth comes from the Phoenician empire, particularly the cult centers of Paphos and Byblus, but Frazer drew on a version of the myth recorded by Apollodorus. According to the myth, there was once a princess in Cyprus named Myrrha, who tricked her father into incest. As punishment for her crime, the gods turned her into a myrrh tree, but she had already conceived a child, and a son sprang fully grown from the tree. His name was Adonis.

The story goes that the goddess Aphrodite, also known by the name Astarte, saw Adonis and immediately fell in love with him. Jealous of anyone else who might look upon him, she locked him in a chest and secreted him away to the underworld. She asked Persephone to guard the chest, not telling her what was inside—but Persephone opened the chest, saw the beautiful Adonis, and immediately fell in love with him as well. The two goddesses competed for Adonis's love, but neither could win his favor, so they asked Zeus to adjudicate. Zeus ruled that Adonis would spend part of the year in the underworld with Persephone, and part of the year in the world above with Aphrodite, eternally dying and being reborn in the love of the two goddesses. Eventually, Adonis was permanently killed in a hunting accident, when he was gored by a wild boar.[18]

In the worship of Aphrodite, there was an annual festival called the *Adonia*, where women would publicly mourn the death of Adonis. Frazer suggested that this seasonal festival was connected to the harvest, and that Adonis was the spirit of the crops; his death was the same as the death of the grain that was cut down.[19]

Frazer adds one more detail to his telling of the story, which is not present in Apollodorus's account. He mentions that in her attempts to persuade Persephone, the goddess Aphrodite personally descended into the underworld to plead her case and to beg that Adonis be returned to the domain of the living.[20] It was

---

17. Frazer, *The Golden Bough*, 301–2.

18. Apollodorus, *The Library, Volume II*, XIV.3-4.

19. Frazer, *The Golden Bough*, 331.

20. Frazer, *The Golden Bough*, 304.

only after this failed that she went to Zeus to demand his divine judgment. This legend of the descent of the goddess is particularly relevant for the parallel it allowed Frazer to draw to the second of his four key myths: the story of Ishtar and Tammuz.

Ishtar and Tammuz

The story of Ishtar and Tammuz comes from further east, in Akkadia. It, in turn, is derived from the Sumerian myth of Inanna and Dumuzi. In discussing this myth, I must offer an important caveat; since the writing of *The Golden Bough*, archaeological evidence has come to light that drastically changes scholars' understanding of the myth, and it's likely that the ancient Akkadians did not tell the story as Frazer recounted it. Tammuz was a shepherd beloved of the goddess Ishtar. In Frazer's interpretation of the story, Tammuz dies annually—it's not clear how—and his soul is taken to the underworld. Ishtar then descends into the underworld to retrieve him, pleading her case before the goddess Ereshkigal, the queen of the dead. Ereshkigal eventually relents, sprinkles Ishtar with the waters of life, and allows her to take Tammuz back to the world above.[21]

Frazer saw this myth as analogous to the story of Aphrodite and Adonis: The Goddess loves a mortal man, who dies and is kept prisoner in the underworld. She descends into the kingdom of the dead to plead her case with the queen of the underworld, and she succeeds in bringing her lover back to life, but only seasonally; eventually, he must die again. However, according to modern interpreters, Frazer got the myth totally backward. The best evidence currently suggests that in the myth of Ishtar and Tammuz, Ishtar *first* descends to the underworld to confront Ereshkigal for reasons that have nothing to do with Tammuz. She is allowed to return to the overworld only on the condition that she find someone to take her place in the land of the dead, and she sacrifices Tammuz, killing him so that she can live.[22] This puts rather a different spin on the myth.

Like Adonis, Tammuz was celebrated with seasonal festivals: one celebrating his marriage to Ishtar and one mourning his death. This latter festival was observed in the middle of summer; in the Mediterranean, summer is the harshest season of the

---

21. Frazer, *The Golden Bough*, 302.
22. Wolkstein and Kramer, *Inanna*, 71.

year.[23] Crops are harvested in the spring, at the end of the rainy season and before the withering heat of summer. This is in contrast to North America or northern Europe, where summer is a time of growth and the harsh season is the winter.

Cybele and Attis

There is yet another annual ritual to mourn the God in the myth of Cybele and Attis. Cybele was a deity originally from Phrygia, in modern-day Turkey, known as the mother of the gods. Her cult spread out across the Mediterranean and eventually took root in Rome, where she was known as *magna mater*, the Great Mother. In 205 BCE, during the second Punic War, the sibylline oracle predicted that any foreign invader would be driven away if the cult of *magna mater* were brought to Rome. A group of ambassadors were sent to Phrygia, and they brought the idol of Cybele back to Rome with them; subsequently, Rome won the war.[24]

According to one version of the myth, Cybele was originally the genderless deity Agdistis, with both male and female genitalia. The rest of the gods feared Agdistis's power, and so they castrated the genderless god, who became the goddess Cybele. On the spot where Agdistis's penis was discarded, an almond tree grew. A princess plucked the fruit from the almond tree and tucked it in between her breasts; immediately, she became pregnant. She gave birth to a son and named him Attis.

Much as in the story of Aphrodite and Adonis, Cybele fell in love with this man born from a tree. In some versions of the story, she made him her priest and demanded a vow of chastity from him; when he broke this vow, she drove him mad and he castrated himself. In other versions of the story, he was killed by a wild boar—again, in parallel to Adonis.[25] When Attis died, Cybele turned him into a fir tree so that he might live forever in another form. Frazer notes that in the Roman cult of Cybele, there was an annual festival in the spring where a fir tree was cut down, processed into the city, and mourned as the embodiment of slain Attis.[26]

---

23. Frazer, *The Golden Bough*, 341.

24. Livy, "History of Rome 29," X.5–XI.8.

25. Pausanias, *Description of Greece, Volume III*, VII.17.9–12.

26. Frazer, *The Golden Bough*, 348.

Isis and Osiris

Finally, I come to the myth of Isis and Osiris, which is probably the best known among modern Pagans and Goddess worshippers. This is another instance where several versions of the myth exist, but Frazer prefers the story as it is told by Plutarch. Osiris was the god-king of Egypt and the consort of Isis, who instructed early Egyptians in agriculture. His brother, Set, was jealous of Osiris's power, and so he tricked Osiris and locked him in a sarcophagus. Isis was already pregnant with Horus at this time, and she had to wander the earth searching for Osiris while she was with child.

Osiris's body had been cast into the river and had drifted to Byblus—one of the sanctuaries of Aphrodite and Adonis. After a series of travails, Isis found the body, which had grown into the trunk of a heather tree. Before she could resurrect it, Set dismembered it and scattered its pieces all over Egypt. Again, Isis went on a quest to recover his body, and she found all of the pieces except for his genitals, which had been eaten by the fish that live in the Nile. She fashioned a new penis for Osiris and resurrected him, and he was installed as the ruler of the kingdom of the dead. Later, an annual festival was celebrated in honor of the myth of Osiris's death and rebirth.[27]

Frazer writes that the myth of Isis and Osiris was explicitly syncretized with the myth of Aphrodite and Adonis in the ancient world because the rituals of the two cults were so similar. People who were initiated into the Mysteries of Osiris would attend the rites of Adonis and find the same mysteries expressed therein. In Frazer's mind, Isis was superior to all the other goddesses and was the culmination of ancient Goddess worship; he wrote that she "is rather late than primitive, the full-blown flower rather than the seed of a long religious development."[28]

Osiris was depicted with a shepherd's crook and a flail, the tool used to thresh grain; together, these linked the mystery of his death with the life cycles of both animals and crops. The death of Osiris was said to occur when the Nile began to flood every year, as the floodwaters were considered the tears of the mourning Isis. Thus again, Frazer connects the dying God with the sacrifice of the grain and the fertility of the land.

---

27. Plutarch, *Moralia, Volume V*, 12–18.
28. Frazer, *The Golden Bough*, 387.

A New Ancient Myth

From these stories, Frazer pieced together what he claimed was the prototypical myth of ancient religion. The Goddess as Aphrodite, Ishtar, Cybele, Isis, or others was eternal and immortal, the source of all life. However, in order to bring forth life, she needed a consort; the fertility of the earth could only be achieved through sexual congress. She "was a goddess of fertility in general, and of childbirth in particular. As such she…needed a male partner."[29] Thus, the Mother Goddess took a lover.

Where the Goddess was immortal, though, her consort was mortal. He may have been human, or he may have been a god, but either way, he was associated with plants and animals, and in many cases he was born out of or grew into a tree—as in the myths of Adonis, Attis, and Osiris. As such, he was the embodiment of the vegetation, which fertilized Mother Earth. Frazer wrote:

> We may conclude that a great Mother Goddess, the person-
> ification of all the reproductive energies of nature, was wor-
> shipped under different names but with a substantial similarity
> of myth and ritual by many peoples of Western Asia; [and]
> that associated with her was a lover, or rather series of lovers,
> divine yet mortal, with whom she mated year by year, their
> commerce being deemed essential to the propagation of ani-
> mals and plants.[30]

Because the crops died annually, so did the God as the spirit of vegetation, and his myth included a seasonal death and rebirth to mirror the cycles of harvesting and planting. Usually, this death was accompanied by a period of mourning on the part of the Goddess, where she would search for her lost love and even descend into the underworld to find him. Through her power, he was then reborn, and the cycle could begin anew.

Frazer explicitly linked seasonal festivals to the life cycle of the dying-and-resurrecting God, suggesting that agricultural holidays were ritual reenactments of the story of the Mother Goddess and her mortal lover. Likewise, he suggested, stories of the immortal Goddess and her dying consort were a seasonal allegory,

---

29. Frazer, *The Golden Bough*, 20.
30. Frazer, *The Golden Bough*, 314.

designed to explain the fertility and the eventual death of livestock, crops, and people. Thus, all of mythology derived from the mystery of sexual union and its creative powers. The Goddess, in all her various aspects, was eternal life; the God was death and rebirth. When they joined in an act of sacred sex, the world became fertile.

Sexuality was key to Frazer's view of the Mother Goddess. Deities like Aphrodite and Ishtar were explicitly linked with love and sex, and Frazer referred to historical accounts suggesting that the cults of these goddesses often featured orgiastic displays of sex. In some temples of the Goddess, he claimed, priestesses were employed as sacred prostitutes.[31] Any man could come to the temple and couple with one of the priestesses as an act of sacred devotion to the Goddess. Moreover, during this sex act, the participants were understood to become the Gods incarnate. The act of sacred prostitution was not a priestess sleeping with an ordinary man; it was the Goddess herself, ritually possessing the priestess and making love to her consort who ritually possessed the man.

Frazer hypothesized that this sacred marriage between the Goddess and the dying-and-resurrecting God was the basis of ancient kingship. Following Bachofen's ideas about matriarchy, Frazer suggested that the divine right to rule was matrilineal in ancient society; the king did not rule in his own right, but merely because he was married to the queen, who was the embodiment of the Goddess herself.

Moreover, the right to rule was only bestowed upon him because his marriage to the Goddess was seen to ensure fruitfulness in livestock and crops: "the Semitic king was allowed, or rather required, to personate the god and marry the goddess, [and] the intention of the custom can only have been to ensure the fertility of the land."[32] As the king, he embodied the divine consort, and may even have been believed to have a magical connection to the weather and the crops—but his rule was understood to be temporary and transient, because only the Goddess was eternal. It was for this reason, Frazer suggested, that the priests of Diana in Aricia were murdered by their successors. As consorts of the Goddess, they were cut down in imitation of the dying God they represented.

There's a great deal more going on in *The Golden Bough* than what I've discussed here—remember, the expanded edition of the book is almost five *thousand*

---

31. Frazer, *The Golden Bough*, 312.
32. Frazer, *The Golden Bough*, 308.

pages—but these are the key points relevant to modern Goddess worship. Frazer synthesized pieces of various myths from the ancient world and turned them into a new, cohesive myth of the Great Goddess. The Goddess of Bachofen's matriarchy had distinct features but threadbare mythology; here, that is remedied with the creation of a robust myth and accompanying ritual. As with Bachofen, remember that Frazer's scholarship is flawed; his myth of the Great Goddess and the dying-and-resurrecting God is not as ancient and universal as he claimed, but is the product of a specific lens of nineteenth-century interpretation of ancient sources. Nonetheless, this new myth was sweeping and grand, and it has become the skeleton for much of the modern mythology of the Goddess.

——— EXERCISE ———
An Herb Garden

One of the best ways to connect to the myth of the Goddess and her vegetative consort is to plant and grow food of your own. If you're like me and you have a gray thumb, this may sound daunting; just about every houseplant I've ever tried to grow has quickly given up on life. Nonetheless, it's worth giving this a try. In the twenty-first century, many people get all of their food from the supermarket rather than growing it themselves. This can lead to a disconnect from the cycles of the earth, and from the sacred experience of growing and harvesting food. I can talk myself blue in the face about the myth of the Goddess symbolizing fertility for the land, but actually experiencing the fertility of the land is something else entirely.

There are several varieties of common kitchen herb that are beginner-friendly and easy to grow at home. Yes, *actually* easy—not easy the way that gardeners say things are easy. These include parsley, basil, mint, thyme, and common sage. For this exercise, you'll be using mint. You'll need:

- A clay pot with good drainage, approximately 10 inches deep
- Enough potting soil to fill the pot
- A package of mint seeds
- A spot indoors that gets decent natural sunlight
- A spray bottle (optional)

Fill the pot with soil. You don't need to add any fertilizer or use a particular fancy soil; regular potting soil is fine. Moisten the soil with a little bit of water. Once the pot is prepared, take a moment to place your hands around it. Hold it, lift it, feel the weight of the pot and the soil it contains. Stick a finger into the soil and feel its texture. Lift it up to your face and smell it, inhaling the rich, earthy scent. Establish your connection with the earth. Say:

> Great Mother, bless this earth and allow it to be fruitful. May it
> bring forth life in your name.

Now, spread your mint seeds over the surface of the soil. Do *not* bury them; they need exposure to sunlight in order to start germinating. If you can, leave a couple inches of space in between the seeds, so that the plants will have room to grow as they mature. Scatter a light dusting of potting soil over the top of the seeds. Say:

> King of vegetation, beloved of the Great Mother, bless this seed and
> allow it to grow. May it bring forth life in your name.

Put the pot in a place where it will get some direct sunlight. If you really want to, you can buy an artificial sun lamp, but that's not really necessary for your purposes here. As long as the mint gets a little bit of sun, it'll be fine, even if it spends a lot of the day in shade.

Leave the pot there and water it every few days, when the soil begins to feel dry. After about ten days, you should start to see some plants germinating. Keep watering them regularly, and turn the pot occasionally so that it gets even sunlight on all sides. If you like, you can use a spray bottle to mist the plants and provide some extra humidity, but that's optional and the mint will grow just fine without it. Your mint plants will be fully mature after about seventy days, but you can start harvesting leaves as soon as they're fully formed.

Whenever you cut leaves from your mint plant, treat the harvest as a solemn affair. Remember, you're killing a god! It may sound silly, but treat this act as seriously as you would treat the death of a person. Tell the plant you are sorry for its loss. Act out the ritual drama of grief as much as you feel comfortable; you may even want to go so far as to wail and sob. Try to work yourself, as much as possible, into seeing this mint plant as a real, living person who has been cut down in his prime. This is the power and the tragedy of Frazer's agricultural myth. When you have finished harvesting your crop of leaves, say:

> *King of vegetation, beloved of the Great Mother, thou art slain.*
> *You have died so that I may live. I thank you for your sacrifice.*
> *It is the promise of the Goddess that you shall live again.*

Do this every time you cut leaves from the plant, to honor the dying God of vegetation. Once you have cut your mint leaves, you can use them in cooking, or dry them and store them for later. As an added bonus, if you practice magic, you can use your freshly grown mint for spellwork or to make incense.

The Laws of Magic

Frazer was a social Darwinist, and he was writing with a particular agenda in mind. He wanted to show a linear progression of human religious thought, from the most "primitive" to the most sophisticated. Part of the project of *The Golden Bough* is a pseudo-historical narrative, charting out Frazer's theory of how religion first emerged and progressed from raw superstition to paganism and eventually to Christianity. Frazer himself was an atheist and believed that society should move past Christianity and into secularism; hiding in the background of *The Golden Bough* is a subtle attempt to undermine Christianity by suggesting that the figure of Christ is just a holdover from the pagan myth of the dying-and-resurrecting God. Frazer saw Christianity as vulgar and primitive, and he believed that by drawing connections between Christian practices and pagan ones, he could discredit the former and make Christianity a thing of the past.

To this day, you'll find memes circulating on Facebook saying that Easter is just a rebranded holiday of Ishtar, that Christmas was originally the Roman festival of Saturnalia, or that Christmas trees are an ancient pagan practice honoring the God of vegetation. These ideas come directly from Frazer. The historical claims are not accurate—Christmas trees, for example, originated in Germany in the Middle Ages, and have nothing to do with ancient tree gods—but Frazer's rebranding of the history of religion has had a lasting impact on popular discourse.[33]

One fascinating aspect of Frazer's story about the development of religion is his theory of magic. Frazer saw magic as a precursor to religion, something that

---

33. Waxman, "How Christmas Trees Became a Holiday Tradition."

emerged in early human society when people were still trying to figure out how they related to the world around them. He imagined that in the early days of human society, people would have tried to use magic to control the weather, the seasons, disease, the life cycles of crops and animals, human fertility, and even death. Only after these magical acts proved ineffective would humans start to conceive of a power greater than themselves—and it was at this stage that the prototypical myth of the Mother Goddess and the dying God would have emerged.

Frazer laid out a theory of magic as a strict mechanistic process with well-defined rules. He was one of the first modern scholars to treat magic seriously as a field of study, and his theory of how magic worked—or rather, how "savage" people would have thought it worked—is still influential to this day. He identified the operating principle of magic as the *Law of Sympathy*: that if two things are connected in some way, then whatever happens to one of them will affect the other. Magic of this sort was called *sympathetic magic*, a term that's still used in magical communities. Under the umbrella of sympathetic magic, Frazer identified two different magical laws.

The first is the *Law of Similarity*: whatever is like a thing *is* that thing. As Frazer puts it, this is the idea that "like produces like, or that an effect resembles its cause."[34] If any two things resemble each other, there is a basic affinity between them. This affinity can be leveraged for the purpose of magic. If I want to affect someone or something, all I need is something that resembles them in some way: a photograph, a doll dressed to look like them, a candle with their name written on it, and so on. Then, symbolically, whatever I do to that object affects the person as well. Frazer calls this kind of magic *homeopathic magic*.

The second law of magic is the *Law of Contact*: "that things which have once been in contact with each other continue to act on each other at a distance after the physical contact has been severed."[35] Once again, the principle relies on a basic affinity between two objects. This time, it's not an affinity based on resemblance, but rather based on their having been in contact with each other. To affect someone with the law of contact, I would need something that had been on or near them: a piece of jewelry they owned, a lock of their hair, a legal document with their signature on it, or something of the sort. All of these things, by virtue

---

34. Frazer, *The Golden Bough*, 26.

35. Frazer, *The Golden Bough*, 26.

of having been in contact with the person, retain some of that person's essence. Therefore, symbolically, I can act on those things and the action will extend to affect the person. This kind of magic is called *contagious magic*.

Frazer surely never intended for modern people to read his book and use it as a guide for how to practice magic. He saw magic as a thing of the past, and he wanted *The Golden Bough* to move society away from magic and religion, not toward them. Nonetheless, a funny thing happened. The book took on a life of its own, and many people reading it were inspired by Frazer's vision of a magical and pagan history. *The Golden Bough* not only inspired atheists and secularists, it also became a guidebook for people looking to rediscover the enchanted past. Frazer's sexual and agricultural mystery of the Goddess and her consort became the foundational myth of a new Pagan revival.

What's more, his theory of magic got folded into that revival, so the new Paganism was populated with people who believed in and practiced sympathetic magic. Frazer's magical laws of sympathy, similarity, and contact allowed this movement to blossom into a magical renaissance as well as a religious one. Thus, the worship of the Goddess in the modern mind became inextricably intertwined with magic and spellcraft. From Frazer forward, the worship of the Goddess would be seen as a fundamentally, inexorably magical religion.

Key Takeaways: Frazer

+ Identification of the Goddess with Aphrodite, Ishtar, Cybele, and Isis

+ Dying-and-resurrecting God as consort to the immortal Goddess

+ Myth of the Goddess tied to agricultural cycles and festivals

+ Sacred sexuality as a key feature of the Goddess cult

+ Formalizing the laws of sympathetic magic and linking magic to Goddess worship

—— RITUAL ——
The King of the Wood

This ritual takes its inspiration from the priesthood of Diana in Aricia and the myth of the king of the wood. It shows life and death as complementary aspects of the Goddess's nature, and it emphasizes that you cannot know one of her gifts without also meeting the other. In the rite, you will install a sacred king as the priest of Diana, defeat him in combat, and pluck the golden bough that signifies the transfer of sacred kingship to someone new.

Group Variation

This version of the rite is a ritual drama where you reenact the myth of the immortal Goddess and her mortal lover, who dies in her service and is symbolically resurrected when another takes his crown. The roles of Diana, the king, and the challengers are all played by participants in the ritual.

You Will Need

+ A small tree or something that looks like it. If you are performing the ritual outdoors, you can use an actual tree; if you are indoors, a plastic Christmas tree works well
+ A wooden dowel, approximately 8 to 10 inches long, that has been spray-painted gold
+ Two quarterstaves
+ A crown

Preparation

Assign ritual roles to the participants. You'll need one person to play Diana, one for the king of the wood, and two challengers. Any additional attendees will have the opportunity to participate in the ritual, but will have no scripted lines. Situate the tree at the edge of your ritual space. Place the spray-painted stick on or in the tree, and secure it with tape or string if necessary; it should be secure enough that it won't fall off, but loose enough that someone could pull it away easily.

Performance

At the start of the ritual, the king of the wood stands in front of the tree, holding the two quarterstaves. Diana stands in the center of the ritual space, holding the crown, and everyone else is arranged around the edge of the space. Diana addresses all participants:

> DIANA: I am the earth from which the forests grow. I am the cave where wild beasts take shelter. I am the mother who gives all life. Who will stand and be my lover?
>
> KING: I will.

The king of the wood takes a step toward her to volunteer himself. She then asks him a series of questions, and as he answers each one, he takes another step toward her:

> DIANA: To be loved by me is no easy thing. Will you guard the gate of my shrine?
>
> KING: I will guard it with my life.
>
> DIANA: Will you keep watch without rest or reprieve?
>
> KING: I will keep watch by night and by day.
>
> DIANA: And will you accept the embrace of death?
>
> KING: I will gladly die if to die is to love you.
>
> DIANA: Then embrace me and know your fate.

They kiss. This can be a kiss on the lips, on the cheek, on the forehead, or elsewhere, depending on the personal comfort of the ritual participants. Diana places the crown on the king's head and directs him back to the tree:

> DIANA: Upon that tree is a golden bough sacred to my name. Take heed, for the day another plucks the golden bough shall be the day of your death. Guard it well in honor of me.

He goes to the tree and turns to face the rest of the participants. Diana raises her hands and proclaims the contest for his crown:

DIANA: The gift of life is the gift of death. All that is born must die. All that grows must wither. Only I am eternal. Therefore, I say: Who dares to step forward and claim the crown of the king of the wood? Who shall slay my love and take his place?

The first of the two preselected combatants steps forward toward Diana, and she greets them with a kiss. The combatant turns to the king of the wood, who gives them one of the two quarterstaves. The two engage in mock combat with the staves, parrying back and forth as they move around the ritual space. Other participants in the ritual should feel free to cheer, boo, or applaud during the combat; this will help keep them engaged and prevent anyone's attention from wandering. Alternatively, at this point the ritual participants may take up a simple chant to set the tone for the combat.

After the combat has gone on long enough to be interesting, the king of the wood strikes the challenger on the chest. The challenger falls, and the king picks up both quarterstaves and returns to the sacred tree. Diana makes her plea once again:

DIANA: I ask a second time. Who shall slay my love and take his place?

The second predetermined combatant steps forward, greets Diana with a kiss, takes a quarterstaff, and engages the king of the wood in combat. Again, they fight for a while, but the king of the wood eventually strikes the challenger on the chest and they fall. The king collects their quarterstaff and returns to the tree. Diana makes her plea a third time:

DIANA: Can no one slay the king of the wood? All of you, I beg you! Who can step forward and take the king's crown?

At this point, any remaining participants who wish to take a more active part in the ritual may step forward. Diana selects one of them, greets that person with a kiss, and passes them off to the king of the wood. They engage in combat again, but this time, there is no predetermined winner. The king and the challenger face off, and whoever can strike the other on the chest first is the victor. If the king wins, he collects the quarterstaff and faces the next challenger—and the next, and the next, as need be.

The king should take care not to defeat *everyone*. If it comes down to the last challenger and the king is still standing, he should make a point to lose his last battle. Likewise, if there are no participants in the ritual other than Diana, the king, and the two initial challengers, then the king should lose his fight with the second combatant.

When the king finally falls, everyone should cheer and applaud. Diana walks over to kneel beside his fallen body. She kisses him and takes his crown, saying:

> DIANA: You served me well, my king, and now your task is done. Go peacefully and know death, as was promised to you.

She stands, takes the hand of the victorious challenger, and leads them over to the sacred tree, motioning for them to pluck the golden bough. When they have done so, she places the crown on their head and offers them a kiss. She turns to the rest of the participants and proclaims the installation of the new king:

> DIANA: Repeat after me: The king is dead! Long live the king!

> ALL: The king is dead! Long live the king!

Everyone continues to chant "Long live the king!" until Diana signals for them to stop. The rite is ended.

Solitary Variation

In this version of the ritual, you take on the role of the challenger who wishes to claim the title of King of the Wood. Rather than fighting against another person, you personify your rival in a coat rack and participate in a symbolic battle for the love of Diana.

You Will Need

- A small tree or something that looks like it. If you are performing the ritual outdoors, you can use an actual tree; if you are indoors, a plastic Christmas tree works well
- A wooden dowel, approximately 8 to 10 inches long, that has been spray-painted gold
- A freestanding coat rack
- A quarterstaff
- A crown

Preparation

Situate the tree at the edge of your ritual space. Place the spray-painted stick on or in the tree, and secure it with tape or string if necessary; it should be secure enough that it won't fall off, but loose enough that you can pull it away easily. Put the coat rack directly in front of the tree, and set the quarterstaff and the crown on the ground next to it.

Performance

At the start of the ritual, stand with the coat rack between you and the tree. Take the crown in your hands and lift it high, saying:

> *Diana is the earth from which the forests grow. She is the cave where wild beasts take shelter. She is the mother who gives all life. Let the king of the wood stand and be her lover!*

Step forward and hang the crown from the top of the coat rack. Say:

> *To be loved by the Goddess is no easy thing. The king shall guard the gate of her shrine with his life. He shall keep watch by night and by day. He will accept the embrace of death, for to die is to know the Goddess in her love. Thus the king of the wood is crowned!*

Step back and pick up your quarterstaff. Thump the staff onto the ground repeatedly, establishing a slow, steady rhythm. Move past the coat rack to the tree, then walk in a circle three times around the edge of your ritual space. The whole time, keep beating the earth with your staff and chant:

> *The king of the wood is crowned! The king of the wood is crowned!*

When you have finished your procession, come back to stand in front of the coat rack. Lifting your staff, point behind the coat rack at the golden dowel in the tree. Say:

> *The gift of life is the gift of death. All that is born must die. Therefore, I come to challenge thee for thy crown. Take heed, o king, for upon that tree is a golden bough sacred to the name of Diana, and the day another plucks the golden bough shall be the day of your death.*

Bring the quarterstaff down in front of you and settle into a mock combat stance. Pretend to fight with the coat rack, stepping in, feinting, stepping back, and making small strikes with your staff. You may feel silly doing this, but it is important to treat it as a serious affair. You are engaged in mortal combat with an enemy, competing for the love of the Goddess. Keep up the play fight until you are winded and exhaustion is starting to creep in. Then, with a dramatic final blow, knock the coat rack over completely. Drop your quarterstaff and say:

> *You have served the Goddess well, king, and now your task is done.*
> *Go peacefully and know death, as was promised to you.*

Walk over to the sacred tree and pluck the golden bough. Then, return to the fallen coat rack, pick up the crown, and place it on your own head. End the ritual by proclaiming:

> *The king is dead! Long live the king!*

3

DIANA, QUEEN OF
THE WITCHES (1899)

IN MY TEEN YEARS, I dabbled in spellcasting, but I was never terribly serious about it. I'd been raised by skeptics, and magic was a big pill to swallow. I felt drawn to ritual and religion, but I clothed it all in a detached, rationalistic respectability; in those early days, I denied believing in the Goddess if anyone asked me, but I talked eagerly about the importance of Pagan deities as archetypes, symbols, and expressions of the collective unconscious. This is an attitude taken by many people in Goddess religions, although my own theology has since trended more toward literal belief. One of the hallmarks of modern Goddess worship is the diversity of theological perspectives: there is no one right way to approach or understand the Goddess.

Because I originally had a psychological, nonliteral view of the Goddess, and I was still clinging to the vestiges of atheism from my childhood, I was not sold on magic and spellcraft. These things, though often presented as a fundamental part of Goddess religion, felt a little too woo-woo for my tastes. In those early years, I would occasionally toy around with the idea of casting spells, but my heart was never in it. I was interested in the religion of the Goddess, but not in the magic that frequently accompanied it.

The turning point came when I was in college. I was a young gay man, still largely in the closet, and I'd been flirting with someone who turned nasty and aggressive. I'd tried to take a step back, but he began to stalk and threaten me. I blocked his phone number, and he created a series of fake numbers with which to keep harassing me. I began to fear for my safety.

With my back up against the wall, unsure where to turn or what to do, I resorted to a course of action I had never tried in earnest before. I decided to cast a spell.

I didn't have much time to think my spell out and plan something elaborate, so I did what felt right. I went to the grocery store and bought a carton of eggs. Coming home, I set up a small altar in my living room and laid an egg on it, then consecrated my space with incense and blessed water. I invited the Goddess to join me, and I asked her for her protection:

> Most gracious Goddess, hear my plea! Safeguard me from the man
> who threatens me. Draw his attentions away from me; let me be
> absent from his mind. Where he would seek me, let him not find
> me. Where he would harm me, let his actions pass me by. Goddess,
> I ask this of you!

I held the egg to my forehead and focused on displacing this man's harmful intentions—so that any ill will he had for me would be diverted to the egg instead. As I did so, I felt a tingling rush up my body, from my feet through my torso and up to my forehead, rushing into the egg. Power flooded from the earth to fuel my spell, and I felt magic.

When I was done, I took the egg to a remote spot and buried it. I placed it into the earth and proclaimed:

> As this egg rots, let his thoughts of me decay. May I be forgotten
> from his mind and absent from his attentions. In the name of the
> Goddess, so mote it be!

I turned and walked away without looking back.

I never heard from him again after that night. He never texted or called, the threats stopped completely, and my life went back to normal. I had cast a spell in a moment of need, and it had worked without qualification. I was safe. What's more, I had opened myself up to an aspect of Goddess worship that had previously been closed to me. I had already been Pagan, interested in the religion and ritual of the Goddess, but that night, I embraced her magic as well. That night, I became a witch.

Witches in Tuscany

In 1899, the American folklorist Charles Godfrey Leland published an unusual and controversial book. He claimed to have discovered a group of pagan witches surviving in Tuscany. In his travels, he had met a woman named Maddalena who belonged to this group. She was unable to introduce him to other witches, nor to bring him to witch rituals, but she managed to collect the witches' body of oral and written lore in a single document, which she passed along to him before breaking off all contact. These witches worshipped Diana, the goddess of the moon. They met on full moons to praise her, to feast, and to cast spells together. Leland purported to have published the sacred lore of the witches, given to him by Maddalena, under the title *Aradia, the Gospel of the Witches*.

The authenticity of the *Gospel of the Witches* was, and remains, highly contested. Some people believe that it's genuine, and that there was in fact a cult of witches worshipping Diana in Tuscany at the end of the nineteenth century. Other people believe that Leland made it all up, that there were no witches and no such person as Maddalena. Still others take a view somewhere in the middle: that Maddalena existed but she was lying to Leland about the witches, or that the *Gospel of the Witches* contained some genuine elements of Italian folk witchcraft mixed in with exaggerations and embellishments.

Among those who believe in the authenticity of the cult laid out in the *Gospel* is Italian historian Carlo Ginzburg. In his 1966 book *The Night Battles*, Ginzburg discussed the *benandanti*, a group of "good witches" who were alleged to operate in Italy toward the end of the medieval period, going on psychic journeys, feasting, and doing battle with evil witches. As part of his study, Ginzburg identified the cult of the *benandanti* with the worship of a Goddess, who was variously known as Perchta, Satia, Abundia, or Diana.[36] Among the skeptics is professor Ronald Hutton, an academic historian studying modern Paganism, witchcraft, and ancient paganism in the British Isles. Hutton notes the historical testimony claiming that witches met in Sabbats led by a woman or goddess, but he dismisses this testimony as folklore rather than historical fact. He maintains that "there is no evidence that groups of people met to adore the Devil, and plan evil, in late medieval and early modern Europe, with or without including figures like Diana."[37] In short, he argues, people talked about witches and witch meetings

---

36. Ginzburg, *The Night Battles*, 42.
37. Hutton, *The Triumph of the Moon*, 151.

constantly, but there is no substantial evidence that these meetings took place in actuality and not merely in the imaginations and stories of ordinary people.

Personally, I confess to being skeptical of the *Gospel*'s origins. There has been no corroborating evidence to support Leland's account, and if there ever was a cult of moon-worshipping Italian witches, they haven't made themselves known before or since. The truth of the matter is, though, that there is no way to verify whether the *Gospel* is or is not what it claims to be. Everyone has their own opinion, but no one will ever be able to know for sure. Additionally, as I've endeavored to show throughout the previous chapters, something does not have to have an ancient provenance in order to be real, legitimate, and powerful. Even if the most hard-line skeptics are right and the *Gospel* is a total fabrication, Leland connected to something larger than himself. Regardless of whether witches were worshipping Diana before the *Gospel*'s publication, it has been an inspiration for thousands of witches and Goddess worshippers since.

Diana, Lucifer, and Aradia

The *Gospel* includes several myths about the goddess Diana, but the chief one is the story of Diana and her brother Lucifer. Diana, the moon goddess, fell in love with Lucifer, the sun god. Although he shares a name with the Christian devil, this Lucifer is far from diabolical. He is, rather, a shining and resplendent solar deity who complements Diana as her other half. She is darkness, night, and the moon; he is light, day, and the sun. This dichotomy between the natures of the Goddess and the God should be familiar from Bachofen, who had written that "in matriarchy the night has primacy, bearing the day from within itself, as the mother bears the son."[38] Diana is described as the primordial darkness at the beginning of all creation, and Lucifer the God of light is born from that darkness: "Diana was the first created before all creation; in her were all things; out of herself, the first darkness, she divided herself; into darkness and light she was divided. Lucifer, her brother and son, herself and her other half, was the light."[39] Some commentators have noted that the role of Lucifer in the *Gospel* is more

---

38. Bachofen, *Myth, Religion, and Mother Right*, 148.
39. Leland, *Aradia*, 21.

akin to Diana's brother in Roman mythology, the sun god Apollo, than to the Christian figure of Lucifer.[40]

The story goes that Lucifer was so beautiful that Diana fell in love with him. She pursued him across the sky, just as the moon chases the sun, "wishing to receive the light again into her darkness, to swallow it up in rapture."[41] This language is, of course, sexual—receiving Lucifer into her darkness is a thin euphemism for sexual penetration—but it also has allegorical significance beyond that. The story of Diana's love for Lucifer expresses the relationship between two opposing natural forces: darkness and light; night and day. Night always follows day, and darkness envelops light. On this reading, darkness should be understood not to be something sinister or evil, but simply primordial. It is the darkness of the womb, or of the tomb; it both precedes and follows the light of human life.

Lucifer, however, fled from Diana's advances, and she decided to resort to deception. Lucifer had a pet cat, which slept on his bed every night. Diana changed her shape, disguising herself as this cat, and waited in Lucifer's bed. When he came to bed, she transformed back into herself and seduced him. Thus, the goddess of the moon and the god of the sun were conjoined, and "light had been conquered by darkness."[42]

It ought to go without saying that the myth of Diana and Lucifer should be in no way a model for human behavior, but I will say it anyway. Mythology expresses itself in symbolic, abstract terms, where the actions of individual figures give voice to some deeper mystery—often about the natural world. In this case, Diana's pursuit and conquest of Lucifer tells a metaphorical story about the cycles of the universe, how day must always yield to night and life must always yield to death. As the *Gospel* notes, "She spun the lives of all men; all things were spun from the wheel of *Diana*. Lucifer turned the wheel."[43] This is a very Frazerian myth of the relationship between the Goddess and the God, with her as the eternal spinning wheel of fate and him as the conquered force of light that spins the wheel. When the relationship between Diana and Lucifer is consummated,

---

40. Spencer, *Aradia*, 13.

41. Leland, *Aradia*, 21.

42. Leland, *Aradia*, 22.

43. Leland, *Aradia*, 22.

Lucifer's power is overtaken because the God is only ever a temporary, mortal consort to the immortal and eternal Goddess.

However, in human terms, Diana's treatment of Lucifer is straightforward sexual assault, and it is a morally horrific act. You can and should be outraged by the assault. Moreover, you can feel that outrage and still understand the transcendent symbolism of the myth. It is simultaneously true that some of the things done in mythology are morally unjustifiable, and that a myth is a symbolic narrative with a deeper meaning than the surface-level actions it recounts. When discussing the myth of Diana and Lucifer, there is room for both layers of understanding.

After consummating her relationship with Lucifer, Diana became pregnant and gave birth to a daughter, whom she named Aradia. The story goes that there came a time in Italy when there was such pervasive injustice among humans that Diana decided she couldn't abide it any longer. She sent Aradia down to earth to liberate the oppressed by teaching them the art of witchcraft:

> 'Tis true indeed that thou a spirit art,
> But thou wert born but to become again
> A mortal; thou must go to earth below
> To be a teacher unto women and men
> Who fain would study witchcraft in thy school.[44]

Aradia came to earth as a messianic figure, lifting up the poor and oppressed, instructing them in magic, and teaching them to worship her mother, Diana. She was the first of all witches, and—according to the *Gospel*—it was through her instruction that the cult of Diana came into existence.

Witchcraft and Revolution

The Gospel of the Witches features one aspect of the modern Goddess that was not seen in Bachofen or in Frazer: Diana is described as a patroness of witches. *Witch* is a powerful word. Witchcraft is not merely magic or spellcasting; it is not the same as the magic of the shaman, the druid, or the temple priest. A witch is someone subversive, dangerous, and frightening. Witches live at the edge of society, untethered from social norms and expectations. In folklore, witches are pow-

---

44. Leland, *Aradia*, 4.

erful women, either exceptionally beautiful or hideously ugly. They can bless or curse the crops, cause enemies to fall in love with each other, render men impotent, and even strike people dead where they stand. The undercurrent of folkloric witchcraft is that it is subversive: witches give power to the powerless or take it away from the powerful, overturning the status quo. A witch's magic may be helpful or harmful, depending on how it is directed, but it is always dangerous.

This attitude toward witchcraft works its way into the *Gospel*. Aradia is sent to earth not only to teach people how to use magic, but also as a political revolutionary. Her goal is to make witches out of the peasants so that they can overthrow their masters. Diana instructs her daughter:

> And thou shalt be the first of witches known;
> And thou shalt be the first of all i' the world;
> And thou shalt teach the art of poisoning,
> Of poisoning those who are great lords of all;
> Yea, thou shalt make them die in their palaces;
> And thou shalt bind the oppressor's soul with power;
> And when ye find a peasant who is rich,
> Then shall ye teach the witch, your pupil, how
> To ruin all his crops with tempests dire,
> With lightning and with thunder terrible,
> And the hail and wind.[45]

The Goddess of witches is not only a deity of magic; she is also fundamentally, inexorably a deity of political revolution. Aradia does not only teach the art of magic. She teaches poisoning, the binding of souls, how to raise tempests and ruin crops—and she directs her witches to use all of these things to overthrow their oppressors. Many of the spells given in *The Gospel of the Witches* are charms to curse or coerce one's enemies. Witchcraft explicitly identifies itself with the poor and the downtrodden, and—at least as it appears in the *Gospel*—it encourages those people to use any means necessary to get a leg up on the people doing them harm.

The rhetoric of the *Gospel* is quite unabashed about encouraging violence and insurrection toward the wealthy and politically corrupt, something which may

---

45. Leland, *Aradia*, 4–5.

be shocking and unsettling to modern sensibilities. Aradia instructs her witches to practice their craft "until the last of your oppressors shall be dead."[46] In today's society, where we often try to focus on nonviolent solutions to conflicts, this can seem extreme, and it may be off-putting for some modern readers. Likewise, some modern practitioners of witchcraft eschew the practice of cursing, choosing to avoid baneful or violent magic; these practitioners may not recognize themselves in the witchcraft taught by Aradia. Nonetheless, it is important to understand that the witchcraft given in Leland's *Gospel* is not nice. It has teeth.

This is a deviation from depictions of the Goddess that Bachofen and Frazer offered. For Bachofen, the Goddess was an essentially peaceful figure, because he considered violence and war to be masculine qualities unbefitting of a female deity. There certainly were violent or warlike goddesses in the ancient world, such as Sekhmet or the Morrigan, but the nineteenth-century imagination tended to focus much more on loving, compassionate mother goddesses. Frazer and Bachofen narrowed their study of goddesses to a particular set who matched their preconceptions about what a goddess should be. Here, with Diana, something a bit darker and more intimidating is reintroduced. The Diana of the *Gospel* is not afraid of violence, and is willing to take—or encourage—extreme measures to achieve justice for her people. With *The Gospel of the Witches*, the forced, stereotyped femininity of the Goddess starts to peel away, revealing a much more complex and nuanced personality.

In order to help the witches throw off their shackles, Diana bestows eleven powers upon them. These are the core magical abilities of the witch as envisaged by the *Gospel*. According to Leland's text, witches who worship Diana can:

+ Bless their friends and curse their enemies.
+ Speak to spirits.
+ Find lost treasures.
+ Summon and speak with the ghosts of dead priests who know where treasure is located.
+ Speak with the wind and understand it in turn.
+ Transform water into wine.

---

46. Leland, *Aradia*, 7.

+ Use playing cards to tell the future.

+ Use palmistry to read a person's fate.

+ Heal sickness.

+ Bestow beauty and glamor.

+ Tame animals.[47]

Some of these items are on the fantastical side; I've never met a single person who could turn water into wine without first mixing it with grape juice and fermenting it, and the power to speak with the ghosts of priests and find the location of buried treasure has always struck me as oddly specific. However, considering the context of witchcraft as a religion for the impoverished, the preoccupation with finding treasure makes a certain amount of sense—as does the conjuration of priests, given the wealth and corruption of the Church in medieval Italy.

For the most part, though, these are practices that are still employed by modern witches today. People who call themselves witches will use magic to heal illnesses, tell the future, draw prosperity, or make themselves more attractive to potential lovers. Some communicate with spirits or have a particular affinity with animals. If you were looking to become a witch today, the powers of Aradia would be an excellent guide to the kind of skills you would want to develop.

Aradia instructs the witches to worship the goddess Diana as the source of their power and their liberation alike. She charges them:

> Whenever ye have need of anything,
> Once in the month, and when the moon is full,
> Ye shall assemble in some desert place,
> Or in a forest all together join
> To adore the potent spirit of your queen,
> My mother, great Diana. She who fain
> Would learn all sorcery yet has not won
> Its deepest secrets, them my mother will
> Teach her, in truth all things as yet unknown.
> And ye shall be freed from slavery,
> And so ye shall be free in everything;

---

47. Leland, *Aradia*, 17.

> And as the sign that ye are truly free,
> Ye shall be naked in your rites, both men
> And women also: this shall last until
> The last of your oppressors shall be dead.[48]

This offers get a few important details about the worship of Diana. First, as I have already mentioned, is the connection with revolution and the overthrow of those in power. Second, she is worshipped specifically on the night of the full moon. Although the Goddess had been associated with the moon by previous authors, this monthly ritual observance is something new, in contrast with the seasonal ritual calendar outlined by Frazer. The idea that the full moon is a night sacred to the Goddess, and is the best night to worship her, would carry forward into the modern Goddess movement. So, too, would the idea of ritual nudity. Some strands of modern Paganism perform their rituals in the nude for exactly the reasons outlined in the *Gospel*: as a sign of freedom and liberation. The practice of ritual nudity, sometimes known as working *skyclad*, also links into the celebration of the body as something sacred and holy, rather than shameful and sinful; the sacred body was associated with the Goddess as far back as Bachofen. Not all Pagans or Goddess worshippers practice ritual nudity, but for those who do, it is a powerful and liberating experience.

The association of the Goddess with witchcraft and political activism has likewise had a lasting effect. As I will show in subsequent chapters, many modern Pagan movements of the twentieth century identified themselves explicitly with witchcraft, tying together the practice of magic with the worship of the lunar Mother Goddess. Moreover, some of these movements—especially the Goddess feminism movement that found voice starting in the 1970s—concerned themselves with political activism as well as religious observance. The worship of the Goddess was seen by some as inextricably linked with political issues like feminist liberation, environmentalism, or socialism. This religious activism has at least partial roots in *The Gospel of the Witches*.

---

48. Leland, *Aradia*, 7.

——— Exercise ———
The Lemon and the Pins

This is a spell taken directly from *The Gospel of the Witches*. There are two variations given: a spell for good luck, which uses multicolored pins, and a curse, which uses black pins. All of the incantations here are the original words from the *Gospel*, with some abridgments and added stage directions on my part. You will need:

+ A lemon or access to a lemon tree
+ Thirteen pins with multicolored heads for the blessing or black heads for the curse
+ 8 ounces of red wine for the curse
+ A heatproof cup for the curse
+ A stovetop and saucepan for the curse

I'll start with the spell for blessing, which is quite simple. At midnight, go to the garden or orchard where your lemon tree is located and pluck a lemon from the tree. If lemon trees don't grow in your climate, buy a lemon at the grocery store and then perform the spell at midnight. Say:

> *Thou who art Queen of the sun and of the moon*
> *And of the stars—lo! I call to thee!*
> *And with what power I have I conjure thee*
> *To grant to me the favor I implore!*[49]

The *Gospel* specifies that it's best to choose an unripe, green lemon for this charm. Holding the lemon in one hand, carefully stick the thirteen multicolored pins into it. As you insert each pin, focus on bringing luck and prosperity for yourself or the person to whom you'll give the charm. When you're done, keep the lemon in your home to draw prosperity to you, or give it as a gift to a friend.

The procedure for the curse is somewhat different. You still pluck the lemon at midnight as before, but this time, you do not insert the pins right away. Instead, take the lemon home with you and wait until noon the next day. At noon, boil red wine on the stovetop, then pour the boiling wine into a cup. The *Gospel* instructs

---

49. Leland, *Aradia*, 37.

that the wine should be boiled by refracting sunlight through a magnifying glass, but this is impractical and unnecessary in an era of gas stoves. Drop the thirteen black-headed pins into the boiling wine, saying:

> *Goddess Diana, I do conjure thee*
> *And with uplifted voice to thee I call,*
> *That thou shalt never have content nor peace*
> *Until thou comest to give me all thy aid.*
> *And thou shalt call for me the fiends from hell;*
> *Thou'llt send them as companions of the sun,*
> *And all the fire infernal of itself*
> *Those fiends shall bring, and bring with it the power*
> *Unto the sun to make this red wine boil,*
> *So that these pins may be red-hot,*
> *And with them I do fill the lemon here,*
> *That unto her or him to who 'tis given is*
> *Prosperity unknown.*[50]

Carefully fish the pins out of the wine and stick them into the lemon, one by one. As you do so, focus on drawing malice into the lemon so that whoever receives it will have suffering and ill luck. When you have finished, leave the lemon on your enemy's doorstep or in another place where they will find it and know it is meant for them. Once you have done so, seal the spell with a final incantation:

> *If this grace I gain from thee*
> *Give a sign, I pray, to me!*
> *Ere the third day*
> *Shall pass away,*
> *Let me either hear or see*
> *A roaring wind, a rattling rain,*
> *Or hail a-clattering on the plain;*
> *Till one of these three signs you show,*
> *Peace, Diana, thou shalt not know.*

---

50. Leland, *Aradia*, 39–40.

Answer well the prayer I've sent thee,
Or day and night I will torment thee![51]

The spell is complete. If your curse has been successful, you will receive a sign in the next three days with sudden foul weather: wind, rain, or hail.

Historical Precedent

Leland's *Gospel* was not the first text to suggest that witches actually existed, nor to identify Diana as their goddess. The idea of an underground witch cult traces back to a man named Jules Michelet, who in 1862 published a book called *La Sorcière*, or in English, *The Witch*. The book was translated into English under the title *Satanism and Witchcraft* a year later. In this book, Michelet argued that the people convicted of witchcraft during the witch hunts of the early modern period were, in fact, witches. He suggested that European peasants, fed up with an economic system that kept them mired in poverty, decided to rebel against that system and the dominant Christian religion that accompanied it. Michelet thought that these peasants would have turned to heresy, worshipping the Christian devil and practicing witchcraft in order to try and escape their social and economic disadvantages.[52]

By the time Leland's *Gospel* was published, then, the idea of the witch as a political and economic revolutionary—of witchcraft as the last resort of the impoverished and oppressed who are trying to seize some control of their lives—is already in place. The association of witchcraft with the overthrow of the wealthy and powerful was firmly entrenched in the nineteenth-century imagination, as was the idea that historical witches really had existed and had been practicing an underground religion. The main point of divergence between Michelet's *Satanism and Witchcraft* and Leland's *Gospel of the Witches* is in the deity that the witches worshipped. For Michelet, witches worshipped Satan, turning themselves against the Christian God. For Leland, they worshipped the pagan goddess Diana, although Lucifer was still in the picture in a highly paganized form. Ronald Hutton notes that "whereas Michelet had accepted the notion that witches had adored the Christian figure of Satan, Leland stated, dogmatically, that this was an invention of churchmen and

---

51. Leland, *Aradia*, 40.
52. Michelet, *Satanism and Witchcraft*, 20.

that Diana had been their true deity."[53] The revolutionary conception of witchcraft was already established by the time the *Gospel* was published, but the great innovation of this new text was the connection between that witchcraft and the lunar goddess Diana.

In fact, that connection has its roots much farther back than Leland's 1899 publication. It originates in official Catholic doctrine. In the year 906, a man named Regino of Prüm wrote a legal and theological opinion where he claimed that witches consorted with Satan, who tricked them into believing that they were actually in the company of the pagan goddess Diana: "They ride upon certain beasts with Diana, the goddess of pagans, and an innumerable multitude of women, and in the silence of the dead of the night to fly over vast spaces of earth, and obey her commands as of their lady, and are summoned to her service on certain nights."[54] In Latin, the text of this legal opinion begins with the word *episcopi*; consequently, it has come to be known as the *Canon Episcopi*.

This text then got picked up in 1140 by a church lawyer named Gratian, who added it to an official body of canon law known as the *Decretum Gratiani*.[55] Thus, it became the official position of the Catholic Church that witches existed and were servants of the devil, but that they *believed* they were servants of the goddess Diana. What's more, the text of the *Decretum Gratiani* adds the name of a second goddess to the charge. Gratian's version of the text adds the words *uel cum Herodiae*, "or with Herodias," to the description of witches consorting with Diana.[56] It's unclear who, exactly, this Herodias is, but the name may be referring to the biblical queen and wife of King Herod.

Notably, Leland provides a commentary on the *Gospel* where he explores the history of this name. He concludes that the name Aradia is an Italianized version of Herodias, and that Aradia is the second witch goddess referred to in the *Decretum Gratiani*: "*Aradia* is evidently enough Herodias, who was regarded in the beginning as associated with Diana as chief of the witches."[57] He then goes on to identify these figures with the "Shemitic [sic] Queens of Heaven"; interestingly enough, the title "Queen of Heaven" was one of the epithets of Inanna and

---

53. Hutton, *The Triumph of the Moon*, 153.

54. Luebke, "Traces of Non-Christian Religious Practices in Medieval Penitentials" [sic].

55. Gratian, "*Decretum Gratiani* (Kirchenrechtssammlung)."

56. Gratian, "*Decretum Gratiani* (Kirchenrechtssammlung)."

57. Leland, *Aradia*, 120.

Ishtar, two of the goddesses who shaped Frazer's theory of the Great Goddess.[58] Leland further writes that "Isis preceded both."[59]

For Leland, at least, there is a clear connection between the Diana of the *Gospel* and various goddesses of the Middle East and Mediterranean—goddesses who are explicitly named by Frazer in the formulation of his prototypical myth of the Goddess. If the *Gospel* is authentic, this connection may be merely an interpretive lens that Leland is applying to it, trying to make sense of the cult of the witches by framing it in the context of established anthropological theories. If the *Gospel* is a forgery, on the other hand, it was evidently written with the Great Goddess in mind. Either way, Leland presented *The Gospel of the Witches* to the world by situating it in a particular context. He introduced Diana, Queen of the Witches, as another face of the Great Goddess herself.

Key Takeaways: Leland

+ The lunar Goddess and her solar consort
+ Association of the Goddess with revolution and political activism
+ The Goddess as a patroness of witches
+ Rituals performed in honor of the Goddess every full moon
+ Historical connections to Diana as a goddess of witchcraft

---

58. Leland, *Aradia*, 120.

59. Leland, *Aradia*, 120.

——— RITUAL ———
LA TREGUNDA

The Gospel of the Witches describes the monthly meeting of the witches, *la tre-gunda*, as a feast held on the night of the full moon. Witches would prepare spe-cial honey cakes in the shape of crescents, drink wine, play music, and then extin-guish all their candles and have sex. The instructions for the *tregunda* given in the *Gospel* focus mainly on the ritual preparation of the honey cakes, which are made with four ingredients: meal, salt, honey, and wine. The *Gospel* doesn't give specific baking instructions, so what follows is my own recipe, with all of the invocations and incantations abridged from those given by Leland. I have added anise to the cakes for flavor because it's difficult to get a cake to taste like anything with just honey and wine. I've also modified the instructions for consecrating salt in the recipe; the Gospel instructs that salt should be consecrated "exactly in the middle of a stream," but this strikes me as impractical for baking in a kitchen.

Group Variation

In this version of the rite, your group will prepare the moon cake all together, focus-ing on a magical goal to be baked into the recipe. Then, you will come together to feast and make merry, consuming the consecrated cake in honor of Diana and in thanks for the blessings she will bestow upon you.

You Will Need

- 4 cups all-purpose flour
- 2 teaspoons ground anise seed
- 1 teaspoon baking soda
- ½ teaspoon salt
- 2 cups honey
- 1 cup unsalted, room-temperature butter
- 1 cup red wine
- 2 large eggs
- An 8-inch square baking pan

Preparation

Decide collectively on the magical goal you want to set for the feast. In the process of making the cake, you are effectively baking your desire into a spell so that when you consume the cake later, you will receive what you asked for. This is one of the most straightforward acts of witchcraft from the *Gospel*.

Begin preparing the cake together at noon on the day of the full moon. Set out all of your ingredients and preheat your oven to 350° Fahrenheit.

Performance

At the start of the ritual, one person places the flour in a large mixing bowl while the others join hands with each other, visualize the agreed-upon magical goal, and say:

> *We conjure thee, O Meal!*
> *Who art indeed our body, since without thee*
> *We could not live, thou who at first as seed*
> *Before becoming flower went in the earth,*
> *Where all deep secrets hide, and then when ground*
> *Didst dance like dust in the wind, and yet meanwhile*
> *Didst bear with thee in flitting, secrets strange!*[60]

The same person then adds the salt to the flour while the rest of the group says:

> *We do conjure thee, salt, lo! Here at noon,*
> *We do indeed desire no other thought,*
> *We yearn to learn the very truth of truths,*
> *For we have suffered long with the desire*
> *To know our future or our coming fate,*
> *If good or evil will prevail in it.*
> *Be gracious unto us!*[61]

Add in the baking soda and anise; mix thoroughly.

---

60. Leland, *Aradia*, 11, modified to the first person plural.
61. Leland, *Aradia*, 13, modified to the first person plural.

Set aside the dry ingredients. In another mixing bowl, whip together the butter and the honey until they are smooth. Whisk in the eggs and wine. When all the wet ingredients are combined, add the dry ingredients a little at a time and mix until smooth. Once the batter is done, pass the bowl around so that every member of the group can hold it, visualizing the magical goal the group has set for the ritual.

Grease an 8-inch square cake pan with butter and pour the batter into the pan. The *Gospel* describes the cakes as being crescent-shaped, but I lack the culinary prowess for shaped cakes, so I settle for a square. If you are more adept in the kitchen than I am, you can experiment with carving the cake into a crescent shape once it's baked.

Bake the cake at 350° Fahrenheit for 80–90 minutes. One person puts the pan into the oven while the others join hands and say:

> *We do not bake the bread, nor with it salt,*
> *Nor do we cook the honey with the wine,*
> *We bake the body and the blood and soul,*
> *The soul of great Diana, that she shall*
> *Know neither rest nor peace, and ever be*
> *In cruel suffering till she will grant*
> *What we request, what we do most desire,*
> *We beg it of her from our very hearts!*
> *And if the grace be granted, O Diana!*
> *In honor of thee we will hold this feast,*
> *Feast and drain the goblet deep,*
> *We will dance and wildly leap,*
> *And if thou grant'st the grace which we require,*
> *Then when the dance is wildest, all the lamps*
> *Shall be extinguished and we'll freely love!*[62]

Remove the cake from the oven and let it cool completely before turning it out onto a serving tray.

That night, at midnight, set out a table with this cake, a goblet of the same wine you used in the recipe, and two small bowls—one filled with water and one

---

62. Leland, *Aradia*, 16, modified to the first person plural.

filled with salt. If you have a private place outdoors where you can do this, so much the better, but you can just as easily do it in the privacy of someone's home. Put on some music you enjoy, eat the cake, drink the wine, and have a bit of a party! If your group is comfortable with nude ritual, I recommend it for this rite. If you have never worked skyclad before, but are curious to try it, this would be an appropriate occasion to be "naked in your rites" in honor of Diana. However, if you are uncomfortable with ritual nudity in a group setting, it is by no means obligatory.

At the end of the ritual, stand in a circle and pass a kiss around the room. This can be a kiss on the lips, on the cheek, or in another manner, depending on the participants' comfort levels and personal boundaries. Once the kiss has been passed all the way around the circle, the rite is officially over.

Solitary Variation

For the solitary *tregunda*, you will prepare the moon cake on your own, focusing on a wish or desire to be baked into the cake. Afterward, you will feast and make merry, consuming the consecrated cake in honor of Diana and in gratitude for the blessings she will bestow upon you.

You Will Need

- 4 cups all-purpose flour
- 2 teaspoons ground anise seed
- 1 teaspoon baking soda
- ½ teaspoon salt
- 2 cups honey
- 1 cup unsalted, room-temperature butter
- 1 cup red wine
- 2 large eggs
- An 8-inch square baking pan

Preparation

Decide on the magical goal you want to set for the feast. In the process of making the cake, you are effectively baking your desire into a spell so that when you consume the cake later, you will receive what you asked for. This is one of the most straightforward acts of witchcraft from the *Gospel*.

Begin preparing the cake at noon on the day of the full moon. Set out all of your ingredients and preheat your oven to 350° Fahrenheit.

Performance

To begin the ritual, place the flour in a large mixing bowl. Extend your hands over it and say:

> *I conjure thee, O Meal!*
> *Who art indeed my body, since without thee*
> *I could not live, thou who at first as seed*
> *Before becoming flower went in the earth,*
> *Where all deep secrets hide, and then when ground*
> *Didst dance like dust in the wind, and yet meanwhile*
> *Didst bear with thee in flitting, secrets strange!*[63]

Add the salt to the flour. As you do so, focus on your magical goal and say:

> *I do conjure thee, salt, lo! Here at noon,*
> *I do indeed desire no other thought,*
> *I yearn to learn the very truth of truths,*
> *For I have suffered long with the desire*
> *To know my future or my coming fate,*
> *If good or evil will prevail in it.*
> *Be gracious unto me!*[64]

Add in the baking soda and anise; mix thoroughly. Set aside the dry ingredients. In another mixing bowl, whip together the butter and the honey until they are smooth. Whisk in the eggs and wine. When all the wet ingredients are combined, add the dry ingredients a little at a time and mix until smooth.

---

63. Leland, *Aradia*, 11.
64. Leland, *Aradia*, 13.

Grease an 8-inch square cake pan with butter and pour the batter into the pan. Bake the cake at 350° Fahrenheit for 80–90 minutes. When you put the pan into the oven, say the following:

> *I do not bake the bread, nor with it salt,*
> *Nor do I cook the honey with the wine,*
> *I bake the body and the blood and soul,*
> *The soul of great Diana, that she shall*
> *Know neither rest nor peace, and ever be*
> *In cruel suffering till she will grant*
> *What I request, what I do most desire,*
> *I beg it of her from my very heart!*
> *And if the grace be granted, O Diana!*
> *In honor of thee I will hold this feast,*
> *Feast and drain the goblet deep,*
> *I will dance and wildly leap,*
> *And if thou grant'st the grace which I require,*
> *Then when the dance is wildest, all the lamps*
> *Shall be extinguished and I'll freely love!*[65]

Remove the cake from the oven and let it cool completely before turning it out onto a serving tray. That night, at midnight, set out a table with this cake, a goblet of the same wine you used in the recipe, and two small bowls—one filled with water and one filled with salt. If you have a private place outdoors where you can do this, so much the better, but you can just as easily do it in the privacy of your own home. Put on some music you enjoy, eat the cake, drink the wine, and have a bit of a party! I recommend experimenting with ritual nudity, just to see how it feels; try being "naked in your rites" in honor of Diana, even if you don't normally practice ritual skyclad. Let loose and enjoy yourself.

When you are done with your feast, kiss your hand and lay it over your heart. With this act, the rite is officially over.

---

65. Leland, *Aradia*, 16.

4

THE WITCH CULT (1921)

WHEN I WAS SEVEN years old, I went to Spain with my parents. We traveled through Madrid and Barcelona, down to Gibraltar, across the western border into Portugal, and up north into the Basque Country. On that trip, we visited the small town of Zugarramurdi. In itself, this town is rather unremarkable; it's a sleepy village in Navarre, with quaint architecture and a few boutique hotels. However, this town has a remarkable history. Between the years 1611 and 1614, Zugarramurdi was the seat of a witch hunt in Navarre, wherein the Spanish Inquisition secured nearly two thousand confessions from accused witches—and implicated the names of five thousand others for the crime of witchcraft.[66] To this day, Zugarramurdi holds the legacy of the witch trials; there is a local field where the witches are supposed to have held their grand sabbats, and a cave called the "witches' cave" where a bonfire is still lit every year to honor the summer solstice. The town also has an unassuming building that holds the *Museo de las Brujas*: the Museum of the Witches.

The museum commemorates the victims of the witch trials, telling the story of the more than two thousand people who were tortured and the eleven people who died at the hands of the Inquisition over the course of the trials. It also features relics from the time: pieces of period clothing, instruments of restraint and torture, and animal skulls and other bizarre paraphernalia that were held as evidence against the accused. On the whole, visiting the museum is a solemn, sobering experience.

---

66. Billock, "Visit the Site of the Biggest Witch Trial in History."

Seeing the exhibit as a child, I didn't entirely understand the weight of the history being presented. Witches, to my mind, were people who existed in books and movies. They were immortal and had magic powers. Witchcraft was something fun, exciting, and wonderful—a game of pretend to be played at recess. I didn't yet know that at one point in the popular imagination, witches had been seen as real and dangerous. I couldn't wrap my head around the notion that witchcraft had been a crime for which thousands of people had been tortured and many had even lost their lives. It was a revelation to me to consider that the word "witch" had ever applied to real people.

Four hundred years after the trials at Zugarramurdi, I call myself a witch. I am now one of those real people. The witchcraft I practice is quite different from what the citizens of Navarre were accused of; the records of the Inquisition paint the witches as a violent cult of clandestine Satanists looking to undermine the church. This is a far cry from the earth-centered, Goddess-worshipping Paganism that I practice. Nonetheless, there is a connection there, an imagined affinity, a mythic history that stretches back from my witchcraft to the trials of the early seventeenth century. Though it is unlikely that any of the accused really thought of themselves as witches, it is certainly true that modern witches have looked to the history of these trials in an effort to build identity for themselves. Many have reimagined witchcraft not as a gruesome parade of Satanism and human sacrifice, but as an exuberant religion that celebrates life, honors the earth, and follows the changing of the seasons. For these people, the witches' goat-horned devil has lost its diabolical terror, and has instead been recast as an animal-headed deity of fertility with deep connections to the land. Looking at the alleged reports of witchcraft from bygone years, many have found a religion of joy buried under a legacy of violence and bloodshed.

The *Museo de las Brujas* is a memorial for the horrors of the past, but that past also contains the seed of the Pagan witchcraft that was to come. Visiting the museum as a child, I was filled with wonder at the witchcraft it portrayed. It felt vibrant, powerful, and deeply alive, and some part of me knew that there was something here for me. That visit set me on a path that would lead me to modern witchcraft and the Goddess. I would not know the Goddess as I do today without the witch trials of Navarre.

From Egyptology to Witchcraft

Charles Godfrey Leland was not the only writer to connect the Goddess with witchcraft. In the late nineteenth and early twentieth centuries, the world fell in love with the idea that witches were actual people who had existed and might still exist, and who were practicing a secret underground religion. From Michelet to Leland, the idea of a hidden witch cult persisted, and it found new expression in 1921 with a woman named Margaret Alice Murray. Murray was an Egyptologist by vocation and was awarded an honorary doctorate from University College London in 1927 in recognition of her contributions to archaeological excavations in Egypt; however, she actually had comparatively little formal academic training as a historian.[67] With the start of the First World War, travel to Egypt became impossible, and so Murray turned her attention to another subject entirely: witchcraft.

In 1921, Murray published a book called *The Witch-Cult in Western Europe*. In it, she claimed—in line with Michelet and Leland—that witchcraft really had existed in medieval and early modern Europe, and that it had been a religious practice of the oppressed lower class. Unlike Michelet, however, Murray suggested that witchcraft was not merely reactionary Satanism; it was, rather, the survival of an ancient pre-Christian fertility cult that had gone underground with the spread of Christianity across the European continent. She combed through records from famous witch trials all across Europe, piecing together testimony from various convicted witches in order to present a picture of what this witch cult would have been like. Who were its gods? What were its rites? What were its central beliefs and practices?

Murray had never done archival research before, having worked primarily with physical artifacts on archaeological digs. As such, her treatment of evidence from the witch trials suffered from serious issues. She went into her investigation with the foregone conclusion that there had been such a thing as a pan-European witch cult, and her goal was simply to discover what it was like—not whether it existed in the first place. She cherry-picked her sources, leaving out any that didn't fit into her narrative, and even admits as much: "I have…confined myself to those statements only which show the beliefs, organization, and ritual of a hitherto unrecognized cult."[68] In so doing, she left out the majority of witchcraft

---

67. Sheppard, *The Life of Margaret Alice Murray*, 98.

68. Murray, *The Witch-Cult in Western Europe*, 10.

accounts from medieval and early modern testimony, presenting a skewed vision of what people in the period thought witchcraft was like.

Moreover, Murray had a habit of taking the testimony of accused witches at face value. If a woman said she had danced naked with the devil, Murray believed that such an event must have actually taken place. The "devil" in question might merely be a man in a costume, but in Murray's eyes, there was no question that the woman had gone somewhere and danced naked with someone. In the first few pages of *The Witch-Cult in Western Europe*, Murray dismisses out of hand the idea that witch testimony might ever be unreliable—either because accused witches were delusional, being prompted by inquisitors from a pre-written script, or confessing to escape torture.[69] All of these, however, are very real concerns, and they make Murray's reading of the records from witch trials far less credible.

Murray's work met with scholarly outcry and outright dismissal immediately upon publication, from her contemporaries who pointed out her misuse of the sources she discussed. In one scholarly review from 1922, the historian George Lincoln Burr wrote that Murray had forcibly imposed a narrative that was not actually present in the evidence she stitched together, and "by hook or by crook these sources are made to confess what their questioner suggests."[70] However, despite its deep flaws, *The Witch-Cult in Western Europe* seized the popular imagination. The wider public fell in love with Murray's narrative, and with the idea that real witches had practiced a secret underground fertility religion well into the seventeenth century. It was an exciting, enthralling narrative. In 1929, Murray was invited to write the entry on witchcraft for the *Encyclopedia Britannica*, and when she did, her place in history was cemented.[71] She had permanently changed the role that people imagined for witchcraft and witches in history.

My presentation of Murray's work may come across as unduly harsh. As a work of scholarship, *The Witch-Cult in Western Europe* fails. The evidence from early modern witch trials simply does not yield the conclusions Murray wanted to draw. However, when talking about Murray's role in the development of modern Goddess worship, *it's okay that she was wrong*. Murray, like all of the figures I've discussed, had flawed ideas and methods that don't stand up to careful his-

---

69. Murray, *The Witch-Cult in Western Europe*, 13–14.

70. Burr, "Reviewed Work(s)," 782.

71. Sheppard, *The Life of Margaret Alice Murray*, 176.

torical scrutiny, but her work has significance independently of whether it's factually correct. Just as Frazer had created a new mythology of Goddess worship, Murray created a new mythology of witchcraft.

Remember, the relationship between the present and the past is not static. It changes as society changes, and the things people think and believe about the past reveal as much about the present moment as they do about history. Murray, like Frazer and Bachofen before her, created a new perspective for the world, shaping what people thought of as ancient and changing what came after her. The story of a prehistoric witch cult that had gone into hiding with the arrival of Christianity is a deeply compelling one, and it resonates strongly with the myth of the Great Goddess. It became the foundation for Wicca and other Goddess-based witchcraft revivals of the twentieth century, as people increasingly blended together the ideas of Goddess worship, witchcraft, and fertility religion. You do not have to credulously accept Murray's historical claims to appreciate the extraordinary role she played in the modern Goddess movement.

Murray's God(dess)

Murray distinguished between what she saw as the practical and religious sides of witchcraft. The practical side of things, which consisted of casting spells and charms, she called *operative witchcraft*. In Murray's usage, this term was interchangeable with magic in general, and anyone who used folk charms or magic of any kind counted as an operative witch. The religious side of things, however, was a pan-European fertility cult. It was dedicated to the service of a patron deity, in whose name witches would gather in groups called "covens" to cast spells, do magic for crops and livestock, curse their enemies, and worship. This deity had both a male and female form. As the God, he was called Dianus; as the Goddess, Diana:

> The deity of this cult was incarnate in a man, a woman, or
> an animal; the animal form being apparently older than the
> human, for the god was often spoken of as wearing the skin
> or attributes of an animal…Such a god is found in Italy (where
> he is called Janus or Dianus), in Southern France, and in the
> English Midlands. The feminine form of the name, Diana, is
> found throughout Western Europe as the name of the female

deity or leader of the so-called Witches, and it is for this reason
that I have called this ancient religion the Dianic cult.[72]

The deity of the witches for Murray was either a Goddess or a God, who
appeared as a person or as an animal. If the "deity" was a person, they were simply
the leader of the coven, whom coven members worshipped as their God. If they
were an animal, they might be the leader of the coven dressed up in costume, or
they might be a pet or farm animal brought in to represent the God(dess) for the
occasion. In this way, Murray explained accounts of witches interacting with gro-
tesque figures and talking animals: these figures were simply coven leaders in dis-
guise, wearing animal masks in their ritual role as the embodiment of their deity.

Although the deity could be a man or a woman, Murray noted that the
majority of witchcraft accounts spoke of witches worshipping a male devil. From
this, she concluded that the worship of the Goddess had been more prevalent in
ancient times, and that the male God had crept in and taken her place over the
centuries.[73] Here, you may catch a whiff of Bachofen's idea of ancient matriarchy. Murray supposed that this male God would have horns through his associations with livestock, most notably sheep or bulls; she suggested that the Christian image of the horned devil was merely a bastardization of this ancient horned
witch deity. Her idea was that the church literally demonized the God of the old
religion, creating the figure of the devil in his image so that followers of this fertility cult could be slandered as devil worshippers.

When the deity appeared as a woman, she was given the title "Queen of the
Sabbat." She was treated as royalty, and everyone present had to genuflect, show
her reverence, and kiss her—even before worshipping the male God, if he was
present as well. According to one account Murray gives, witches made offerings
of bread, eggs, and money to their Goddess.[74] As part of their rites, the witches
would have ritual sex with the Goddess or God incarnate, especially during seasonal festivals—the idea being that sexual congress with the deity would increase
the fertility of the land. Murray writes that witches "would insist upon it as their
right, and it probably became compulsory at certain seasons, such as the breed-

---

72. Murray, *The Witch-Cult in Western Europe*, 11.
73. Murray, *The Witch-Cult in Western Europe*, 12.
74. Murray, *The Witch-Cult in Western Europe*, 36.

ing periods of the herds or the sowing and reaping periods of the crops."[75] This idea—that the God(dess) of fertility ensured the life of the land by ritually possessing the body of a priest or priestess and then coupling with a worshipper—should be familiar from Frazer's theory of the Great Goddess cult. In fact, Murray was in direct correspondence with Frazer, communicating with him while she formulated her witch cult hypothesis. Frazer's Great Goddess was a direct influence on Murray's theory of the witch cult.[76]

Murray even picked up on Frazer's idea of the dying-and-resurrecting God. She suggested that the ritual sacrifice of the witch deity, either as a person or as an animal, was a regular feature of witch rituals. The God was burned alive, and his or her death ensured the fertility of the crops. She writes, "We have here a sacrifice of the god of fertility. Originally the sprinkling of the ashes on fields or animals or in running water was a fertility charm."[77] She even went so far as to claim that the practice of burning witches at the stake in Europe was a survival of the ritual sacrifice of the dying-and-resurrecting God, and that famous accused witches like Joan of Arc submitted to their executions willingly as part of this ritual sacrifice.[78]

Murray's great divergence from Frazer, and from the other authors I have examined thus far, is that she did not draw a sharp distinction between the Goddess and the God. For Frazer, there was a clear mythology of the immortal Goddess and her mortal consort, who died and was reborn with the reaping and sowing of crops. For Murray, however, there seems to have been only one witch deity, who could equally appear as a Goddess or a God. Rather than the Great Goddess and her consort, she presented one witch God who was essentially genderless. As a person or an animal, this God embodied the principle of fertility in nature, which was the focus of the witches' worship.

In this witch God, you can see many of the traits that had been associated with the Goddess from Bachofen up to Murray's time. This deity is associated with the earth, crops, animals, sacred sexuality, and magic—and has the name Diana or Dianus, just like Leland's witch Goddess and one of the faces of Frazer's

---

75. Murray, *The Witch-Cult in Western Europe*, 132.

76. Sheppard, *The Life of Margaret Alice Murray*, 172.

77. Murray, *The Witch-Cult in Western Europe*, 119.

78. Murray, *The Witch-Cult in Western Europe*, 209.

Great Goddess. Murray acknowledges that the witch religion may have its roots in "the Mother-Goddess worshipped chiefly by women."[79] However, with *The Witch-Cult in Western Europe* this Goddess figure is essentially divorced from conceptions of gender. In Murray's witch cult, this embodied force of nature may be called both Goddess and God by its worshippers, and it need not be restricted to one gender. This is a powerful idea that would return with the polemics of radical feminism in the late twentieth century, when feminist thinkers vocally questioned the Christian conception of God the father as being only male.

——— EXERCISE ———
FLYING OINTMENT

One of the appendices of *The Witch-Cult in Western Europe* lists the recipes for so-called "flying ointments." These are topical ointments made with psychoactive herbs, which witches would rub into their skin before going to their rituals. Murray hypothesized that the entheogenic effect of the flying ointment would induce a feeling of religious ecstasy, cause hallucinations, and even give people the illusion that they were flying—thus giving rise to the pervasive myth that witches flew to their sabbats.[80]

The flying ointment recipes given by Murray all contain highly toxic ingredients that, in the wrong dosage, could easily kill someone. Therefore, allow me to say in no uncertain terms: *DO NOT experiment with poisonous herbs.* They will kill you if you don't know what you're doing.

The following recipe uses mugwort and wormwood, which are both plants in the artemisia family. They contain thujone, the same psychoactive chemical compound found in absinthe.[81] Thujone is alcohol-soluble, so when these plants are infused into alcohol, they can have a mild psychoactive effect similar to cannabis. There is some evidence linking thujone to seizures, so if you suffer from epilepsy or seizures, don't use this recipe.[82] Avoid using flying ointments while nursing or

---

79. Murray, *The Witch-Cult in Western Europe*, 12.

80. Murray, *The Witch-Cult in Western Europe*, 213.

81. National Toxicology Program, "NTP Technical Report on the Toxicology and Carcinogenesis Studies of $\alpha\beta$-Thujone," 16.

82. National Toxicology Program, "NTP Technical Report on the Toxicology and Carcinogenesis Studies of $\alpha\beta$-Thujone," 20.

pregnant, or if you have other medical conditions that may be contraindicated. When in doubt, consult with your doctor.

The following recipe is my own, and it is nontoxic. It's not nearly as psychoactive as Murray's recipes are, but it also won't land you in the hospital. You will need:

+ ½ ounce dried wormwood
+ ½ ounce dried mugwort
+ 2 quart-sized mason jars
+ 2 cups isopropyl alcohol (91 percent)
+ ¾ cup distilled water
+ ¾ cup baby oil
+ ¾ cup emulsifying wax pellets
+ A cheesecloth
+ A blender

First, make a mugwort and wormwood tincture. Sterilize one of the mason jars with soap and hot water. Add the mugwort, wormwood, and isopropyl alcohol to the jar. Stir gently to get rid of any air bubbles, then cover the jar. Store it at room temperature and out of direct sunlight for six weeks, swirling the contents occasionally. This will allow the thujone from the herbs to extract into the alcohol. If you want to observe the lunar cycle in preparing your flying ointment, you can start making the tincture on a new moon; it will be ready on a full moon.

Once your tincture is ready, sterilize your blender and the remaining mason jar with soap and hot water. Using a cheesecloth, strain 1 cup of the tincture into the blender. You will have extra; if you like, you can strain this off and reserve it for other magical purposes.

Add the distilled water to the blender. In a small saucepan, mix together the baby oil and the emulsifying wax. Heat on low, stirring constantly, until the wax is melted. Then, pour the combined oil and wax into the blender. Cover and blend on high for one minute; immediately wipe out the saucepan with paper towels. Pour the mixture from the blender into the sterilized mason jar. Cover and refrigerate overnight to allow the ointment to set. Store the ointment in the refrigerator when you're not using it.

This recipe is completely safe for external use, and you don't risk poisoning yourself when you apply it, but that also means it's not going to give you the same intense entheogenic experience as some commercially available flying ointments. You may choose to buy a flying ointment instead if you're looking for more of a kick, but you should always use caution and discretion when vetting a vendor. Remember: *if you are purchasing a flying ointment made with toxic ingredients, only buy from experienced herbalists.* I cannot emphasize enough how potentially dangerous it is to mess around with poisonous plants.

The result will be a thick, greasy, pale-green ointment. Due to the high alcohol content, the mixture will liquefy quickly when it comes in contact with your skin. To use the flying ointment, rub it into the parts of your body where there are major arteries and your skin is thin: your throat, underarms, inside your wrists and elbows, and on your upper thighs near the groin. This should be done shortly prior to ritual or magic on special occasions. This flying ointment is safe if you use it for ritual once every three to four weeks, but don't use it every day; while perfectly safe in small doses, thujone is not great for you if it builds up in your system over time.

Witch Ritual and Theology

What did the rituals of the witch cult look like according to Murray? She distinguishes between two kinds of ritual. *Sabbats* were seasonal holidays taking place four times per year: May 1, August 1, November 1, and February 1.[83] These were agricultural festivals dedicated to the fertility of crops and livestock, and they were the major holidays of the religion. According to Murray, the sabbats always took place at night. However, the sabbats were not the only times witches convened. They also met at *esbats*, which had no fixed date or time. Esbats were the working occasions of the coven.[84] These were the times that witches would gather together to cast spells, report on coven business, and worship their God. The terminology of sabbats as seasonal holidays and esbats as working occasions is still used today by Wiccans and various other witches or Pagans.

Murray broke the structure of witch meetings down into a few core components. Everything was lit by candlelight, and the witch deity was identified by wear-

---

83. Murray, *The Witch-Cult in Western Europe*, 82.
84. Murray, *The Witch-Cult in Western Europe*, 84.

ing a hat or crown with a lit candle on it.[85] At the beginning of witch rituals, witches would pay homage to their God: "The homage consisted in renewing the vows of fidelity and obedience, in kissing the Devil [i.e., the witch God] on any part of his person that he chose to indicate, and sometimes in turning a certain number of times widdershins."[86] After everyone had given the deity their due, there was a discussion of magic—both of spells that had been performed since the previous sabbat and of ones that had yet to be performed. If the meeting was an esbat, the coven would take this time to do those spells all together.[87] On sabbats, there would be a seasonal ritual and a religious sacrament, which involved a blessing of bread and wine similar to the act of Christian communion and may also have entailed some form of sacrifice.[88] Finally, the ceremony concluded with feasting, music, dancing, and sexual revelry.[89]

Nowhere in *The Witch-Cult in Western Europe* does Murray mention Leland's *Gospel of the Witches* directly, and it is not even certain that she ever read it, but there are some thematic parallels. Either Murray read the *Gospel* and was influenced by it, or she independently came to similar ideas about what witches do. Both Murray and Leland give an account of witch festivals as joyous and rowdy occasions, with music, banquets, dancing, and a healthy dose of sex. Both also saw witches as morally ambiguous figures who were just as happy to curse their enemies as to bless their friends. Murray added an explicit agricultural connection to her version of the witch cult, incorporating Frazer's ideas about the dying-and-resurrecting God and the seasonal ritual cycle accompanying that myth.

These accounts provide a strong picture of how witchcraft and paganism came to be viewed in the late nineteenth and early twentieth centuries. The two were inextricably intertwined, as witchcraft was understood to be a survival of ancient paganism into the modern world. Thus, whatever was true of witchcraft would be considered true of paganism more broadly, and vice versa. Whether with Leland's Diana or Murray's genderless witch God, this version of Paganism was centered on a deity who celebrated life, and whose rituals were boisterous, raunchy, and *fun*. The primary deity of witchcraft is associated with fertility, the earth, and magic,

85. Murray, *The Witch-Cult in Western Europe*, 107.
86. Murray, *The Witch-Cult in Western Europe*, 93.
87. Murray, *The Witch-Cult in Western Europe*, 93.
88. Murray, *The Witch-Cult in Western Europe*, 111.
89. Murray, *The Witch-Cult in Western Europe*, 93.

yes—but above and beyond that, is simply associated with having a good time. Witch rituals as presented by Leland and Murray alike are excuses for a party. Thus, Paganism, witchcraft, and Goddess worship are life-affirming, celebratory, and unburdened by a sense of shame or sin.

Murray's great innovation is in designating the witch God not as some abstract deity, but as being physically present in witch rituals. Leland's Aradia was a messianic deity who had walked among humans at some point in the mythic past, but who was no longer physically present among the worshippers of Diana. For Murray, however, the God was present at every witch meeting, whether as an animal or as a member of the coven who ceremonially assumed the role for the purposes of the rite. This put the witches in direct contact with the life-force of nature they worshipped. Deity was no longer something abstract and intangible; it was immediate, real, and physically present.

Moreover, it carried with it the seed of a deep theological significance, which has since blossomed in the Goddess movement: Every body is the body of the Goddess. Every person is a manifestation of the divine, and is sacred simply by virtue of existing in the physical world. If a member of the witch coven—an ordinary person—could become the witch God(dess) for the purposes of a ritual, that meant there had to be a divine spark already present in ordinary people. With Bachofen and Frazer, the Goddess was already associated with the sacred body and with reverence for the physical world. Murray's description of the witch deity allowed for an even deeper expression of this theology. If any person or animal could act as deity incarnate, then every person and animal was sacred and worthy of veneration. Murray's witches had a direct, personal connection to the divine, and that theology has carried over into modern Goddess worship.

The Queen of Elfhame

In *The Witch-Cult in Western Europe*, Murray notes a second title sometimes given to the queen of the sabbat: the Queen of Elfhame.[90] The word *elfhame* comes from *elf* and *hame* ("home"); it's another word for the kingdom of the fairies. Murray noted a close link between the belief in witches and the belief in fairies, and she hypothesized that witchcraft had originated as the worship of fairies: "That there was a strong connexion between witches and fairies has been known to all students of fairy lore. I suggest that the cult of the fairy or primitive race

---

90. Murray, *The Witch-Cult in Western Europe*, 34.

survived until less than three hundred years ago, and that the people who practised it were known as witches."[91] Under this guise, the witch deity was the fairy queen, the spirit of the land who embodied wild and mischievous nature.

Murray draws on testimony about fairies from various witch trials, and the information given in this testimony is quite interesting. Some of it differs drastically from the other lore she had amassed. Murray identified the God of the witches with the "devil" mentioned in a great deal of witch testimony, but the devil is practically nowhere to be found in the testimony about fairies.

Emma Wilby, a contemporary historian of early modern witchcraft, has suggested that in some cases, at least, there is good reason for the unique descriptions of fairies in these records. Wilby conducted a close analysis of one famous witch trial: the trial of Isobel Gowdie in Scotland in 1652. She read Gowdie's confessions in detail and looked at the historical context, including the nature of witch trials at the time, pervasive beliefs about witches, common torture techniques used on accused witches, and the tradition of oral storytelling common in seventeenth-century Scotland. Ultimately, she concluded that material in the confession having to do with the devil was most likely Gowdie trying to tell her interrogators what they wanted to hear, but that the parts of her confession referencing fairies may have reflected genuine Scottish folklore and beliefs about fairies in the 1650s.[92]

There is no credible evidence for the widespread pan-European witch fertility religion that Murray had hypothesized, but that does not mean that all of the testimony from historical witch trials is completely useless. Some of the details included in that testimony may reflect genuine folk beliefs about magic, fairies, or the spirits of the land. The descriptions of fairies given in the witch trials are plausibly quite close to the way that people in that period genuinely thought about them, and to the folk stories that were told about fairies. Isobel Gowdie testified that the queen of fairy was richly dressed in white and brown, and that the king of fairy was a strong, broad man. She said that the fairies had whisked her away to a kingdom beneath a local hill, where they had feasted and given her more food than she could eat; further, she described the fairies as fickle, mischievous spirits who delighted in spoiling milk and laming cattle.[93] All of these details align with stories about the fairies that are told to this day.

---

91. Murray, *The Witch-Cult in Western Europe*, 176.

92. Wilby, *The Visions of Isobel Gowdie*, 95.

93. Wilby, *The Visions of Isobel Gowdie*, 40.

Murray's description of the witch cult, and of its deity, is rooted partially in such descriptions of the fairy queen and king. This connection extends beyond Murray's own work and touches on modern Goddess worship as well. Thanks in large part to the work Murray did in pointing out the place of the fairies in historical witch trials, modern witches and Goddess worshippers often draw extensively on fairy lore. The Goddess is commonly imagined as a beautiful woman decked in flowers, wearing ethereal white or earthy colors of green and brown. She may even present herself in different aspects depending on the seasons, appearing as a beautiful young maiden in the springtime and an ugly old woman in the winter. Depictions of fairies in popular culture, such as Shakespeare's Titania or the fairy godmother from Cinderella, strongly influence the picture many people have in their heads when they talk about the Goddess.

Would pre-modern Europeans have seen the fairy queen as an aspect of the universal Great Goddess? Almost certainly not. But with the publication of *The Witch-Cult in Western Europe*, Murray drew a link between the two. She drew on the existing connections between fairies and witchcraft in the popular mind, and she added the idea of a universal fertility deity at the center of the witch cult. This deity had its roots in historical accounts of Diana as the Goddess of witches, as well as in Frazer's Great Goddess theory and his universal myth of the dying-and-resurrecting God. From there, these figures became associated with the queen and king of the fairies. Murray established a link between them, which has lasted over a century into the modern day. Although there are still people today who do *not* link fairies to the Great Goddess, fairy lore has continued to inform how the world thinks and talks about the Goddess. She would not be who she is today if not for the connection Murray made between the Goddess and the fairy queen.

Key Takeaways: Murray

- Witchcraft as the survival of ancient pagan fertility religion
- Diana/Dianus as a deity who could have any gender
- Individuals assuming the role of the deity in ritual
- Emphasis on the sacred nature of revelry
- Identification of the Goddess with the queen of the fairies

——— RITUAL ———
The Esbat

For this ritual, you will reenact the witches' esbat according to Murray's framework. This is a ritual of light, where the abundant blessings of the Goddess are signaled by the progressive lighting of candles. In keeping with Murray's accounts, the ritual is followed by a feast and revelry.

Group Variation

Murray's accounts of witch religion always deal with covens, and she describes witch rituals as being community affairs. Here, you will reenact the esbat in the manner that Murray describes it, with one person taking the role of the queen of the sabbat and acting as the Goddess for the duration of the rite.

You Will Need

- A crown with candles in it
- A white robe for the queen of the sabbat
- Candles for all participants to hold
- A table
- A sheet or other cloth
- Food and drink for a feast: cold cuts, cheese, fruit, bread, etc.
- Musical instruments or a smartphone hooked up to a speaker

Preparation

The most difficult part of the setup for this ritual is the candle crown. You want a wreath with lit candles set into it, which can be placed upon the queen's head. If the wreath can be decorated with fresh greenery, so much the better, but that's not as important as the candles. If you search online, you can find a variety of sources with instructions for constructing a Santa Lucia's crown, a candle crown used in Sweden for the winter festival of St. Lucia; this is exactly the sort of thing you'll need for this rite. Alternatively, there are instructions for making a candle crown given in Janet and Stewart Farrar's book *A Witches' Bible*.[94] If you are

---

94. Farrar and Farrar, *A Witches' Bible*, 66–67.

uncomfortable using actual lit candles for this ritual because of the potential fire hazard, electric candles will work just as well.

At the start of the ritual, the table should be pushed to one side of the ritual space, opposite the door. All of the food for the feast should be laid out upon it and covered with the sheet. The queen waits in a separate room, along with one other person whom I call the officer, using a term borrowed from Murray.[95] All other participants wait inside the ritual space, holding unlit candles. They are in darkness.

In her room, the queen dresses in a white robe and puts on the crown, lighting the candles. She should be a striking figure, and should stand out from the crowd. One way to ensure this is to make sure that the queen's costume contrasts visually with everyone else's—for example, by dressing the queen in white and everyone else in black.

Performance

When the queen is ready, the officer takes a candle for themselves, lights it from one of the candles on the queen's crown, and enters the ritual room. If electric candles are being used, the officer should hold their candle to one of the queen's as if they were lighting a real candle, then turn on the switch to light it.

> OFFICER: Attend! Attend! The queen of the sabbat is coming!

If people have been talking, they all fall silent now. The queen enters the ritual space, moving slowly and regally. This will have a dramatic effect, and it has the added benefit of keeping her candles from going out. As she passes, people bow and avert their eyes. The queen walks across the room until she gets to the table, then turns and addresses the participants:

> QUEEN: I am your Goddess. I am your God. I give fruit to the field and beasts to the forest. Through me the womb quickens and the seed sprouts. Adore me and be blessed with life.

> ALL: We adore you.

---

95. Murray, *The Witch-Cult in Western Europe*, 138.

QUEEN: I am the feast at your table and the song that calls you from your bed. I am the cry of lovers in the dark. Adore me and be blessed with ecstasy.

ALL: We adore you.

QUEEN: Mine are the secrets of blessing and blight. This is my gift to you: to cause love or hate, to make men rich or poor, to bring rain or sun. Adore me and be blessed with power.

ALL: We adore you.

OFFICER: Come all ye before the God of the witches! Come and adore!

Each ritual participant comes before the queen in turn. They kneel before her and kiss her hand, and she offers them each a blessing:

PARTICIPANT: All my fealty to thee, my queen. *[kisses hand]*

QUEEN: It is accepted gladly. What boon do you seek?

PARTICIPANT: *[names blessing]* [96]

QUEEN: It is granted.

Once the participant has been granted their blessing, they stand and light their candle from one of the candles in the queen's crown. They then step away and let the next person come for a blessing.

When everyone has been blessed, all members of the ritual should be holding lit candles. The queen raises her hands and proclaims:

QUEEN: Behold! From darkness, I have given you light. I have come like the dawn to illumine your world and bring you joy. Night gives birth to day, silence to song, winter to spring, and I am at the center of it all.

OFFICER: We rejoice in your bounty!

QUEEN: Then let us feast and make merry!

---

96. The blessings should be simple and abstract, things like "health" or "prosperity"—not specific requests like "for my ex-wife to renegotiate our custody agreement" or "to get an A on my biology exam."

With the assistance of the officer, the queen removes the covering from the table, revealing the food and drink that have been laid out. At this point, anyone may come forward to eat and drink. Music should be played, either electronically or on live instruments, and people should dance and mingle freely. The ceremonial part of the ritual is over; what remains is just a good, old-fashioned party. If the queen wishes, she may remove her crown at this time and join the rest of the ritual participants. Likewise, the others may choose to extinguish their candles and flip a light switch in order to make it easier for them to eat, drink, and dance.

Solitary Variation

The witch cult as Murray described it was structured around covens and group ritual; Murray did not give any attention to the possibility of solitary practitioners. However, you can adapt this esbat ritual for solitary use with a candelabrum and an effigy as stand-ins for the queen of the sabbat.

You Will Need

- A candelabrum with three dinner tapers
- A statue, drawing, poppet, or other image of the Goddess
- A fourth candle and a candleholder
- A table
- A sheet or other cloth
- Food and drink for a feast: cold cuts, cheese, fruit, bread, etc.
- A musical instrument or an MP3 player hooked up to a speaker

Preparation

Place the food and drink on one end of the table and cover them with the sheet. Put your candelabrum on the other end of the table and light the central candle, leaving the other two unlit. Set your image of the Goddess in front of candelabrum and put your fourth candle and its candleholder off to one side. Have a musical instrument or an MP3 player on hand for the end of the ritual.

Performance

Stand in front of your table at the end with the candelabrum. Raise your hands and proclaim the start of the ritual:

Attend! Attend! The queen of the sabbat is coming!

Lift the lit central candle out of the candelabrum. Holding the candle high over your head, process slowly in a circle around your table. As you walk, say:

You are my Goddess. You are my God. You give fruit to the field
and beasts to the forest. Through you the womb quickens and the
seed sprouts. I adore you, to be blessed with life.

Replace the lit candle in the center of the candelabrum. Pick up your representation of the Goddess and kiss it, then set it back in place on the table. Take one of the unlit candles from the candelabrum and light it from the central one. Holding this new candle high above your head, process around the circle a second time, saying:

You are the feast at my table and the song that calls me from my
bed. You are the cry of lovers in the dark. I adore you, to be blessed
with ecstasy.

Replace the candle in the candelabrum. Pick up your representation of the Goddess and kiss it again, then set it back in place. Take the third candle from the candelabrum and light it from the central one. Holding it high above your head, process a third time around the circle, saying:

Yours are the secrets of blessing and blight. This is your gift to me:
to cause love or hate, to make men rich or poor, to bring rain or
sun. I adore you, to be blessed with power.

Replace the candle in the candelabrum. Pick up your representation of the Goddess and kiss it a third time, then lift it above your head. Exalting this image, say:

I come before the God of the witches! I come and adore! All fealty to
thee, my queen.

Replace the image on the table, then kneel and prostrate yourself in front of it. Kiss the ground before you and focus on the Goddess. Spend some time in prayer and meditation. When you are done, lift yourself up and take the fourth candle in your hand. Light it from the candelabrum, touching its wick to all three of the lit candles. As you do so, ask the Goddess for a blessing:

> *My queen, I come before you to ask a boon. Bless this humble witch*
> *with [your wish].* [97]

When your candle is lit, hold it in one hand and walk to the other end of the table. With your free hand, pull back the sheet and reveal the feast you have laid out. Say:

> *Behold! From darkness, the queen of the sabbat has given me light.*
> *She has come like the dawn to illumine the world and bring joy.*
> *Night gives birth to day, silence to song, winter to spring, and she is*
> *at the center of it all. I rejoice in her bounty! I shall feast and make*
> *merry!*

At this point, the ceremonial part of the ritual is over, and what remains is time for you to eat, drink, play music, and dance. You may put your lit candle back in its candleholder so that you have both hands free. Eat heartily and partake in the bounty of the Goddess. When you are done eating, quietly extinguish the candles to mark the end of the esbat.

---

97. The blessings should be simple and abstract, things like "health" or "prosperity"—not specific requests like "for my ex-wife to renegotiate our custody agreement" or "to get an A on my biology exam."

5

THE NEW AEON (1904)

AT ONE MEMORABLE RITUAL I attended, the priestess presiding over the rite had decided to experiment with oracular trance. She stood in front of the altar with a cup of wine held in both hands and invoked the Goddess, asking her to provide a message for each of the ritual participants. Then, one by one, each of us came in front of the priestess and she spoke to us, delivering personalized missives that she felt moved by the Goddess to share with us.

As I came before her, she smiled at me. Clouds of incense smoke wreathed around her, illuminated by flickering candlelight. The whole scene had an otherworldly quality to it, like something from a dream. Her red hair caught the light and shone like a flame, and I thought I could see twinkling stars behind her eyes. She was the very image of a Pythian oracle, transcendent and filled with a divine light that was much greater than her or any individual person in the room.

She swayed back and forth, lifting her cup to me. I reached out for it, so that my hands and hers were both clasped around the cup, and she pulled me toward her. In a low, soft voice, she spoke into my ear and told me what the Goddess wanted to say.

"You must delight in lust and joy and rapture," she said, "And you must always drink deeply from my cup. Do not fear excess, but abandon yourself to my love, for I am the Goddess of ecstasy. All sensual delights are sacred to me. Worship me in joy!"

She said other things to me that night, some of which were deeply personal, but those words in particular have stuck with me. Ever since that night, whenever

I attend a ritual and there is a component of sacred feasting and drinking, I make a point to take a long draught from the cup, savoring the gifts of the Goddess.

I am, by nature, a fuddy-duddy. I don't drink, smoke, or do drugs, and I even avoid caffeine because it takes too much of a toll on my body's circadian rhythm. Left to my own devices, I like to be in bed by ten and I don't indulge in vices more hardcore than the occasional ginger ale. The members of my coven jokingly call me "Grandpa" because I can't keep pace with them on a night out. I am not prone to excess.

The Goddess, on the other hand, is.

She does not require drunkenness and gluttony of her worshippers. If she did, that would be a huge problem for anyone who struggled with addiction or disordered eating. What the Goddess does require, however, is a willingness for people to embrace life fully and allow themselves to experience the delights of the senses. She is the Goddess of life and of the love for life. To worship her, I had to learn how to abandon myself to life's pleasures and to enjoy myself unreservedly.

Now, I drink deeply whenever my cup is filled in honor of the Goddess, although it contains fruit juice rather than wine. The simple act of accepting all that she has to offer is one of the deepest, most profound forms of worship I know. It is a form of letting go, giving myself over to the Goddess in her entirety, and not trying to hold back or limit what she gives to me. I accept all of her—and in doing so, I find the dissolution of my own ego, as I am transformed by the ecstasy of the divine. In the cup of the Goddess I taste eternity, and for just a moment I experience the rapture of her infinite, all-encompassing love.

Do What Thou Wilt

I am now going to rewind in time to a point before Murray had ever published about the witch cult. At the same time that Leland and Murray were building the idea of Pagan, Goddess-worshipping witchcraft, another strain of Goddess worship was developing. This was a more formal, structured approach to the Goddess, rooted not in ideas about folklore and witchcraft but rather in high ceremonial magic as it was practiced by the occultists of the late nineteenth and early twentieth centuries. Occultism in this period was dominated by initiatory secret societies, which were often organized into lodges modeled on Freemasonry. The magic worked in these lodges was inspired by Rosicrucianism, astrology, and Hermetic Qabalah, with other influences including tarot and medieval

Solomonic magic. Because the occult community was quite small, these lodges often interconnected; one organization would be started by former members of another, and individual people would belong to multiple secret orders at once.

One of the most famous magical practitioners to come out of this period was a man named Aleister Crowley. In 1904, Crowley was visiting Egypt with his wife at the time, Rose Edith Crowley (née Kelly). While they were there, he put her into a hypnotic trance, and she told him—as the story goes—that the god Horus was waiting for him. Subsequently, over three days from April 8 to April 10, a spirit named Aiwass dictated a series of mystical revelations, and Crowley and Kelly recorded these revelations in a text called *Liber AL Vel Legis: The Book of the Law*. This book would become the foundational text for a new religion of the twentieth century, which Crowley called *Thelema* after a Greek word meaning "will."

The central focus of Thelema is the concept of *true will*: the individual's alignment with their own higher self, and the discovery and pursuit of what that higher self truly desires. This is expressed in a core Thelemic maxim: "Do what thou wilt shall be the whole of the Law. Love is the law, love under will."[98] The charge to "do what thou wilt" is not merely license for people to selfishly do whatever they want; rather, it is a direction for people to discover what they *truly* will and to pursue that. True will is understood as something deep, spiritual, and inescapably individual. It transcends base impulses and desires, and is instead a matter of what a soul yearns for on the highest level. One person's true will may not be the same as another's, and each Thelemite has an obligation to discover their true will for themself. No one else can tell another person what their true will is. It's something that falls upon the individual.

Thelema is a magical religion built around this core philosophy. All of the Thelemic rituals that Crowley wrote incorporate occult symbolism and techniques, blending religious ritual with ceremonial magic. An important part of Thelema is the achievement of knowledge and conversation with the Holy Guardian Angel, a personal tutelary spirit who guides the Thelemic practitioner and is aligned with the practitioner's higher self. Crowley identified his own Holy Guardian Angel as the spirit Aiwass, who had dictated *The Book of the Law* to him. He wrote a ritual adapted from earlier occult sources, called the Bornless

---

98. Crowley, *Liber AL Vel Legis*, 13.

Ritual, which was designed to help bring the practitioner into conversation with their own personal Holy Guardian Angel. In addition to the Bornless Ritual, Crowley wrote magical rituals that drew on the energies of the four elements, the seven planets of traditional astrology, angels, demons, the Qabalistic Tree of Life, and much more besides. All of these rituals were geared toward what Crowley called the Great Work: discovering and then achieving one's true will.

Thelema is a highly individualistic religion and has no central authority beyond the writings of Aleister Crowley. However, there are various Thelemic organizations that offer public and private rituals, training, and magical initiations. One such organization is called the A∴ A∴ (*Argentium Astrum*, "the silver star") and was founded by Crowley. The most famous Thelemic body is called the *Ordo Templi Orientis*, or O.T.O.; the O.T.O. predates Crowley, but he reformed it drastically and turned it into a Thelemic organization when he took over its leadership. Beyond these two organizations, there are smaller bodies, as well as many Thelemites who practice on their own and do not belong to any group or governing body.

The legacy of Thelema has been long-lasting. Thelema as a religion is still alive today, but Crowley has had an effect even beyond Thelema. He was an extraordinarily influential magician, and he changed the face of modern occultism. Many of his books are cornerstones for magicians even today, with titles such as *Magick Without Tears* or *Magick in Theory and Practice*. He employed a convention of spelling "magick" with a K when talking about occult work; this, too, remains popular among magic(k)al practitioners. Crowley's effect on contemporary occultism truly cannot be overstated; the occult world was forever changed after him. The same is true for Goddess worship, as the view of the Goddess in Thelema became a major tributary to the larger Goddess movement.

The Three Aeons

I can now turn my attention to the deities of Thelema. *The Book of the Law* is divided into three chapters, each of which is narrated in the voice of a different Thelemic deity. These deities are named Nuit, Hadit, and Ra-Hoor-Khuit. Additionally, the three chapters of *The Book of the Law* reflect three periods of human history, each lasting approximately two thousand years. These three aeons are known as the aeons of Isis, Osiris, and Horus—and they can be understood to align with the three Thelemic figures given voice in *The Book of the Law*.

The first Thelemic deity is the goddess Nuit. Crowley describes Nuit as "Space—that is, the total of possibilities of every kind...This idea is for literary convenience symbolized by the Egyptian Goddess Nuit, a woman bending over like the Arch of the Night Sky."[99] Nuit is the original deity in Thelema, the source from which all other divine manifestation comes. She is, above all else, a goddess of possibility and potential. She contains within herself the beginnings of all things, not yet actualized, but ready to spring into existence. Crowley visualizes her as a sky goddess; she is a celestial, all-encompassing being, the backdrop against which all of the world is set.

Nuit is identified with the Egyptian goddess Isis; Crowley wrote that the first aeon of history was the aeon of "Isis, the mother, when the Universe was conceived as simple nourishment drawn directly from her; this period is marked by matriarchal government."[100] Thus, in Nuit, there are traces of the great Mother Goddess discussed by figures like Frazer and Bachofen, and there is also Bachofen's familiar claim that ancient civilization was originally matriarchal. For Crowley, matriarchy and the Mother Goddess are the first of three stages of human religion and civilization.

After the aeon of Isis comes the aeon of "Osiris, the father, when the universe was imagined as catastrophic; love, death, resurrection, as the method by which experience was built up; this corresponds to patriarchal systems."[101] Crowley draws on Frazer's familiar myth of Osiris as the dying-and-resurrecting God, marking these themes as the defining features of the second phase of human religious development—moving from the worship of the Mother Goddess to her consort, the God of death and resurrection. This aeon lasted from 500 BCE up to the year 1904, and Osiris can be connected to Hadit just as Isis connected to Nuit. Where Nuit was a goddess of potentiality, Hadit is a god of actuality; Crowley describes him as "any point which has experience of these possibilities," referring to the infinite possibilities contained within Nuit.[102]

Finally, beginning with the revelation of *The Book of the Law* in 1904, there is the aeon of Horus, the son of Isis and Osiris. Horus is linked to Ra-Hoor-Khuit,

---

99. Crowley, *Liber AL Vel Legis*, 10.

100. Crowley, *Liber AL Vel Legis*, 16.

101. Crowley, *Liber AL Vel Legis*, 16.

102. Crowley, *Liber AL Vel Legis*, 10.

a new god for the modern world.[103] Crowley saw the writing of *The Book of the Law* as a defining moment that would usher in a new period of human civilization, and he designed Thelema to be the religion of this new age. Ra-Hoor-Khuit is also called the Crowned and Conquering Child; he is the child born from the union of Nuit and Hadit, ushering in something new and greater than both of them. Where the era of Isis was matriarchal and the era of Osiris was patriarchal, the era of Horus is meant to be fiercely individual, where "there is no law beyond Do what thou wilt."[104]

Because I am most concerned with discussing the Goddess here, I am going to focus on Nuit. In Nuit, there are some familiar elements from previous iterations of the Goddess. She is labeled as the original Mother Goddess and aligned with an imagined prehistoric matriarchy, and her mythos is overlaid on the story of Isis and Osiris, which contributed to Frazer's theory of the Great Goddess. However, there are also traits in Nuit that were not previously part of the Great Goddess's mythos. For Bachofen and Frazer, the Goddess had been associated with the fecund power of the earth; for Crowley, she is beyond the earth and the material world. Nuit offers for the first time a transcendent, cosmic Goddess. Nuit exists beyond the physical world. It is a part of her, rather than her being a part of it. She also contains within herself the possibility for countless worlds other than our own, and the limitless expanse of time and space.

This transcendent Star Goddess is a face that the Goddess did not have before. With Crowley, the discussion of the Goddess pivots from the Earth Mother to a more mysterious, sublime deity. Nuit exists beyond the world of the senses, and because of that, she is not immediately present in the world the way that Bachofen's Earth Mother was understood to be. *The Book of the Law* states that if the universe is imagined as a sphere, "she, the circumference, is nowhere found"; she is at the outer reaches of everything, beyond anyone's ability to know directly.[105] Nuit is the Goddess as infinity. Coming face-to-face with her is the experience of contemplating the infinite expanse of the universe and realizing just how small you are. This experience is summed up beautifully in a passage of *The Book of the Law*:

---

103. Crowley, *Liber AL Vel Legis*, 16.
104. Crowley, *Liber AL Vel Legis*, 64.
105. Crowley, *Liber AL Vel Legis*, 38.

Then the priest answered & said unto the Queen of Space,
kissing her lovely brows, and the dew of her light bathing his
whole body in a sweet-smelling perfume of sweat: O Nuit, continuous one of Heaven, let it be ever thus; that men speak of
Thee not as One but as None; and let them not speak of thee
at all, since thou art continuous! [106]

Nuit is the ineffable, inexpressible Goddess. She is the infinite expanse of
space and time, stretching out to eternity in all directions. As Crowley describes
her, she may be known through a feeling of religious ecstasy, but as soon as you
try to put that feeling into words, you have failed, because she exists beyond all
words. This is a far cry from the physical, embodied Goddess worship presented
by thinkers like Bachofen. With Thelema, for the first time, the Goddess is
unearthly and transcendent.

Babalon and the Great Beast

Nuit is not the only face of the Goddess found in Thelema. There is another
Thelemic figure named Babalon, who is sometimes called the Scarlet Woman or
the Mother of Abominations. Her name is taken from the biblical book of Revelation:

Then the angel carried me away in the Spirit into a wilderness.
There I saw a woman sitting on a scarlet beast that was covered with blasphemous names and had seven heads and ten
horns. The woman was dressed in purple and scarlet, and was
glittering with gold, precious stones, and pearls. She held a
golden cup in her hand, filled with abominable things and the
filth of her adulteries. The name written on her forehead was
a mystery: BABYLON THE GREAT, THE MOTHER OF
PROSTITUTES AND OF THE ABOMINATIONS OF
THE EARTH.[107]

In the Bible, Babylon is described as profane and disgusting; for Crowley,
however, she was a divine figure. In her book *The Eloquent Blood: The Goddess*

---

106. Crowley, *Liber AL Vel Legis*, 28–29.

107. Revelation 17:3–5 (New International Version).

Babalon and the Construction of Femininities in Western Esotericism, Dr. Manon Hedenborg White describes Babalon as "a goddess symbolizing the magical formula of passionate union with all of existence, and the initiatory goal of ego death through ecstatic communion with the divine."[108] Babalon is a liberated, sexual goddess who revels in divine ecstasy; she is also the Earth Mother encountered in previous narratives about the Goddess. Where Nuit is transcendent and fundamentally beyond this world, Babalon is immanent and fundamentally of this world. She is the Goddess embodied.

Babalon's exact status in Thelema is complicated and somewhat unclear. In one sense, she is a goddess unto herself, another deity in the Thelemic pantheon. In another sense, Babalon is an aspect of the same divine principle that manifests as Nuit; she is the worldly counterpart to the all-encompassing cosmic Goddess. In yet another sense, the name is a reference to a particular ritual role held by priestesses within Thelema, as they ceremonially play the part of the Scarlet Woman in certain rituals. And in yet another sense, the name is a title given by Crowley to the various women with whom he had sexual and magical partnerships, the same way that artists would sometimes refer to a lover as their "muse." Babalon is all of these things at once: she is a goddess, a face of the Great Goddess, a ritual role, and a title used to refer to specific individuals.[109] Because of this, conversations about Babalon can be difficult, as commentators have to navigate who exactly they are talking about.

Just like Nuit, Babalon has a consort. This is Τo Μεγα Θηριον (*to mega thērion*, "the great beast"), whose name is taken from the beast ridden by Babylon in the book of Revelation; sometimes, he is also called Chaos. Crowley often referred to himself as "The Beast 666," a title given to him by his mother when he misbehaved as a child.[110] Later in his career, when he considered himself to have achieved magical adepthood, Crowley assumed the title "Master Therion." Thus, in one sense, Therion is simply another name for Crowley himself, just as Babalon was a name for his female lovers. Beyond that, however, the Great Beast is understood as a divine principle that complements the Goddess as Babalon. According to Crowley, "She rides astride the Beast; in her left hand she holds the

---

108. White, *The Eloquent Blood*, 2.

109. DuQuette, *The Magick of Aleister Crowley*, 76.

110. DuQuette, *The Magick of Aleister Crowley*, 76.

reins, representing the passion which unites them. In her right hand she holds aloft the cup, the Holy Grail aflame with love and death."[111] He awakens her sexuality and serves as her lover. He feeds her appetites and gives himself over to her divine ecstasy.

Babalon is an incredibly complex figure in Thelema, and this short chapter cannot do her justice. In a very crude sense, she is a sacred prostitute, embodying a highly sexualized view of womanhood and emphasizing women's receptive role in penetrative sexual intercourse. In this sense, Babalon and Therion are sometimes described as the partnership of passive and active.[112] Babalon is often represented by a cup or other vessel being filled with the power of Therion. She is the vagina and he is the phallus; she is the cup, and he is the wine that fills it. However, there is much more to Babalon than just this sexual dimension, and one would be remiss to reduce her to a misogynistic parody of womanhood. The cup of Babalon can symbolize the vagina in a superficial way, but it is much more besides; Crowley writes that "the Cup [is] an expansion—into the Infinite."[113] Babalon's cup represents the intuition and understanding of the magical practitioner, which liberate the magician's consciousness and allow for the discovery of one's true will. It is a symbol of divine love, not merely in a sexual sense, but in the sense of universal interconnectedness.

Thus, Crowley writes, "This is the danger of the Cup; it must necessarily be open to all, and yet if anything is put into it which is out of proportion, unbalanced, or impure, it takes hurt."[114] Babalon is the bliss of ecstatic union with the divine, awakening the magician to their will and the callings of the Great Work. The description of her as a sacred prostitute is not merely a warped view of women's sexuality, but rather a metaphorical expression of this deeper magical truth: Babalon accepts all sacrifices, and she turns nothing and no one away. Thelemic author Lon Milo DuQuette explains that "She eventually receives unto Herself the totality of the life of the evolving universe…This She shares with the Beast, and they unite in drunken ecstasy. Thus she is called the Great Whore for in her 'shamelessness' she receives all and refuses none."[115] Babalon is an undiscriminating power of divine

---

111. Crowley, *The Book of Thoth*, 94.

112. White, *The Eloquent Blood*, 208.

113. Crowley, *Magick*, 78.

114. Crowley, *Magick*, 78.

115. DuQuette, *The Magick of Aleister Crowley*, 77.

love, which allows the magician to experience magical transcendence; while this love can manifest as sexuality, it is no way limited to sexual expression. The title of "the Great Whore" is not merely a sexual pejorative, but rather an attempt to portray the universality with which she embraces all life.

Babalon presides over the mysteries of love, sacrifice, intoxication, transformation, and bliss. She is "the Divine Power and the underlying and secret force permeating all creation," and there is an evident connection between her and the more familiar, embodied worship of the Great Mother from Bachofen and Frazer's writings.[116] But she is also much more. It is through union with her that Thelemites are awakened to their true will and their ability to work magic and seek alchemical transformation.

——— EXERCISE ———

A Purifying Bath

The process of identifying and attaining one's true will is a long and involved one. Crowley identifies three principal stages in this process, and in all magical operations: purification, consecration, and initiation.[117] The final stage—initiation—is accomplished with the Bornless Ritual, where the Holy Guardian Angel is invoked by the powers of the four elements to reveal itself to the practitioner. However, this initiation must be preceded by a long process of ritual cleansing. The exercise given here offers a simple two-step purification and consecration, which you can use prior to most magical or ritual operations. You will need:

- A bathtub
- A cheesecloth
- A 6-inch length of twine
- 1 tbsp dried hyssop
- 7 drops olive oil
- 8 drops cinnamon essential oil
- 4 drops myrrh essential oil
- 2 drops galangal essential oil

---

116. DuQuette, *The Magick of Aleister Crowley*, 77.
117. Crowley, *Magick*, 184.

First, make the anointing oil and the herb sachet. In a small dish, mix together all of the oils in the proportion listed above.[118] Set the mixture aside. Cut the cheesecloth into a 6-inch by 6-inch square. Put the hyssop in the middle of the square, then fold the cheesecloth over the hyssop and tie it with the twine, making a sachet.

Fill your bathtub with hot water and add the sachet. Immerse yourself in the water, using your hyssop sachet to gently scrub at your skin. Take some time to meditate and allow yourself to feel the water washing you clean. As you bathe, you are scrubbing away the miasma of the ordinary world, leaving yourself in a state of ritual purity where you are fit to do magic. While you bathe, repeat the following words:

> Thou shalt purge me with hyssop, O Therion, and I shall be clean;
> thou shalt wash me, and I shall be whiter than snow.[119]

This prayer of purification is adapted from Psalm 51, with the name of the Thelemic deity Therion substituted in. It is Therion who purifies you so that you can undergo the initiatory ordeal presented by Babalon. Crowley gives the prayer in Latin: *Asperges me, Therion, hyssopo, et mundabor; lavabis me, et super nivem dealbador.* If you prefer, you can use the Latin, but if trying to speak Latin will distract you from your meditation, stick to the English.

Bathe for as long as you feel you need to, until you achieve a sense of peace and cleanliness. When you feel you have washed away the ordinary world, get out of the bath and drain the tub.

After toweling off, dip a finger into your prepared anointing oil and anoint your forehead, saying:

> Inflame in us, Therion, the fire of your love, and the flame of eternal devotion.[120]

This phrase is taken from the Catholic mass. Again, if you wish, you may use the Latin that Crowley gives: *Accendat in nobis Therion ignem sui amoris et flammam aeternae caritatis.* However, if the Latin is going to make you stumble over

---

118. Crowley, *Magick*, 739.
119. Crowley, *Magick*, 214.
120. Crowley, *Magick*, 215.

your words, you can keep to the English. Due to the cinnamon essential oil present in the mixture, the anointing oil will sting your skin and turn it red. This is intentional; Crowley writes that "when placed upon the skin it should burn and thrill through the body with an intensity as of fire."[121] Nonetheless, be careful with the oil. Don't use too much, and be sure not to get any in your eyes.

Anoint your right shoulder, saying the same "Inflame in us..." words as you did above. Then anoint your left shoulder, your right wrist, your left wrist, the center of your chest, your right knee, your left knee, the spot just above your pubic hair, and finally your feet. With each anointing, repeat the words of consecration.

When you have finished anointing yourself, wash your hands to get rid of any excess oil. Then don a fresh robe or any other ritual attire you use. You are now ready to proceed with your ritual work. If you were planning to perform the Bornless Ritual, you would undergo a much more extensive period of ritual purification. This might include baths and anointing such as the ones described, but it would also include other forms of purification such as a vegetarian diet, sexual abstinence, and extended prayer.[122] For ordinary ritual or magical purposes, however, this exercise is more than enough.

Thelema, Sex, and Samadhi

Much of the language, ritual, and symbolism of Thelema is sexual in nature. The deities of Thelema are never presented on their own, but rather relative to a sexual coupling. Ra-Hoor-Khuit is the divine child produced by the union of Nuit and Hadit; the Great Work of the magician's initiation is accomplished through the symbolic coupling of Babalon and Chaos. This overt sexual symbolism is not merely a result of Crowley's high libido. There is, rather, something deeper at work here, a yearning for higher mystical truth that finds expression through sexual language.

Crowley's use of sexual imagery is inspired in part by a fascination with non-European mysticism. Crowley lived at the height of the British Empire in a time when British control extended over much of the Middle East and South Asia. When *The Book of the Law* was revealed, Egypt was subject to British rule, as European imperial powers encroached upon the Ottoman Empire's sphere of

---

121. Crowley, *Magick*, 60.

122. Crowley, *Magick*, 211–12.

influence in the buildup to the First World War. Part of Crowley's fascination with Egyptian magic and religion stemmed from a colonial interest in extracting the wisdom of the "Orient" and bringing it back to Britain.

Outside of Egypt, Crowley's main source of eastern inspiration was yoga, specifically tantra. India was also part of the British Empire, and Crowley had spent an extensive period of time traveling through it, particularly on mountaineering expeditions in the Himalayas.[123] While there, he acquired an acute interest in Hinduism and tantric mysticism. In particular, Crowley was fascinated with the sexual element of tantra and the idea that sex could be something mystical and sacred rather than profane or merely animalistic. He was taken with the yogic notion of samadhi, a state divine bliss and dissolution of the self. Crowley described this dissolution by writing that "in *samādhi* the Many and the One are united in a union of Existence with non-Existence."[124] There are many ways to achieve samadhi, but the one that seized Crowley's imagination the most was the experience of sexual rapture. He saw this as the key to accomplishing the Great Work, allowing the magician to experience transcendence of their individual self through sexual union with another—and, thereby, to achieve communion with their Holy Guardian Angel.

It was a sexual experience with his lover Victor Neuberg that allowed Crowley to fulfill the Great Work himself and, he felt, bestowed upon him the status of Master of the Temple. From there, Crowley built much of his magic around sexual symbolism, trying to point the way for others to achieve samadhi as well. As biographer Alan Richardson notes, Crowley "had already known that the sexual act did not detract from the glory of God, but it was only in this moment that he realised it could actually be done to the glory of God and made a sacrament."[125] Crowley's own experience of sexuality opened him up to a transformative magical and mystical experience; it helped him to achieve samadhi and to dissolve his individual consciousness in something infinitely larger than himself. In writing the rituals of Thelema, he then used the language of sex to try to communicate that same experience to others.

---

123. Kaczynski, *Perdurabo*, 96.
124. Crowley, *Magick*, 38.
125. Richardson, *Aleister Crowley and Dion Fortune*, 128–29.

It would be reductive and incorrect to say that Thelema is all about sex. Rather, the sexual symbolism pervasive in Thelema is a way of hinting at an experience that is fundamentally inexpressible. For Crowley, sexual ecstasy was the closest analogue to the divine ecstasy that marked the fulfillment of the Great Work. The sexual pairings of Nuit and Hadit, or of Therion and Babalon, were manifestations of a much larger magical principle. He saw that the world was artificially divided into self and other, lover and beloved, me and thee, and that the true path to initiatory transformation required dissolving these boundaries and allowing the self and the other to become one. Hedenborg White notes that "Crowley writes in the commentary that…Babalon's formula entails 'constant copulation or *samādhi* on everything.'"[126] In order to achieve their true will, magicians must sacrifice all of themselves to the Goddess, draining their blood into the cup of Babalon so that they may be reborn. They give themselves over entirely to her and lose themselves in her. This is the great mystery of Thelema.

Crowley's theoretical writings and the rituals of Thelema point to sexual magic as one way of achieving this dissolution of the self. What Crowley took from tantric mysticism was the idea that sexual bliss is merely an expression of divine bliss, and that by losing oneself in the act of sex, magicians could also open their understanding to the transformative power of the divine. Thus, mystical union with Babalon could be accomplished through sexual union with a human lover.

Sex is, importantly, not the only path to accomplishing the Great Work. Sex is a smaller manifestation of a larger divine principle, not the other way around. Although Crowley presented sexual ecstasy as one way of achieving samadhi, sex and samadhi are not the same thing, and there are other ways for the magician to experience this transcendence. However, sexual symbolism and language run throughout Crowley's Thelemic writings, and when they appear, you would do well to understand that he is not just talking about sex. Rather, sex is a convenient shorthand for him to hint at a larger, indescribable experience: the initiatory death of the ego and the mystical union of the magician with Babalon, which allow for knowledge and conversation with the Holy Guardian Angel.

---

126. White, *The Eloquent Blood*, 58.

Key Takeaways: Crowley

+ Individual actualization and the doctrine of true will
+ The three aeons of Isis, Osiris, and Horus
+ Nuit and Babalon as the transcendent and immanent faces of the Goddess
+ Babalon as the power of universal, indiscriminate divine love
+ Union with the Goddess as the key to magic and the Great Work

―――― RITUAL ――――
OPENING THE VEIL

One of the central rituals of Thelema is the *Ecclesiae Gnosticae Catholicae Canon Missae*, or the Gnostic Mass. Crowley penned this ritual in 1915, while he was in Moscow. The full Gnostic Mass is an elaborate ritual, with complex specifications for the dimensions of the altar and the temple, the use of secondary altars, additional ritual roles, and so on; many of these specifications have Qabalistic significance and add to the symbolism of the rite.

Due to its complexity, I am unable to offer Crowley's Gnostic Mass as a ritual for you to perform on your own. What I offer instead is a simplified version of one portion of the original ritual: section IV of the Gnostic Mass, titled "Of the Ceremony of the Opening of the Veil." I have modified some of the stage directions and ritual actions for the sake of performance, but all of the spoken lines are preserved from Crowley's original. If you live near an O.T.O. chapter and are able to attend a Gnostic Mass, I highly encourage you to do so; it is a beautiful ritual, and a pared-down version cannot do the original justice.

Group Variation

In this ritual, a priest embodying Hadit enthrones a priestess on the altar and invokes Nuit into her body. From behind a veil, Nuit then speaks to the ritual participants, delivering a speech taken from *The Book of the Law*. Afterward, the priest pierces the veil with his lance, symbolizing the sexual union of Nuit and Hadit as well as the priest's own discovery of mysteries beyond his individual consciousness.

You Will Need

+ An altar sturdy enough for the priestess to sit on
+ A red altar cloth
+ A dais with three steps leading up to it; if a dais is unavailable, you may use three stepping stones arranged in a line
+ Two pillars, one white and one black; in a pinch, these can be made out of painted refrigerator boxes
+ A veil or curtain that can stretch between the two pillars, and a rod on which to hang it

+ A copy of *The Book of the Law*
+ A censer and incense
+ A ewer full of salt water
+ A lance

Preparation

Assign roles for the priestess, priest, a deacon, and an assistant. Crowley refers to the assistant as a "child," but the role can be played by an adult. Arrange the ritual space with the altar in the east on top of the dais, or with the altar in the east and three stepping stones leading up to it. Place the altar cloth over the top of the altar. Put the pillars slightly in front of the altar and to either side of it, with the white pillar on the right and the black pillar on the left; hang the veil on a rod between them so that it can be drawn closed to conceal the altar. Place *The Book of the Law* on the altar.

Performance

At the start of the ritual, the priest stands in the far west of the room, holding a spear in his right hand. The priestess, deacon, and child stand in front of him, facing him. The child holds a ewer of salt water in one hand and a lit censer with incense in the other hand. All other participants are seated around the edge of the room so that they can see the altar in the east, but so that the veil will obscure the altar from their view when it is drawn between the two pillars. The priest says:

> PRIEST: Thee therefore whom we adore we also invoke. By the power of the lifted Lance!

He raises the lance. All participants raise their hands in salute. The priest takes the priestess by her right hand with his left, keeping the lance raised. He says:

> PRIEST: I, PRIEST and KING, take thee, Virgin pure without spot; I upraise thee; I lead thee to the East; I set thee upon the summit of the Earth.

He leads the priestess to the altar and enthrones her upon it. The deacon and child follow behind him. The priestess takes *The Book of the Law*, resumes her seat, and holds it open on her breast with her two hands, making a descending triangle with her thumbs and forefingers. The priest gives the lance to the deacon to hold, takes the ewer from the child, and sprinkles the priestess, making five crosses over her forehead, shoulders, and thighs. He hands the ewer back to the child and takes the censer, making five crosses over the priestess as before, then hands the censer back to the child.

The priestess kisses *The Book of the Law* three times. The priest kneels in front of her in adoration, with his hands joined together. Then he rises and draws the veil in front of the altar. All participants stand. The priest takes the lance from the deacon and holds it uplifted. He walks around the perimeter of the ritual space three times, followed by the deacon and the child. On the last turn, the deacon and the child leave him and go to the center of the ritual space, where they kneel facing the altar. All other participants kneel in the same way.

The priest returns to the east and mounts the first step of the dais or the first of the three stepping stones, saying:

PRIEST: O circle of Stars whereof our Father is but the younger brother, marvel beyond imagination, soul of infinite space, before whom Time is Ashamed, the mind bewildered, and the understanding dark, not unto Thee may we attain, unless Thine image be Love. Therefore by seed and root and stem and bud and leaf and flower and fruit do we invoke Thee.

He continues the invocation, quoting *The Book of the Law*:

PRIEST: "Then the priest answered & said unto the Queen of Space, kissing her lovely brows, and the dew of her light bathing his whole body in a sweet-smelling perfume of sweat; O Nuit, continuous one of Heaven, let it be ever thus; that men speak not of thee as One but as None; and let them speak not of thee at all, since thou art continuous."

While he speaks, the priestess behind the veil disrobes, so that she is sitting nude on the altar. Once the priest has finished speaking, she responds, quoting *The Book of the Law*:

PRIESTESS: "But to love me is better than all things; if under the night-stars in the desert thou presently burnest mine incense before me, invoking me with a pure heart, and the serpent flame therein, thou shalt come a little to lie in my bosom. For one kiss wilt thou then be willing to give all; but whoso gives one particle of dust shall lose all in that hour. Ye shall gather goods and store of women and spices; ye shall wear rich jewels; ye shall exceed the nations of the earth in splendour and pride; but always in the love of me, and so shall ye come to my joy. I charge you earnestly to come before me in a single robe, and covered with a rich head-dress. I love you! I yearn to you! Pale or purple, veiled or voluptuous, I who am all pleasure and purple, and drunkenness of the innermost sense, desire you. Put on the wings, and arouse the coiled splendour within you: come unto me!" "To me! To me!" "Sing the rapturous love-song unto me! Burn to me perfumes! Wear to me jewels! Drink to me, for I love you! I love you. I am the blue-lidded daughter of sunset; I am the naked brilliance of the voluptuous night-sky. To me! To me!"

The priest mounts the second step and says:

PRIEST: O secret of secrets that art hidden in the being of all that lives, not Thee do we adore, for that which adoreth is also Thou. Thou art That, and That am I.

He quotes *The Book of the Law* again:

PRIEST: "I am the flame that burns in every heart of man, and in the core of every star. I am Life, and the giver of Life; yet therefore is the knowledge of me the knowledge of death." "I am alone; there is no God where I am."

The deacon rises to their feet, and everyone else follows suit. The deacon delivers instructions to the other participants, taken from *The Book of the Law:*

DEACON: "But ye, O my people, rise up and awake.
Let the rituals be rightly performed with joy and beauty.
There are rituals of the elements and feasts of the times.
A feast for the first night of the Prophet and his Bride!
A feast for the three days of the writing of the Book of the Law.

A feast for Tahuti and the children of the Prophet—secret, O Prophet!
A feast for the Supreme Ritual, and a feast for the Equinox of the Gods.
A feast for fire and a feast for water; a feast for life and a greater feast for
   death!
A feast every day in your hearts in the joy of my rapture!
A feast every night unto Nu, and the pleasure of uttermost delight!"

The priest mounts the third step and invokes Ra-Hoor-Khuit, the god of the new aeon, saying:

PRIEST: Thou that art One, our Lord in the Universe the Sun, our Lord
   in ourselves whose name is Mystery of Mystery, uttermost being whose
   radiance enlightening the worlds is also the breath that maketh every
   God even and Death to tremble before Thee—by the Sign of Light
   appear Thou glorious upon the throne of the Sun. Make open the path
   of creation and of intelligence between us and our minds. Enlighten our
   understanding. Encourage our hearts. Let thy light crystallize itself in our
   blood, fulfilling us of Resurrection.
   A ka dua
   Tuf ur biu
   Bi a'a chefu
   Dudu nur af an nuteru.

During this speech, the priestess may remain nude or don her robe depending on her comfort level. When the priest has finished speaking, she responds with the law of Thelema as given in *The Book of the Law*:

PRIESTESS: "There is no law beyond Do what thou wilt."

The priest parts the veil with his lance, revealing the priestess enthroned on the altar.[127]

---

127. Crowley, *Magick*, 587–90. Lines from the Gnostic Mass reproduced with permission of the O.T.O.

Solitary Variation

The Gnostic Mass is designed for a group performance. You can enact a version of it on your own by enthroning a cup to represent the Goddess in the priestess's stead, but you will need to deliver Nuit's speech yourself since there is no one else to speak on her behalf. Thus, you act both as the Goddess and as the priest who invokes her.

You Will Need

- An altar
- A red altar cloth
- Two pillar candles, one white and one black
- A chalice
- A veil or handkerchief that can cover your cup
- A copy of *The Book of the Law*
- A censer and incense
- A ewer full of salt water
- A lance

Preparation

Place your altar in the east of your ritual space and cover it with the altar cloth. Set the two pillar candles on the altar, with the white one on your right and the black one on your left. Light the candles. Light the censer and add incense to it; place it, the ewer, and the veil on the ground near the altar, taking care not to place the censer on or next to anything flammable. Set *The Book of the Law* on the altar between the two candles.

Performance

To start the rite, stand in the west of your ritual space, holding your lance in your right hand and your chalice in your left hand. Say:

> *Thee therefore whom I adore I also invoke. By the power of the lifted Lance! I, PRIEST and KING, take thee, Virgin pure without spot; I upraise thee; I lead thee to the East; I set thee upon the summit of the Earth.*

Walk to the altar and place your chalice on it, between the two pillars and behind *The Book of the Law*. Set your lance down on the ground and pick up the ewer, sprinkling five crosses over the cup. Set the ewer down and pick up the censer, making five crosses as before. Set the censer down and take *The Book of the Law* from the altar, holding it open on your breast with your two hands, making a descending triangle with your thumbs and forefingers. Hold it there for a moment, then kiss it three times and set it back on the altar. Place your veil or handkerchief over the chalice so that it is obscured from your vision.

Pick up your lance and hold it aloft in your right hand, then walk around the perimeter of your ritual space three times. When you have finished your procession, stand in front of your altar, about three paces back from it. Take a step forward and kneel, saying:

> *O circle of Stars whereof our Father is but the younger brother,*
> *marvel beyond imagination, soul of infinite space, before whom*
> *Time is Ashamed, the mind bewildered, and the understanding*
> *dark, not unto Thee may I attain, unless Thine image be Love.*
> *Therefore by seed and root and stem and bud and leaf and flower*
> *and fruit do I invoke Thee.*

Continue the invocation, quoting from *The Book of the Law*:

> *"Then the priest answered & said unto the Queen of Space, kissing*
> *her lovely brows, and the dew of her light bathing his whole body*
> *in a sweet-smelling perfume of sweat; O Nuit, continuous one of*
> *Heaven, let it be ever thus; that men speak not of thee as One*
> *but as None; and let them speak not of thee at all, since thou art*
> *continuous."*

Place a hand over your eyes and recite the words of the Goddess Nuit. Because your eyes are covered for this portion of the ritual, you will have to memorize this speech, even if you refer to a script for the rest of the rite. As an alternative, you can pre-record yourself reading this speech and play the recording back at this point in the ritual. Say:

> *"But to love me is better than all things; if under the night-stars in*
> *the desert thou presently burnest mine incense before me, invoking*

me with a pure heart, and the serpent flame therein, thou shalt
come a little to lie in my bosom. For one kiss wilt thou then be
willing to give all; but whoso gives one particle of dust shall lose all
in that hour. Ye shall gather goods and store of women and spices;
ye shall wear rich jewels; ye shall exceed the nations of the earth in
splendour and pride; but always in the love of me, and so shall ye
come to my joy. I charge you earnestly to come before me in a single
robe, and covered with a rich head-dress. I love you! I yearn to you!
Pale or purple, veiled or voluptuous, I who am all pleasure and
purple, and drunkenness of the innermost sense, desire you. Put on
the wings, and arouse the coiled splendour within you: come unto
me!" "To me! To me!" "Sing the rapturous love-song unto me! Burn
to me perfumes! Wear to me jewels! Drink to me, for I love you! I
love you. I am the blue-lidded daughter of sunset; I am the naked
brilliance of the voluptuous night-sky. To me! To me!"

Uncover your eyes. Stand, take a step forward, and kneel again, saying:

O secret of secrets that art hidden in the being of all that lives, not
Thee do I adore, for that which adoreth is also Thou. Thou art
That, and That am I.

Continue, quoting The Book of the Law again:

"I am the flame that burns in every heart of man, and in the core
of every star. I am Life, and the giver of Life; yet therefore is the
knowledge of me the knowledge of death." "I am alone; there is no
God where I am."

Stand and spread your arms wide. Recite the holy days of Thelema, as given
in The Book of the Law:

"But ye, O my people, rise up and awake.
Let the rituals be rightly performed with joy and beauty.
There are rituals of the elements and feasts of the times.
A feast for the first night of the Prophet and his Bride!
A feast for the three days of the writing of the Book of the Law.

*A feast for Tahuti and the children of the Prophet—secret, O
Prophet!*
*A feast for the Supreme Ritual, and a feast for the Equinox of the
Gods.*
*A feast for fire and a feast for water; a feast for life and a greater
feast for death!*
A feast every day in your hearts in the joy of my rapture!
A feast every night unto Nu, and the pleasure of uttermost delight!"

Take a third step forward. You should now be standing immediately in front
of the altar. Invoke Ra-Hoor-Khuit, the god of the new aeon, saying:

*Thou that art One, my Lord in the Universe the Sun, my Lord in
myself whose name is Mystery of Mystery, uttermost being whose
radiance enlightening the worlds is also the breath that maketh
every God even and Death to tremble before Thee—by the Sign of
Light appear Thou glorious upon the throne of the Sun. Make open
the path of creation and of intelligence between me and my mind.
Enlighten my understanding. Encourage my heart. Let thy light
crystallize itself in my blood, fulfilling me of Resurrection.*
A ka dua
Tuf ur biu
Bi a'a chefu
Dudu nur af an nuteru.

Lower your lance until it is touching the veiled chalice. Pronounce the law of
Thelema, as given in *The Book of the Law*:

"There is no law beyond Do what thou wilt."

Using the tip of your lance, gently remove the veil from the chalice, revealing
the holy grail of the Goddess on the altar.[128]

---

128. Crowley, *Magick*, 587–90. Lines from the Gnostic Mass reproduced with permission of
the O.T.O. and modified to the first person singular.

6

ALL GODDESSES ARE
ONE GODDESS (1938)

THERE ARE FEW TEMPLES to the Goddess in today's world. Building temples requires land, money, and a sizable population of worshippers. Goddess religion, on the whole, has none of these things. There are a few Pagan and Goddess-oriented organizations, but Goddess worship is decentralized, with no formal body that can pool the resources to purchase or develop land. Goddess worshippers tend to be scattered geographically as well, making it difficult to find a location where there would be enough pilgrims to support a temple in the long run. There is one Goddess temple in Glastonbury, which I had the privilege to visit on a recent trip to the United Kingdom, but beyond that, it's difficult to find sacred sites dedicated specifically to the Goddess.

Most of the time, if I want to feel the presence of the Goddess, I go out into nature. Wandering alone through a forest path or watching the moon rise over a lake, it is easy to feel her immanence in the world. An offering of fresh water poured out upon the earth, a spoken prayer, a hand laid upon the trunk of a tree, and the Goddess is with me. Sometimes, though, I want something more concrete—not just the pervasive presence of the Goddess in the world, but a sacred site that has been specifically built by human hands in her honor. On these occasions, I make a pilgrimage to New York City and visit the Metropolitan Museum of Art.

At the far end of the Egyptian Wing of the museum stands the Temple of Dendur. It is a complete temple from Roman Egypt, built in approximately 15 BCE. In 1965, the temple was deconstructed stone by stone and shipped to America as a gift from the Egyptian government. There, it was rebuilt in its entirety, dominating an open chamber in the Fifth Avenue mansion that houses the Met's main collection. The temple stands on an elevated platform at the center of the chamber, its entrance flanked by two stone pillars. A pool of water sits before the temple, so anyone approaching the site must go around to the side and mount the steps onto the platform before turning to the entrance of the temple itself.

The Temple of Dendur was dedicated to the goddess Isis at the time of its construction. Now, no incense is burned there, no libations are poured, and no hymns are sung, but the site still feels holy. Every time I walk through the Egyptian Wing and step into the final chamber where the temple is held, I am awash with tranquility. Here is a place of stillness, outside the passage of time. Thousands of people flood through this room every day, ebbing and flowing like the tide, but the temple sits fixed on its platform, constant and unchanging. Whether in America or in Egypt, the Temple of Dendur has stood for thousands of years, and I know it will continue to stand long after I am gone from the world.

Each time I visit, I peer through the entrance into the inner sanctum of the temple. A chill passes through me, and I know that Isis is still here, inhabiting the sacred house that was built for her on the other side of the world. She watches over the tides of human civilization, and though the temple is no longer in active use by a priesthood, it is still very much alive with her presence. As I climb the steps to stand before the temple of Isis, I come before her as another postulant among the countless thousands who have worshipped her.

A second certainty settles over me, as well: This is my Goddess, the same Goddess that I saw stretched out across the sky that night in Bryant Park. I may know her by a different name, but as I stand in awe of Isis, I have no doubt that she is one and the same as the Goddess I know. Over the millennia, her rites have been lost and reimagined, her names have changed, even her stories have been rewritten—but the Goddess herself is the same. I'm not much of a soft polytheist, and this kind of syncretism goes against my theological sensibilities; I *know* that the Goddess is a modern deity, that the way I worship her now is simply not the same as how Isis was worshipped in the year 15 BCE.

But when I feel the presence of Isis in her own temple, those sensibilities don't matter. The Goddess doesn't have to make sense to me, doesn't have to shrink herself to fit the limits of what my rational mind can allow. She is greater than that, and what she is does not depend upon what I know. And somehow, yes, she is ancient Isis even at the same time that she is something decidedly new.

The Magic of Gender

Crowley was not the only ceremonial magician to have an impact on modern Goddess worship. Another key figure in the Goddess movement was an occultist named Dion Fortune. Born as Violet Firth, Fortune adopted a pseudonym for her occult work. The name was based on her magical motto, *deo non fortuna* ("God, not fate"), which in turn came from her family motto. She and Crowley had both been members of a British secret society called the Hermetic Order of the Golden Dawn before leaving the order to pursue their own interests. Crowley founded the religion of Thelema; meanwhile, Fortune started an occult society called the Fraternity of Inner Light, later renamed the Society of Inner Light. With this society, she carried on many of the magical teachings of the Golden Dawn along with her own additions and innovations.

Fortune was an extraordinarily influential magician, and her book *The Mystical Qabalah* is the landmark text of modern hermetic Qabalah. She was fascinated by the magic of gender, and she wrote at great length about the respective roles that men and women could perform in occult ritual. Like the other thinkers I've presented, Fortune had reductive ideas about gender that are now outdated. She believed that reality was divided into several planes, and that men and women formed a polarity of active and passive—but that this polarity alternated between the material and subtle planes. Thus, in Fortune's view, men are physically active but psychically receptive, while women are physically receptive but psychically active:

> While the male gives the physical stimulus which leads to
> reproduction, he does not realise that on the inner planes he is by
> virtue of the law of reversed polarity, negative, and is dependent
> for emotional completeness upon the stimulation given by the
> female. He is dependent upon her for emotional fertilisation.[129]

To Fortune's mind, this gender polarity extended beyond the relationship between individual practitioners; it was a fundamental feature of all reality, up to and including the gods. In her 1938 novel *The Sea Priestess*, she wrote "that at the dawn of manifestation the gods wove the web of creation between the poles of the pairs of opposites, active and passive, positive and negative, and that all

---

129. Fortune, *The Mystical Qabalah*, 141.

things are these two things in different ways and upon different levels."[130] Fortune envisioned the magical and divine world as inexorably gendered, built up of male and female pairs in various guises. This extended to the gods themselves; Fortune is perhaps most famous for her claim that "all the gods are one god, and all the goddesses are one goddess."[131] For Dion Fortune, all the various deities of world mythology were just different faces and names given to the two primordial powers, a Goddess and a God.

There were syncretic attitudes in other authors who wrote about the Great Goddess, many of whom had the idea that the universal myth of the Goddess and her consort would appear under various guises across world mythology. However, Dion Fortune provides the clearest and sharpest articulation of this theological position. Fortune saw all deities as facets of the same gendered divine energy, which she often articulated in Qabalistic terms. Thus, for her, every goddess and every myth was more or less interchangeable, merely providing a different point of view on the one Great Goddess. This is a stronger claim than found in previous authors; even Frazer cherry-picked his sources for the myth of the Goddess, focusing on Mediterranean myths that fit his narrative and excluding the various myths that did not. Part of the reason for this aggressive syncretism may be an expanding interest in non-European cultures, as like Crowley, Fortune was fascinated by the so-called wisdom of the Orient.

In 1936, Fortune set herself up in an abandoned church in London.[132] She converted this church to a ritual space, which she used to stage a series of rites dedicated to the Great Goddess and God. These rituals were called the Rites of Isis and Pan, respectively—as the goddess Isis and the god Pan were the two figures that Fortune most often used as stand-ins for her universal Goddess and God. The rites were performed for an audience that included non-occultists, although attendance was invitation only. In performing her rituals this way, Fortune brought her vision of the Great Goddess to a wider audience, introducing it to people who had never encountered the world of ceremonial magic and secret societies.

Fortune's work did a great deal to popularize the modern idea of a syncretic Goddess who subsumed all others. Like Crowley, she brought the Goddess into the twentieth century and wrote rituals that allowed modern people to worship

---

130. Fortune, *The Sea Priestess*, 124.

131. Fortune, *The Sea Priestess*, 169.

132. Fortune, *Dion Fortune's Rites of Isis and of Pan*, 8.

her, rather than just reading accounts of how the Goddess might have been worshipped long ago in faraway places. Also like Crowley, Fortune took inspiration from the Egyptian goddess Isis, drawing on her myth and symbolism as one of the primary sources for her eternal Goddess figure.

Her work in popularizing the Goddess was not limited to ritual and magic. Fortune also wrote a series of esoteric novels intended for the general public, which incorporated symbolism and concepts from her occult work. In this way, she hoped to make her ideas more accessible to the world at large. She wrote, "It is because my novels are packed with such things as these…that I want my students to take them seriously. The 'Mystical Qabalah' gives the theory, but the novels give the practice."[133] Her novels were meant to be an introduction to the world of occultism, magic, and the Gods.

The most famous and significant of Fortune's occult novels is *The Sea Priestess*. Published in 1938, it tells the story of an asthmatic real estate agent who meets a mysterious and powerful woman. This woman, it turns out, is a priestess dedicated to the Great Goddess, and she enlists the novel's protagonist to help her accomplish her ritual work. *The Sea Priestess* includes long discussions of the nature of the Goddess and Fortune's thoughts about gender in magic and religion, as well as extended ritual sequences that are lifted directly from Fortune's own Rite of Isis. *The Sea Priestess* brings the Goddess to life in narrative form, showing exactly how Fortune thought the Goddess should be worshipped and the effects that this worship should have on the people who dedicated themselves to its service. This novel has served as inspiration for generations of Goddess worshippers, shaping their ideas about who the Goddess is and how they can invoke her.

The Sea Priestess

The protagonist of *The Sea Priestess* is Wilfred Maxwell, a real estate agent in the parochial English town of Dickford. At the start of the novel, Wilfred is asthmatic and foul-tempered, a bachelor living with his domineering mother and sister. He is frequently incapacitated by his asthma attacks, and he is dependent upon morphine to ease his asthma. Right at the beginning of the book, Wilfred has a divine revelation of the hidden mystical nature of the moon, while he is suffering a particularly acute asthma attack and is out of his mind on morphine:

---

133. Fortune, *The Sea Priestess*, xiii.

> She ruled over a kingdom that was neither material nor spiritual,
> but a strange moon-kingdom of her own. In it moved tides—
> ebbing, flowing, slack water, high water, never ceasing, always
> on the move; up and down, backwards and forwards, rising and
> receding; coming past on the flood, flowing back on the ebb; and
> these tides affected our lives. They affected birth and death and
> all the processes of the body…if I could only learn the rhythm
> and periodicity of her tides I should know a very great deal.[134]

Wilfred's encounter with the moon instills in him a deep yearning for the mystical. This yearning is answered when a woman named Vivien Le Fay Morgan moves to Dickford. Wilfred subsequently starts calling her Morgan Le Fay, after the figure from Arthurian myth. She reveals to Wilfred that she is a former lady's servant who inherited a large fortune from her mistress; she and her mistress had conducted a series of occult experiments, and through divination they had learned of a hidden cave where ancient Britons had performed human sacrifices to appease the sea in times of flood.[135] Morgan enlists Wilfred to help her discover the cave so that she can perform a ritual in it.

Wilfred acquires an estate for Morgan, located out on the coast. They begin the process of restoring the building, turning it into a sea temple for Morgan's ritual. As they undertake this restoration work, Wilfred and Morgan develop a deep magical partnership, and Wilfred slowly realizes that he has fallen in love with her, although she has told him there is no chance they will ever be romantic or sexual partners.[136]

Along the way, they learn that Morgan is the reincarnation of a priestess from Atlantis, who was brought to ancient Britain to help the locals in a time of severe flooding. Wilfred, in parallel, is the reincarnation of one of the men she had sacrificed in her previous life. Their mission in this lifetime is to rediscover the sea cave and complete the magical work she had once done there in honor of the Great Goddess of the moon and the tides. Part of the purpose of this work is to revive the worship of the Goddess in the modern world. As Morgan tells Wil-

---

134. Fortune, *The Sea Priestess*, 5.

135. Fortune, *The Sea Priestess*, 39.

136. Fortune, *The Sea Priestess*, 91.

fred, "If you and I can do this thing…we shall bring back into modern life something that has been lost and forgotten and that is badly needed."[137]

At the climax of the novel they discover the hidden cave, and on the night of the full moon they enact their ritual. They perform an elaborate invocation of the Great Goddess, to whom they give many names including Diana, Levanah, and Persephone—but the principal name they give her is Isis. Over the course of the invocation, they describe the Goddess as the Great Mother, the Lady of the Moon, and the ruler of the sea, whose rhythm in the tides is parallel to the rhythm of increase and decrease in human life. After the invocation, Morgan is ritually possessed by the spirit of Isis, who speaks through her and instructs Wilfred in her mysteries. Wilfred, acting as a priest of Isis in the rite, experiences an initiatory death and rebirth. Finally, Morgan departs without a word after the ritual, and Wilfred never hears from her again.[138]

After this ritual is complete, Wilfred's life is changed forever. His asthma improves and he becomes more confident, happier, and more engaged in his community. His relationship with his family improves, he begins to enjoy work more, and he falls in love and marries a local girl. All of this, the reader is given to understand, is a psychological transformation brought about by the magical work he and Morgan had undertaken, a consequence of his initiation into the Mysteries of Isis. At the end of the novel, Wilfred's wife Molly receives a piece of ceremonial jewelry as a gift left by Morgan Le Fay, and Wilfred begins to train her in magic just as Morgan had trained him, so that the two of them can continue their ritual work in honor of the Great Goddess.

——— EXERCISE ———
THE FIRE OF AZRAEL

About halfway through *The Sea Priestess*, Wilfred and Morgan participate in a divinatory ritual, in order to understand the nature of the magical work they are undertaking. They construct a special ritual bonfire made out of three types of wood, which allows them to receive a divinatory vision of the mythic past. Fortune refers to this ritual as the fire of Azrael.[139] For this exercise, you can reconstruct the fire of Azrael to perform your own divination. You will need:

---

137. Fortune, *The Sea Priestess*, 130.

138. Fortune, *The Sea Priestess*, 161–70.

139. Fortune, *The Sea Priestess*, 95–96.

+ A firepit or other place where you can safely build a fire

+ Ordinary firewood and kindling

+ A handful of cedar chips

+ A handful of sandalwood chips

+ Several dried twigs of juniper

+ A fire extinguisher in case of emergency

For best effect, do this on the night of the full moon. Build a fire in your firepit using whatever firewood is easily available to you. When you've got a good fire going, add the cedar and sandalwood chips.

Take two of your juniper twigs and hold them in an X shape over the fire. If you have a particular divinatory question you want to ask, hold that question in your mind. Otherwise, keep your mind blank, and open yourself up to the possibility of whatever the fire will show you. Say:

> *Take two twigs of the juniper tree.*
> *Cross them, cross them, cross them.*
> *Look in the coals of the fire of Azrael*
> *To see _____.*[140]

Here, you may declare your question; for example, you might say "To see what awaits me in my love life" or "To see inspiration for my novel." If you don't have a particular question, simply say "To see what the Goddess will show."

Add all of your juniper twigs to the fire. Be careful when you do so; juniper is not an easy wood to burn, and it tends to spark and sputter. When you have added all of your wood, sit and watch the fire, holding your question in mind or keeping your mind blank the whole time. Try not to let your mind wander, nor to look away from the fire. You want to be intently focused on the fire and the question for a prolonged period of time.

As the fire begins to die down, your eyes will fatigue, and you will begin to see shapes and images in the embers. What you see may be elaborate, or it may be quite simple and understated—a flame that looks like a tree, a twig that curls in a heart shape. Whatever you see or don't see is fine; don't feel like you have to force

---

140. Fortune, *The Sea Priestess*, 95.

it, or like you're failing if you don't have an intense psychic vision. You may see images in your mind's eye, or you may just notice shapes in the flames and embers themselves. If you look into the flames for long enough, your eyes will start to play tricks on you, and you will see *something*. Allow that something to be whatever it is, and don't try to impose a certain expectation of what you think it should be.

Stare into the fire until it dies all the way down or until you feel like you've seen enough and your question has been answered. Then, write down everything you saw so that you don't forget it. If you conclude your divination before the fire is out, make sure to extinguish it; never leave a fire unattended. Take some time to interpret the images you received in your divination. Some of them may be very clear—for example, if you saw the face of someone you know—but most will be abstract and symbolic.

For each image, write down all the various things you might associate with it. Any association is fair game, even if it doesn't immediately seem relevant to the question you asked. For example, if you saw a rose, you might think about love, but you might also think about *Beauty and the Beast* or the perfume your aunt Dorothy used to wear. Write all these associations down; at this stage in the process, you're just looking to generate as much material as possible, not to filter out what you think is or isn't useful.

When you've done this for every image, look through the lists of associations you've come up with. What are the parallels or similar themes that emerge across all the images? Are there any surprising commonalities? Find the themes that are associated with all or most of the images you recorded, and circle or highlight them in your written notes. You may even find that there are multiple overlapping themes; perhaps you saw five images, and four of them share theme A, while a different set of four share theme B. Write down, as succinctly as possible, what these unifying themes are. This is the answer to your question.

Depending on the question you've asked, the answer may require some further elaboration. If you've asked to see what's going to happen in your love life and you see images associated with romance and love, that's a pretty clear answer, but you may get a more puzzling, obscure answer instead. Divination often gives answers in riddles or mysteries, and these answers can take some time to figure out. If you have identified a clear theme among the images you saw in the fire of Azrael, but you can't figure out how it answers your question, don't fret. Take some time to reflect on it, meditate, and even sleep on it. When in doubt, you can discuss your divination with someone else, and a second pair of eyes may see something you've missed. The answer will reveal itself in time.

Divination is a skill like any other, and it takes practice. The first time you use the fire of Azrael, it will likely be difficult to figure out how to interpret your visions, unless you have some other prior experience with divining. That's normal. The more you do this kind of psychic work, the easier it will get, so don't be too discouraged if you have difficulty with it at first.

Dion Fortune's Goddess

The description of Isis in *The Sea Priestess* has some features that are already familiar, but it also brings new qualities to the figure of the Great Goddess. Up to this point, the Goddess hadn't been associated with the sea at all. On the contrary, the sea was masculine for Bachofen, as the symbolic semen that fertilizes the earth. Moreover, ancient sea goddesses are relatively few and far between, with sea deities from Neptune to Manannán Mac Lir being depicted as male. Dion Fortune makes an altogether different connection, identifying the tides of the sea with the cyclical nature of the Goddess and her mysteries. With Fortune, the sea is coded feminine, and it becomes the domain of the Mother Goddess.

Part of this shift comes from a new understanding of the origins of life. Bachofen identified the Goddess with the earth, which was seen as the origin of life. By the late 1930s, however, the theory of evolution had placed the source of life not on the earth, but in the primordial waters of the ocean. It was understood that life had originated somewhere in the dark, unknown depths of the sea, before animal organisms had gradually evolved the ability to survive on land. As such, the Great Mother needed to be a deity not only of the earth and the crops, but of the deeper, older source of life that predated them. She became the Sea Goddess, and the waters of the sea were identified with the life-giving amniotic fluid of the womb.

More than that, the perpetual ebb and flow of the tides aligned with the cyclical nature of the Goddess as she had already been described by other authors. The Goddess of Bachofen and Frazer is eternal; she presides over the process of death and rebirth, but she herself is untouched by it. Likewise, the Sea Goddess presides over the changing tides: The water on the shore rises and falls, but the sea itself is forever. For Fortune, the ebb and flow of the tides was a natural metaphor for the cycle of death and rebirth, an easy extension of the symbolism already associated with the Goddess.

These tides are a consequence of the gravitational pull of the moon, and as I have already discussed, the moon and the Goddess have been associated more or less since the beginning. Bachofen's Goddess was lunar and nocturnal, and the witch Goddess of Leland and Murray was identified with the Roman moon deity Diana. The collective imagination of Europe in the late nineteenth and twentieth centuries gendered the moon as female, in part because the twenty-nine-day lunar cycle nearly corresponds to the menstrual cycle of sexually mature humans. Dion Fortune notes that "these lunar tides play a very important part in the physiological processes of both plants and animals, and especially in the germination and growth of plants and the reproduction of animals, as witness the twenty-eight day lunar sexual cycle of the human female." [141] Thus, the moon was already tied to growth, fertility, and sexuality—and particularly women's fertility and sexuality. In extending her vision of the Goddess to include the sea and its tides, Fortune draws on this preexisting lunar association, making the Sea Goddess and the Moon Goddess one and the same.

In the ritual given in the climax of *The Sea Priestess*, which is itself closely inspired by Fortune's Rite of Isis, Morgan invokes the Goddess Isis as follows:

> O thou most holy and adorable Isis, who in the heavens art the
> Supernal Mother, and upon earth Our Lady of Nature, and in
> the airy kingdoms between heaven and earth the ever-changing
> Moon, ruling the tides of flux and reflux upon the earth and
> in the hearts of men. Thee, thee we adore in the symbol of the
> Moon in her splendour, ever-changing. And in the symbol of
> the deep sea that reflects her. And in the symbol of the opening
> of the gates of life. [142]

Fortune weaves together several strands of symbolism, forming one coherent picture of the Great Goddess. She is identified with the earth, the moon, and the sea—and she is understood to be all three of these things at once. Moreover, she is identified as the Supernal Mother, a term taken from Qabalistic magic. This moniker not only aligns the Goddess with the matriarchal Goddess described by Bachofen, Frazer, and Murray; it also situates Fortune's Goddess in the context

141. Fortune, *The Mystical Qabalah*, 242–43.
142. Fortune, *The Sea Priestess*, 162.

of ceremonial occultism. Moreover, it draws a parallel with the figure of Babalon from Thelema, as Fortune's reference to the Supernal Mother is a name for the same Qabalistic concept expressed by Crowley's Mother of Abominations.[143] *The Sea Priestess* offers a vision of the Goddess as nature, as the Great Mother, and as one half of a gender-based energetic circuit, upon which Fortune's system of Qabalistic magic depends.

The Goddess as described in *The Sea Priestess* is also aggressively syncretic. She is given more than a dozen names over the course of the novel: Aphrodite, Ashtoreth, Astarte, Binah, Diana, Ea, Ge, Hathor, Hecate, Hera, Isis, Levanah, Luna, Marah, Persephone, Selene, and Shaddai el Chai. Many of these names are of goddesses associated with the moon, as with Diana, Hecate, and Selene. "Levanah" and "Luna" are simply words meaning "moon" in Hebrew and Latin, respectively.

Likewise, there are several names here that should already be familiar from previous discussions of the Great Goddess: Diana is the witch Goddess in *The Gospel of the Witches* and *The Witch-Cult in Western Europe*. The story of Aphrodite and Persephone is one of the chief examples given for the myth of the Goddess in *The Golden Bough*. Moreover, Fortune writes of the connection between Aphrodite and Persephone, "Herein is a great mystery, for it is decreed that none shall understand the one without the other."[144] Likewise, Isis, Astarte, and Ashtoreth are all figures named by Frazer as incarnations of the Great Goddess.

Many of these names are familiar already and have helped build the myth of the Goddess up to this point, but seeing them all looped together is astonishing. Dion Fortune emphatically proclaims that all of these goddesses are in fact one and the same, that there is only one Goddess behind all of them, and that the names are immaterial to her worship.

The Golden Ass

Dion Fortune's radical syncretism is groundbreaking in a modern context, but it is not without ancient precedent. Just as there is a great diversity of theological perspectives in modern Goddess worship, ancient paganism had practitioners with a variety of views of their gods. As different cultures and empires came into contact with each other, it was common for people to identify foreign deities with similar

---

143. DuQuette, *The Magick of Aleister Crowley*, 77.
144. Fortune, *The Sea Priestess*, 165.

figures in their own pantheons, reaching for a familiar analogue to the gods they encountered abroad. This was particularly common in the Roman Empire, where the practice was known as *interpretatio romana*: "the Roman interpretation."[145]

Though widespread, this syncretism was still more limited than the soft polytheism espoused by Dion Fortune. People associated deities with similar traits, as, for example, the gods Hermes and Thoth were frequently syncretized as patrons of writing—but this is a far cry from Dion Fortune's stance that "all the gods are one god, and all the goddesses are one goddess."[146] There were limits to this ancient syncretism: It was organized around the principle of finding similarities in two deities' myths or traits, not around a general background assumption that all deities were really one and the same. Thus, Hermes was frequently syncretized with Thoth, but not with Set or Horus.

There is, however, one place in the ancient world with the sort of all-encompassing syncretic soft polytheism expressed by Fortune. Appropriately enough, it is found in a record of the initiatory Mystery cult of Isis. This record is called *The Golden Ass*; it's a fictional narrative published in late antiquity by the author Apuleius. It is at once a sex comedy, a social satire, and a piece of religious propaganda promoting the worship of Isis. Apuleius himself was a priest of Isis's Mystery cult, and he had even been put on trial for witchcraft because it was believed that he had used his secret mystical knowledge to magically seduce a rich widow.[147]

The Golden Ass tells the story of a wealthy young Roman citizen named Lucius, who has an unhealthy curiosity and an interest in magic. After he secretly observes a witch practicing her art, he steals one of her magical ointments and gets turned into an ass. The rest of the book follows Lucius's increasingly desperate attempts to change himself back to his original form, as he comes up against bandits, abusive children, sexually promiscuous priests, and much more. Along the way, several smaller tales are told, recounting pieces of mythology and stories of goddesses from all over the Roman Empire—including such familiar faces as Cybele and Aphrodite. Only at the end of the book is Lucius restored to his body, when Isis appears to him in a vision and promises his salvation if he worships her. In this vision, Isis explicitly identifies herself as the Great Goddess who subsumes all others:

---

145. Hornblower and Spawforth, *The Oxford Classical Dictionary*.

146. Fortune, *The Sea Priestess*, 169.

147. Apuleius, *The Golden Ass*, x.

> I, the mother of the universe, the mistress of all the elements, the firstborn offspring of the world of time; I, the highest of the powers above, the queen of the shades below, the first of all who dwell in the heavens; I, the one true face and manifestation of all the gods and goddesses…and the Egyptians, those paragons of ancient lore and learning, who worship me in ceremonies that are truly my own, call me by my true name, QUEEN ISIS.[148]

Isis appears to Lucius and identifies herself as the true Goddess who stands behind the face of every goddess known in the world. She is worshipped in every temple, under a multitude of names, and every goddess is in fact none other than the one Great Goddess. All the stories Lucius heard while he was transformed into an ass are, in reality, stories of Isis in her various guises.

It's interesting to note this connection between Dion Fortune's theology and the way that Isis was historically worshipped in the second century CE. Even as modern thinkers innovate and build a new language for the worship of the Goddess, those same thinkers are reaching back through time to find ancient precedent for what they do. There is a constant interplay between the past and the present, where thinkers in the present look to the past and often reinterpret it to suit their own ends, even as they are creating something new that will shape the future. Fortune's syncretic Sea Goddess under the name of Isis was in some ways uniquely modern, and could only have come about in a twentieth-century context where budding Paganism and Qabalistic ceremonial magic met; nonetheless, it has a resonance with the ancient past.

Key Takeaways: Fortune

+ The Goddess as one half of a gendered divine polarity
+ Connecting the lunar Goddess to the sea and tides
+ Synthesizing Pagan conceptions of Goddess-as-nature with ceremonial occult principles
+ Radical syncretism—all goddesses are one Goddess
+ Inspiration drawn from the historical cult of Isis

---

148. Apuleius, *The Golden Ass*, 236–37.

—— RITUAL ——
A New Rite of Isis

Dion Fortune's Rite of Isis is a poetic ritual where a priest invokes the Goddess into the body of the priestess and the Goddess speaks in verse. In the original Rite of Isis, she is invoked in three aspects: as Isis, Persephone, and Aphrodite. What follows is my own ritual, inspired by the language and meter of Fortune's original rite.

Group Variation

The original Rite of Isis is a ritual drama performed by a priestess and a priest, with the rest of the attendees observing. This variation is designed the same way: the ritual actions are performed by a priestess and priest in the center of the ritual space, and everyone else observes the symbolic death and rebirth of the priest at the Goddess's hands.

You Will Need

+ An altar draped with a blue cloth
+ A bell
+ A cup filled with salt water
+ A silver-colored coin
+ A silver-colored crown
+ A veil

Preparation

The temple should be arranged with a central altar covered by a cloth in shades of sea blue. The cup of salt water, the bell, and the coin are placed on top of the altar. At the start of the ritual, the priestess and priest stand across the altar from each other, facing one another. She wears a silver crown, and over the crown there is a veil that obscures her face. The other participants are seated in chairs at the edge of the room with a good view of the altar.

Performance

The priestess takes the bell from the altar and circumambulates the temple space, ringing the bell and proclaiming:

PRIESTESS: Heke babaloi! Begone, ye profane. Let this temple be purified
that it may be a fit place for the Goddess to enter.

She then replaces the bell on the altar and returns to her spot opposite the
priest. She stands with her arms folded across her chest. The priest invokes:

PRIEST: I am the priest who stands at the shore of the sea;
    The waves caress, embrace, and call to me.
    O lunar Isis, Marah, Hecate,
    Come now unto the priest who calls to thee.
    Come unto me, for I am he!

    Thy lunar fire shines ever radiantly
    Upon the waves of the primordial sea.
    I sing the song of Rhea, Binah, Ge,
    Supernal Mother of all mystery,
    Demeter and Persephone.

    Thou shining silver queen of destiny
    Behind whose veil no living man may see,
    Fire of the heavens, water of the sea,
    I invoke in all thy majesty.
    I am thy priest. Come unto me!

The priest rings the bell nine times. The priestess takes the silver coin and
places it inside the cup, then lifts the cup over the altar, offering it to the priest:

PRIESTESS: I am Isis above and Hathor below,
    I guard the things no mortal man may know.
    From my unsounded depths all life did grow;
    I am the tides of life that ebb and flow.
    I raise you up and bring you low.

    I alone the power of life bestow.
    The secrets of the soul are mine to show:
    Mine the moon with silver flame aglow,
    Mine the salted tears of joy and woe,
    And mine the tomb to which you go.

Circe have I been called, and Calypso;
Great heroes past did seek my love to know,
But all were felled with but a single blow.
I am she who reaps all that you sow:
Behold the might of Isis, lo!

The priest rings the bell three times. He takes the cup from the priestess, then kneels in front of the altar. He lifts the cup toward her and invokes a second time:

PRIEST: O lift thy veil and let me see thy face,
Supernal mother, unsurpassed in grace!
Eternal, mighty queen of time and space,
Before thy shrine I humbly do abase
Myself and all my mortal race.

PRIESTESS: No mortal man may see my face and live.

PRIEST: My life is thus the price I gladly give.

The priest lifts the cup to his lips and takes a sip. He replaces the cup on the altar and prostrates himself. The priestess removes her veil and speaks again:

PRIESTESS: To look upon my face is to know death:
Astarte, Aphrodite, Ashtoreth.
I am she who takes a man's last breath
And stands upon the banks of the river Lethe.
Shaddai el Chai, Levanah and Aemeth,
Release from life: my shibboleth.

PRIEST: I die! I die!

PRIESTESS: But know this too, the mystery of birth,
For so my tides replenish all the earth.
Through me all mortal lives are given worth,
And pains are eased in promise of rebirth,
That all who die find joy and mirth.

The priest stands once more and faces the priestess. She extends her hands and he takes them so that the two are holding hands across the altar. She says:

PRIESTESS: The sea tides flow and ebb, and flow again;
   So too the seasons of the lives of men.
   I rule the ocean's unknown depths; and when
   My worship in the world is found again,
   My secrets are uncovered then.

   There are two deaths, the lesser and the great;
   The death of the body must ye all await.
   To die the greater death, pass through the gate
   Of my initiation. On that date
   Ye have fulfilled your soul's true fate.

   I am the eternal and unchanging sea.
   All life comes from and then returns to me.
   Diana, Luna, and Persephone,
   I go by many names but all are me.
   I am the Mother. I am she!

   I am the Mother who gives birth to thee
   And only by my hand may you be free,
   So come beneath the moon to worship me
   And call my name to the primordial sea:
   Isis and Rhea, Binah, Ge!

The priest takes the bell from the altar and circumambulates the temple space, ringing the bell and proclaiming:

PRIEST: Hear one, hear all! The Great Goddess is returned to earth! She has opened the gate of initiation. May we restore that which has been lost to the world!

Solitary Variation

In this version of the rite, you will play both the priestess and the priest, offering an invocation of the Goddess and then allowing her to speak through you in order to reveal her mysteries. When the face of the Goddess is revealed, you will hold up a mirror and see yourself as the embodiment of Isis.

You Will Need

- An altar draped with a blue cloth
- A bell
- A cup filled with salt water
- A silver-colored coin
- A silver-colored crown
- A hand mirror
- A veil

Preparation

Place the altar in the center of your ritual space and cover it with a cloth in shades of sea blue. Put the cup of salt water, the bell, and the coin on top of the altar, and set the mirror face down next to them. Put on the crown and wear the veil over the crown so that it obscures your face.

Performance

Take the bell from the altar and circumambulate your ritual space, ringing the bell and proclaiming:

> *Heke babaloi! Begone, ye profane. Let this temple be purified that it*
> *may be a fit place for the Goddess to enter.*

Return to the altar and set the bell down. Cross your arms over your chest and invoke the Goddess:

> *I am the one who stands at the shore of the sea;*
> *The waves caress, embrace, and call to me.*
> *O lunar Isis, Marah, Hecate,*
> *Come now unto the one who calls to thee.*
> *That am I; come unto me!*
>
> *Thy lunar fire shines ever radiantly*
> *Upon the waves of the primordial sea.*
> *I sing the song of Rhea, Binah, Ge,*
> *Supernal Mother of all mystery,*
> *Demeter and Persephone.*

> *Thou shining silver queen of destiny*
> *Behind whose veil no living man may see,*
> *Fire of the heavens, water of the sea,*
> *I invoke in all thy majesty.*
> *I am thy servant. Come to me!*

Ring the bell nine times. Take the silver coin and place it into the cup of salt water, then lift the cup high over your head. Invoke the Goddess a second time:

> *Thou art Isis above and Hathor below,*
> *Thou guard'st the things no mortal man may know.*
> *From thy unsounded depths all life did grow;*
> *Thou art the tides of life that ebb and flow*
> *To raise me up and bring me low.*
>
> *Thou alone the power of life bestow.*
> *The secrets of the soul are thine to show:*
> *Thine the moon with silver flame aglow,*
> *Thine the salted tears of joy and woe,*
> *And thine the tomb to which I go.*
>
> *Circe hast thou been called, and Calypso;*
> *Great heroes past did seek thy love to know,*
> *But all were felled with but a single blow.*
> *Thou art she who reaps all that I sow:*
> *Behold the might of Isis, lo!*

Place the cup back on the altar and kneel before it. Ring the bell three times. Then, crossing your hands over your chest again, invoke a third time:

> *O lift thy veil and let me see thy face,*
> *Supernal mother, unsurpassed in grace!*
> *Eternal, mighty queen of time and space,*
> *Before thy shrine I humbly do abase*
> *Myself and all my mortal race.*
>
> *No mortal may look on thy face and live;*
> *My life is thus the price I gladly give.*

Lift the mirror and look at your reflection. Take a moment to feel the presence of the Goddess descend into your body. Then, allow her to speak through you, watching your reflection speak from behind the veil:

> *To look upon my face is to know death:*
> *Astarte, Aphrodite, Ashtoreth.*
> *I am she who takes a man's last breath*
> *And stands upon the banks of the river Lethe.*
> *Shaddai el Chai, Levanah and Aemeth,*
> *Release from life: my shibboleth.*

Set down the mirror and take a sip from the cup. As you do so, cry out:

> *I die! I die!*

Remove your veil and set it on the altar. Pick up the mirror again and look at your reflection once more, now unveiled. As you behold the face of the Goddess, let her continue to speak through you:

> *But know this too, the mystery of birth,*
> *For so my tides replenish all the earth.*
> *Through me all mortal lives are given worth,*
> *And pains are eased in promise of rebirth,*
> *That all who die find joy and mirth.*
>
> *The sea tides flow and ebb, and flow again;*
> *So too the seasons of the lives of men.*
> *I rule the ocean's unknown depths; and when*
> *My worship in the world is found again,*
> *My secrets are uncovered then.*
>
> *There are two deaths, the lesser and the great;*
> *The death of the body must ye all await.*
> *To die the greater death, pass through the gate*
> *Of my initiation. On that date*
> *Ye have fulfilled your soul's true fate.*

I am the eternal and unchanging sea.
All life comes from and then returns to me.
Diana, Luna, and Persephone,
I go by many names but all are me.
I am the Mother. I am she!

I am the Mother who gives birth to thee
And only by my hand may you be free,
So come beneath the moon to worship me
And call my name to the primordial sea:
Isis and Rhea, Binah, Ge!

Set down the mirror on the altar. Remove your crown and set it on the altar as well. Then, take the bell and circumambulate your ritual space, proclaiming:

The Great Goddess is returned to earth! She has opened the gate of
initiation. May she restore that which has been lost to the world!

THE TRIPLE MUSE (1948)

EACH PERSON IN GODDESS religion finds their own relationship with the Goddess. There is a shared language in the way that people approach and talk about her, but everyone who worships the Goddess also forms a private relationship with her, something special that's untouched by anyone else. In my personal, individual practice, I know her as a threefold deity.

The notion of the Triple Goddess is widespread in the Goddess revival. She has three faces—the maiden, the mother, and the crone—and these faces are supposed to correspond to the stages of a woman's life and the cyclical nature of all creation. This, however, is not the threefold Goddess as I worship her. Although the myth of the maiden, mother, and crone is a powerful one that speaks to many people, it has never spoken to me, and it does not feature in my personal relationship with the Goddess. Rather, I pray to the Goddess under three other aspects: beauty, goodness, and truth.

As beauty, she governs everything pleasant and alluring. All forms of art, creativity, love, happiness, and desire are sacred to her.

As goodness, she is the Goddess of human behavior and people's treatment of each other. Things sacred to her include virtues like kindness, charity, loyalty, courage, and justice.

As truth, she offers knowledge in all its forms. She is the patroness of science, philosophy, mathematics, history, and language.

To the best of my knowledge, no one else worships the Goddess in this way. You won't find these three aspects listed in any other book; in fact, they're drawn from principles of medieval Christian philosophy, which in turn have their roots in the works of Plato and Aristotle. Nonetheless, even though this understanding of the Goddess is not shared by the wider world, it is incredibly meaningful to me. Looking at the world around me, I see everything as enchanted with beauty, goodness, and truth, sacred to the Goddess for having one or more of those qualities.

Of course, these aspects of the Goddess don't always coexist. A beautiful thing may be illusory, good deeds are often unglamorous, and sometimes the truth can do more harm than good. But wherever I can find one of these qualities, I have found the Goddess—and because of that, I see her everywhere I look. Having come to know her in this way, I find that the whole world is pregnant with her presence. Every moment, every thing, every person is sacred.

Is this version of a Triple Goddess the "correct" way to see her? Of course not. There is no one absolute truth when it comes to the Goddess. This vision of her is sacred and special for me, but that doesn't mean it would have any meaning or weight whatsoever for someone else. It does, however, underscore an important point: at the end of the day, everyone has to form their own conception of the Goddess.

I've read many books about the Goddess and performed rituals written by myself and others. All of that was good, and it helped me to build a deeper understanding of who she is, but it was not enough on its own. I had to discover not just who the Goddess was for the world, but who she is for me, specifically. I had to open myself up to her and find my own way of knowing her, as does everyone who walks this path. Over the years, as I allowed myself to form that personal relationship, I developed a deep understanding of the Goddess that is mine alone, a revelation that carries me forward in my practice. I asked the Goddess for a deeper connection, and she gave it to me. In the religion of the Goddess, divine inspiration guides us all.

Inspired by the Goddess

The Second World War devastated the world in more ways than one. The bloodiest war in human history, coupled with the horror of the Holocaust, left a scar that affected not just politics, but also the economy, the arts, science, history, and religion. People had to wrestle with atrocities that had previously been considered unimaginable, and those atrocities threw the rest of society into sharp relief. The unquestioned assumptions upon which civic, political, and religious institutions were built suddenly seemed all too precarious, as the world had seen first-hand how easy it was for those institutions to be swept away by totalitarianism. The aftermath of the war was a time of reckoning and painful doubt as the world tried to rebuild itself.

It is in this context that I turn my attention to a strange tome called *The White Goddess*, published in 1948 by the British poet Robert Graves. Graves is famous as the author of *I, Claudius* and *The Golden Fleece*, but *The White Goddess* is altogether different from his other works. It is neither poetry nor a novel; rather, it's a work of poetically inspired nonfiction, where Graves puts forward his views about religion, history, paganism, and the nature of poetry. Graves picked up on the familiar idea of an ancient Goddess associated with the moon, whose worship was the original religion of human civilization, and he proposed a return to this religion as the solution to the religious and moral crisis of the twentieth century.

Beyond this, however, Graves added his own spin. For him, the Goddess was first and foremost associated with poetry and artistic inspiration. He claimed that "the language of poetic myth anciently current in the Mediterranean and Northern Europe was a magical language bound up with popular religious ceremonies in honour of the Moon-goddess, or Muse...and that this remains the language of true poetry."[149] Graves identified the Goddess chiefly with the ancient Greek figure of the Muse. For him, the Goddess was a goddess of creative inspiration, and the chief act of devotion to her was the creation of poetry or art dedicated to her name. Just as classical poets had dedicated their work to the Muse, Graves suggested, all true poets throughout history were inspired by the Goddess under various names and guises.

The White Goddess itself is a work of poetic inspiration; as the story goes, Graves was struck by an all-consuming creative vision and wrote the first draft of the book in only six weeks. Although this story is likely embellished and years' worth of research underpins the book, *The White Goddess* is in many ways more a work of religious epiphany than a work of scholarship.[150] Graves was moved by direct religious revelation and a need to share his vision of the Goddess with the world. He was not writing a work of rigorous academic study. Although *The White Goddess*, like many other works before it, is riddled with factual inaccuracies

---

149. Graves, *The White Goddess*, 6.
150. Carter, *Stalking the Goddess*, 11.

and errors of historical interpretation, it is important to approach this book with the understanding that Graves was never really trying to be a historian at all. He was, rather, a poet and a prophet. His language was one of metaphor and symbolism, and he had no qualms about bending historical fact to fit his aesthetic and creative sensibilities.

Graves's picture of the Goddess, then, is a modern myth—something that claims ancient provenance, but that really isn't designed to hold up to close historical scrutiny. He was strongly inspired by James Frazer and Margaret Murray, and he suggested that the worship of the Goddess was an ancient fertility cult with seasonal festivals, which was "secretly preserved as religious doctrine in the covens of the anti-Christian witch-cult."[151] Like Frazer, Graves attributed a consort to the Goddess. This consort was a dual God whose life cycle was divided amongst the summer and winter months; he was both son and consort to the Goddess, and his death and resurrection were the pervasive theme of Goddess-centric mythology and poetry:

> The Theme, briefly, is the antique story, which falls into thirteen chapters and an epilogue, of the birth, life, death, and resurrection of the God of the Waxing Year; the central chapters concern the God's losing battle with the God of the Waning Year for love of the capricious and all-powerful Threefold Goddess, their mother, bride, and layer-out. The poet identifies himself with the God of the Waxing Year and his Muse with the Goddess.[152]

The story of the eternal Goddess and her dying-and-resurrecting consort is thoroughly familiar by now. Of particular note with Graves, however, is that the story of the consort is changed somewhat. For Graves, the God is not only the Goddess's lover; he is also her son. He is born from her, consummates a sexual relationship with her, and then is slain by a rival and buried by her. This is an elaboration of the seasonal mythic cycle that had previously been associated with the Goddess, providing more detail and establishing an incestuous relationship

---

151. Graves, *The White Goddess*, 20.
152. Graves, *The White Goddess*, 20.

between the Gods that had not appeared before. Graves claimed that all poetry was an elaboration of this central mythic theme.

As the source of his mythic structure, Graves was primarily focused on two Welsh poems called *Hanes Taliesin*, "the tale of Taliesin," and *Câd Goddeu*, "the battle of the trees." *Hanes Taliesin* recounts a riddle told by the medieval bard Taliesin; *Câd Goddeu* tells the story of a battle where the magician Gwydion enchants the trees of a forest to fight on his behalf against Arawn, the king of the otherworld. Gwydion is a son of Dôn, a Welsh mother goddess; thus, Graves claimed that Gwydion was fighting on Dôn's behalf against Arawn's patriarchal rule: "The Battle of the Trees was fought between the White Goddess ('the woman') for whose love the god of the waxing year and of the waning year were rivals, and 'the man'…who challenged her power."[153] Graves saw these poems as containing a secret code that revealed the mystery of the Goddess: that her worship was the ancient and true religion, but that she had been supplanted by patriarchal religions like Christianity. Based on phonetic similarities to Dôn's name, Graves identified her with the Irish goddess Danu, the Greek Danaë, and the Roman Diana. All of these, he said, were cross-cultural manifestations of the same ancient Goddess cult—and the Goddess was the source of art and culture wherever she was found.

If you feel like there was a bit of a leap in the reasoning here, you're not alone. *The White Goddess* is a maddening book, and Graves turns jumping to conclusions into an Olympic sport. Nonetheless, this is the conclusion he draws. Graves had a vision of human civilization built not on war, science, or law, but rather on art, beauty, and creativity. These were the things he considered foundational to human society, and he attributed them to the universal worship of the Goddess in her many forms.

The Tree Alphabet

In his interpretation of the *Hanes Taliesin*, Graves suggests that the poem contains a cipher for an ancient Irish alphabet based on the names of trees—the same trees animated by Gwydion in the *Câd Goddeu*. According to Graves, this alphabet was one of the great mysteries of the Goddess, because it was the key to language and, thereby, to poetry.

---

153. Graves, *The White Goddess*, 331.

Graves imagined that the *Hanes Taliesin* encoded the secrets of pre-Christian Druidic wisdom, and that it had been purposefully jumbled and obfuscated in order to conceal these secrets from outsiders. He attempted to decipher it, and in so doing, he presented his own version of the ogham, an Irish alphabet. Graves claimed that each letter in the ogham came from the name of a tree, and that these trees all had mystical significance for the worship of the Goddess. He suggested that this system would have been used not only for writing, but also for divination and as a sort of calendar. As author Mark Carter notes, "Each ogham letter was assigned a symbolic tree and various other seasonal associations, which allowed ogham to serve as an alphabet and calendar…Each letter represented a single lunar month and each month was symbolized by a tree, which bloomed or thrived within that month." [154]

However, one should be cautious in approaching Graves's tree alphabet. Contemporary scholarship is at odds with the various historical claims Graves made about the ogham and its use, and there is no real evidence to suggest that it was ever used for divination or that there was any such calendar as Graves had proposed. Moreover, ogham is an Irish alphabet, and the *Hanes Taliesin* is a Welsh poem; the Welsh and Irish languages come from different linguistic families, and it is unlikely that a Welsh poem would have contained a coded Irish alphabet. Remember that Graves was a poet, not a historian, and his ideas about ancient ogham stem more from his creativity than from historical evidence. Like the scholars who discussed the Goddess prior to him, Graves was flawed, and his historical claims—about the tree alphabet as much as about the Goddess—were often unfounded.

One of the uses Graves suggests for the tree alphabet is a sort of hidden Druidic calendar: That each of the thirteen consonants in the alphabet corresponded to one lunar month, and that thirteen lunar months of twenty-eight days would add up to an almost perfect 365-day year. He suggested that this lunar calendar was associated with the Goddess because of the similarities between lunar cycles and human menstrual cycles: "The Moon, being a woman, has a woman's normal menstrual period…of twenty-eight days." [155] Unfortunately for Graves, this is not entirely true. The moon's phases do not fit a neat twenty-eight day cycle,

154. Carter, *Stalking the Goddess*, 96.
155. Graves, *The White Goddess*, 161–62.

and in fact, a lunar cycle averages twenty-nine-and-a-half days.[156] Graves's lunar calendar doesn't work in practice, and so he assigned dates on the solar Gregorian calendar to each of his tree months.

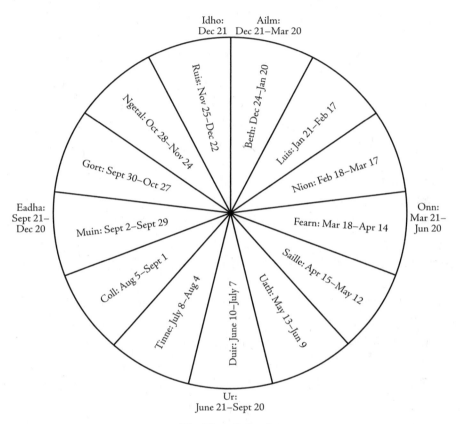

The Tree Calendar

B: Beth (Birch)

The birch tree grows its leaves in the dead of winter, and as such, Graves associated it with purification and new beginnings, writing, "The birch is the tree of inception."[157] The dates given for Beth in the tree calendar are December 24 through January 20.

---

156. Nemiroff and Bonnell, "Astronomy Picture of the Day Index."

157. Graves, *The White Goddess*, 161.

L: Luis (Rowan)

The rowan is associated with protection from accident and malefic witchcraft. According to Graves, it had the power to bestow life or take it away: "The quick-beam [rowan] is the tree of quickening…Since it was the tree of quickening it could also be used in a contrary sense."[158] The dates for Luis are January 21 through February 17.

N: Nion (Ash)

Graves associates the ash tree with flooding, water, and sailors. He also assigns it to the power of resurrection, noting, "In British folklore the ash is a tree of re-birth."[159] The dates for Nion are February 18 through March 17.

F: Fearn (Alder)

The alder tree doesn't burn cleanly in a fire, but it can be made into an efficient charcoal. Its resin is also useful for waterproofing. As such, Graves suggested that "principally the alder is the tree of fire."[160] Graves associated alder with fire and all its purifying and protective properties. The dates for Fearn are March 18 through April 14.

S: Saille (Willow)

Graves identifies the willow tree with witches, death, and the moon, suggesting that "its connexion with witches is so strong in Northern Europe that the words 'witch' and 'wicked' are derived from the same ancient word for 'willow.'"[161] The dates for Saille are April 15 through May 12.

H: Uath (Hawthorn)

Graves saw the hawthorn as a dangerous, malevolent tree, associated with harm and ill luck. He considered it particularly bad for love and sex, calling hawthorn "the tree of enforced chastity."[162] The dates for Uath are May 13 through June 9.

---

158. Graves, *The White Goddess*, 162–63.
159. Graves, *The White Goddess*, 163.
160. Graves, *The White Goddess*, 166.
161. Graves, *The White Goddess*, 168.
162. Graves, *The White Goddess*, 170.

D: Duir (Oak)

The oak is a tree of strength and power, associated with thunder gods like Zeus. Graves also draws on the work of James Frazer, who identified the oak tree as the mark of sacred kingship. Thus, for Graves, oak is "the tree of endurance and triumph."[163] The dates for Duir are June 10 through July 7.

T: Tinne (Holly)

As the year passes midsummer and begins the descent to winter, it goes from growth to decay. Graves saw the holly as a twin to the oak, which marked the shift from life to death. He called holly "the tree of murder" and identified it with the theme of sacrifice.[164] The dates for Tinne are July 8 through August 4.

C: Coll (Hazel)

Graves identifies the hazel and its nutritious nuts as "an emblem of concentrated wisdom: something sweet, compact, and sustaining enclosed in a small hard shell."[165] The hazel tree, then, is the tree of wisdom, science, and knowledge. The dates for Coll are August 5 through September 1.

M: Muin (Vine)

Although he uses the word "vine," Graves actually identifies Muin with the blackberry bush. He says very little about it, except to call it "the tree of joy, exhilaration, and wrath" and to identify it with sacred drunkenness.[166] The dates for Muin are September 2 through September 29.

G: Gort (Ivy)

The ivy is associated with Dionysus, the Greek god of drunkenness and revelry who was—in some versions of the myths—slain and then reborn. As such, Graves links ivy to intoxication and says that it is "dedicated to resurrection."[167] The dates for Gort are September 30 through October 27.

---

163. Graves, *The White Goddess*, 171.

164. Graves, *The White Goddess*, 179.

165. Graves, *The White Goddess*, 176.

166. Graves, *The White Goddess*, 178.

167. Graves, *The White Goddess*, 178.

NG: Ngetal (Reed)

Graves notes that some other scholars of the ogham list a different tree here: P for Peith, the dwarf elder. However, he chooses to use the reed. He calls the reed "an ancient symbol of royalty," identifying it with both Jesus and the Egyptian Pharaoh.[168] He associates it with sovereignty, authority, and dominion. The dates for Ngetal are October 28 through November 24.

R: Ruis (Elder)

The final consonant in the alphabet and the final month in the calendar is the elder. Graves rather melodramatically labels elder as "the tree of doom," identifying it with death, ill luck, and despair.[169] The dates for Ruis are November 25 through December 22, with December 23 as an intercalary day before the start of the new year.

A: Ailm (Silver Fir)

Graves associates the vowels of his alphabet with seasons, not months. He identifies the silver fir as "a birth-tree," linking it to the rebirth symbolism of the winter solstice.[170] It rules the time from the winter solstice to the spring equinox.

O: Onn (Furze)

The furze tree is identified with the mystery of initiation, which Graves says is made salient by lighting furze fires, "burning away the old prickles…to make tender new ones sprout on the stock."[171] Onn rules the time from the spring equinox to midsummer.

U: Ur (Heather)

For Graves, the heather is a tree of love and marriage, "sacred to the Roman and Sicilian love-goddess."[172] He notes its role in the legend of Isis and Osiris as an

168. Graves, *The White Goddess*, 179.
169. Graves, *The White Goddess*, 180.
170. Graves, *The White Goddess*, 186.
171. Graves, *The White Goddess*, 187.
172. Graves, *The White Goddess*, 187.

instance of a love myth connected to the tree. Ur rules the time from midsummer to the autumn equinox.

E: Eadha (White Poplar)

Graves calls the white poplar "the shield-maker's tree" and identifies it with wisdom and repose.[173] He further suggests that it symbolizes the power to conquer death. Eadha rules the time from fall equinox to the winter solstice.

I: Idho (Yew)

According to Graves, the yew is "the death-tree in all European countries."[174] He links it to funerary customs, poison, and witchcraft. Idho completes the cycle of the seasons at the winter solstice, linking its symbolism of death with the rebirth found in Ailm.

——— EXERCISE ———
Your Own Tree Alphabet

You can reconstruct Graves's tree alphabet and use it yourself for divination, meditation, or to conceal secret writing. You will need:

- Eighteen popsicle sticks
- Paint and a paintbrush, a wood-burning tool, or some similar way to mark your pieces

The tree alphabet that Graves presents is historically muddy, and there is no reason to believe that there ever was a tree calendar such as he suggests. However, that does not mean that you can't use Graves's tree alphabet today! So long as you keep in mind where it came from and take care not to spread misinformation, the tree alphabet and its complementary calendar may prove interesting and useful to contemporary Goddess worshippers.

---

173. Graves, *The White Goddess*, 188.
174. Graves, *The White Goddess*, 189.

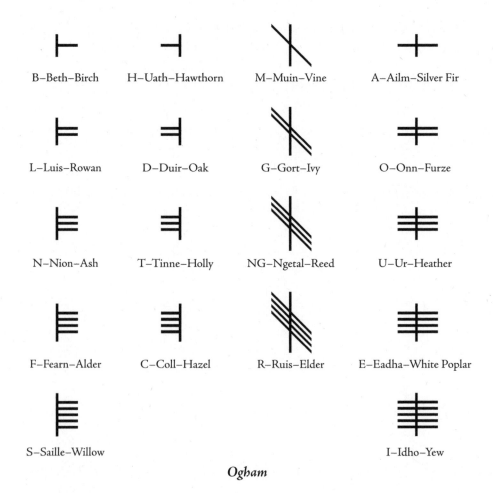

Ogham

Each letter in the ogham is made with a central vertical line marked by a number of horizontal or diagonal lines. When letters are strung together to form a word, the ends of their vertical staves are connected so that the word is read from top to bottom along the central line. On a set of wooden popsicle sticks, paint the symbols shown above; alternatively, you can use a wood-burning tool to mark the symbols. You can then use these for divination by placing the sticks in a bag, asking a question, and pulling one at random to receive your answer; refer to the list above for the themes associated with each tree. You may also find value in measuring time by Graves's seasonal calendar, or in using the tree alphabet as a coded writing system for your personal journal or ritual writings.

The Triple Goddess

Aside from strengthening the Goddess's connection to art and poetry, Graves is noteworthy for introducing one other major concept into modern Goddess worship: the Triple Goddess. Graves conceived of the Goddess as having three aspects, three different faces which she showed to the world. These three faces were cyclical, representing different stages of human life: youth, maturity, and old age. Likewise, they were connected to the cyclicality of nature, and in particular to the phases of the moon, so that the Goddess's young aspect was associated with the waxing moon, her mature aspect with the full moon, and her aged aspect with the waning moon: "As the New Moon or Spring she was girl; as the Full Moon or Summer she was woman; as the Old Moon or Winter she was hag." [175]

These three aspects—the girl, the woman, and the hag—came to define discussions of the Goddess in the back half of the twentieth century. Over time, the names of the three aspects solidified as the maiden, the mother, and the crone. [176] The three phases, in turn, came to be overlaid with biological phases associated with sexual maturity. The maiden is often described as the Goddess prior to menarche (first menstruation), when she is still too young to bear children; the mother is the menstruating Goddess, who is sexually mature; and the crone is the postmenopausal Goddess, who is no longer capable of conception. [177] Sometimes, the Maiden is assigned a larger portion of the Goddess's lifespan, taking her up through sexual maturity but before she starts to have children.

Although the three aspects of the Triple Goddess are now broadly associated with menstruation, Graves didn't conceive of her in such biological terms. Rather, he saw the Triple Goddess as embodying youth, maturity, and old age, construed more broadly. Because the Goddess for Graves was a patroness of poetry, he was primarily concerned with the intellectual and metaphorical facets of the Goddess's three phases; his interest was not in biological growth, but in the ways these themes played out in artistic development. For Graves, the faces of the Triple Goddess were not stages of physical development, but three central themes for the poet to explore in his work: "Death, Birth, and Beauty—formed a triad of Goddesses who presided over all acts of generation whatsoever: physical, spiritual,

---

175. Graves, *The White Goddess*, 378.

176. Farrar and Farrar, *The Witches' Goddess*, 29.

177. Allen, *Jailbreaking the Goddess*, 25–26.

or intellectual."[178] The Goddess's central role was to provide artistic inspiration on these three themes of death, birth, and beauty. Elsewhere, Graves expanded on these themes, and he identified five principal mysteries sacred to the Goddess: birth, initiation, marriage, repose, and death.[179]

Again, Graves's picture is a stark innovation on the views of the Goddess that came before him. For previous historians like Bachofen or Murray, the Goddess was a decidedly literal figure: She presided over the fertility of the earth and of her worshippers, bestowing life and the promise of renewal in death. She was a real, concrete manifestation of the life-giving forces of nature, not an abstract poetic principle. Occultists like Crowley or Fortune had taken a more abstract view of the Goddess, but even they had described her as a real magical power. For Graves, it seems, the Goddess was none of these things. His Goddess was much more a deity of wisdom and art than of nature, more closely linked to Athena or Calliope than to Frazer's Cybele, Leland's Diana, Crowley's Nuit, or Fortune's Isis. Yes, she was connected to the mysteries of birth and death, but only instrumentally so; her chief role was to bestow artistic vision, and her connection to nature was simply a means by which she provided this vision to her favored poets.

Reading Graves, it is difficult to tell whether he really believed in the Goddess as a deity, or whether he was simply describing her as an elaborate metaphor for his creative process. Probably the reality lies somewhere between the two. Certainly he speaks with something like religious devotion. At the close of the book, he describes the worship of the Goddess as "the future of religion in the West," framing it as a reckoning with and solution to the horrors of the Second World War.[180] In a postscript to the book written in 1960, he concludes with a rallying cry: "None greater in the universe than the Triple Goddess!"[181] But at the same time, he speaks of his devotion to her only in terms of poetry and creation. He adorns no shrine, pours no libation, erects no temple, and writes no ritual. In this way, he is unlike the occultists and practitioners I have discussed up to this point, ranging from Dion Fortune with her rite of Isis to the witches of Leland's *Gospel*.

---

178. Graves, *The White Goddess*, 8.
179. Graves, *The White Goddess*, 132.
180. Graves, *The White Goddess*, 465.
181. Graves, *The White Goddess*, 483.

He professes his devotion to the Goddess, but does not propose to enact this devotion with any rite of worship other than his poetry.

Another extraordinary difference between *The White Goddess* and the texts I've discussed up to this point is that Graves divides the Goddess into separate aspects. In the myth of the Goddess as it has manifested previously, she is eternal and unchanging. She may have a consort who dies and is reborn, but the Goddess herself is the ground of all being, untouched by age or death. Graves, however, presents the Goddess as cyclically aging, growing old and young again in time with the changing phases of the moon. In a sense, this is in line with what others had said about the Goddess; it reinforces the Goddess's connection with the cycles of life and death, making that connection much more immediate. Much like Dion Fortune, who gave the Goddess governance over the ebb and flow of the tides, Graves expands on her lunar associations and emphasizes her cyclicality. Nonetheless, the ascription of three faces to the Goddess, rather than one, is a profound new development in her modern myth.

Critiquing the Triple Goddess

Graves's conception of the Triple Goddess is not without its problems. It became pervasive in twentieth-century Goddess worship, but more recent thinkers have taken a critical eye to it, pointing out various ways in which it presents a reductive, essentializing, or harmful view of the Goddess and of women. Graves wrote about the Goddess exclusively from a man's point of view. In his imagination of her, she was a patron of poetry and the arts, but the poet was always a man. The role of the Goddess was functionally inert; she was an object for the poet to look upon in order to find inspiration for his own artistic endeavors. The Goddess herself did not make any art or write any poetry. She was not a creator, merely a source of ideas for the men who create.

Not only that, but the three aspects of the Triple Goddess are phases of life defined through her relationship to men. To look at Graves's original aspects of girl, woman, and hag is to see her through a man's eyes. Elsewhere in the book, Graves identifies her as "mother, bride, and layer-out," but this description comes up against the same problem.[182] She is defined in terms of the relationship she holds to a particular man. As the bride, she is his sexual partner. As the mother,

---

182. Graves, *The White Goddess*, 20.

she is a nurturer and comforter. As the layer-out, she is the one who mourns him. In all of these cases, *he* is the focus; the poet is at the center, and the Goddess is merely defined in terms of who she is for him or what she can provide him. The Triple Goddess never gets to stand on her own two feet and simply be herself.

In recent decades, many figures in the Goddess movement have argued that the Triple Goddess is actually quite a sexist way to depict the Goddess. It seems that—whether with Graves's original aspects or the later, more ubiquitous Triple Goddess as the maiden, mother, and crone—she is always reduced to her relationship to someone else. She is defined by other people, outside of herself, and what's more, those people are often men. A defining feature of the Goddess's three aspects is her sexual availability: the girl is too young to be a sexual prospect, the hag is too old, and the woman alone is a suitable object for the poet's sexual affections.

This objectifying gaze is further reinforced by the link between the Triple Goddess and menstruation. Such a link associates the Goddess, and womanhood more broadly, with the ability to bear children. As contemporary Goddess feminist Lasara Firefox Allen notes in their book *Jailbreaking the Goddess: A Radical Revisioning of Feminist Spirituality*, "In the maiden, mother, and crone archetypal system, mother means woman. If a woman cannot or will not bear children, she may not easily see her face in this goddess."[183] If the three phases of the Goddess are associated with premenarche, menstruation, and menopause, these biological processes are also taken—implicitly or explicitly—to be the three phases of a woman's life. Consequently, women are defined more or less as walking uteruses, whose value and role in the world is determined by their sexual availability to men and their ability to get pregnant.

Conceptualizing the Goddess this way is potentially alienating for a couple of reasons. For one thing, it immediately excludes trans women from the category of womanhood, and it disregards the existence of trans men, nonbinary people, and intersex people. The common picture of the Triple Goddess is founded on a simplistic and reductive understanding of sex and gender, where the words "woman" and "uterus" are more or less interchangeable. The reality is much more complex, and there are good reasons to want Goddess religion's understanding of deity to align with the current scientific understanding of these issues.

---

183. Allen, *Jailbreaking the Goddess*, 24.

More broadly, the Triple Goddess describes a particular narrative about the life of a woman: she starts as a young, sexually immature girl, then immediately becomes a mother and bears children until she is an old, unsexual hag. This is a narrow vision of a woman's life, and it can be alienating to those who don't fit it. A middle-aged woman who chooses not to have children is neither maiden, mother, nor crone. A mother who adopts is still a mother, despite having no biological link to her children. A postmenopausal woman with an active sex life doesn't fit the stereotype of the hag or crone. A young adult who isn't thinking about children may find herself too mature to be a maiden, but not interested in becoming a mother. The Triple Goddess divides life into neat categories, but the realities of life are variegated and individual. There are plenty of people who simply don't fit.

Perhaps most importantly, the Triple Goddess doesn't leave much room for all the other things a woman can be. Whether trans or cis, mother or childless, old or young, women—and, for that matter, goddesses—are far more than just maiden, mother, or crone. They are warriors, artisans, politicians, scientists, philosophers, and more, but none of these things are encompassed by the three phases of the Triple Goddess. The Triple Goddess is a fairly superficial understanding of who the Goddess can be, and it leaves a great deal to be desired.

None of this is to say that the Triple Goddess is an inherently bad way to understand the Goddess, or that people should not worship the Goddess in this way if they feel called to do so. The maiden, mother, and crone have been overwhelmingly influential in modern Goddess worship. Countless lives have been touched by the Triple Goddess, and countless people have been forever changed by this approach to the divine. The Triple Goddess carved out a space for women to see themselves as divine, to worship God the mother rather than God the father; this would become extremely important, particularly for the development of Goddess feminism. Many devotees of the Triple Goddess will argue that her biological associations are overstated: that the biological language is used as an easy point of access to understanding her, but that her symbolism is really much deeper. In this view, the maiden represents everything that is growing and coming into its own; the mother governs all acts of creation, not just procreation; and the crone rules over wisdom and peace in all their forms. In this way, the Triple Goddess can be a scholar, a carpenter, a lawmaker, and much more besides. She need not be constrained to a particular narrow conception of womanhood.

Nonetheless, the critique that has arisen in recent decades is simply that the Triple Goddess is described in fraught language. Generations of Goddess worshippers found the Triple Goddess inspiring and liberating, but others have found her alienating and constrictive. The language used to identify the Triple Goddess at least implicitly condones a fairly essentialist, reductive view of womanhood, to which many people have struggled to connect. Contemporary practitioners can acknowledge how life-changing and powerful the Triple Goddess has been, but still take the time to think critically about their language and their concepts. Graves had a particular vision of the Goddess, which has colored everything that came after him. You should be mindful of how important and historically significant the Triple Goddess has been, but you can also take a step back and realize that she is not the only way the Goddess has been—or can be—understood. For those who relate to the Triple Goddess, the three-phased deity can be a wonderful thing. For those who don't, though, there are other ways to find the Goddess.

Key Takeaways: Graves

+ The Goddess as a source of artistic inspiration
+ A less literal, more metaphorical conception of the Goddess and her worship
+ Ogham reimagined as a tree calendar sacred to the Goddess
+ The Triple Goddess as girl, woman, and hag—or maiden, mother, and crone
+ Three principal mysteries: death, birth, and beauty

—— RITUAL ——
THE TRIPLE GODDESS

This ritual invokes the Triple Goddess as the source of poetic inspiration. Even if you do not identify strongly with the Triple Goddess figure, it is worth your time to explore some of her symbolism. This rite avoids the biological picture of the Triple Goddess, instead focusing on the more abstract, symbolic Goddess as Graves understood her.

Group Variation

In this version of the ritual, you will select three members of your group to play the Triple Goddess. You will invoke the Goddess, then perform a group divination to determine which of her three aspects will join you in the ritual. Then, each participant in the ritual makes an offering of poetic inspiration.

You Will Need

+ Three masks: one white, one red, and one blue
+ Pieces of poetry prepared by all members of the group
+ A red rose

Preparation

Prior to the ritual, select three people to play the aspects of the Triple Goddess. Only one aspect of the Goddess will be invoked in the ritual, but you won't know which until after the ritual begins, so each person should be willing to take on the responsibility. Everyone else will act as poets dedicated to the Goddess.

Everyone, including the three people playing the Goddess, should choose a piece of poetry to read aloud during the rite. These can be poems they've written for the occasion, or each participant may choose an already-published poem that has personal significance to them. Be attentive to length; because everyone will be reading their poem aloud in ritual, none of the pieces should be too long. Agree together on a maximum length for the poems you recite; I'd recommend somewhere about thirty lines as a good limit, but you may go longer or shorter depending on the needs of your group.

You'll need three masks for this ritual in the colors red, white, and blue. These can be as simple or as fancy as you like; you can pick up cheap plastic Halloween masks and paint them, adding any embellishments you see fit. At the start of the ritual, the three actors playing the Goddess stand in the center of the ritual space with their backs to each other, facing outward. The poets stand around them. The maiden holds the white mask in her hands, the mother holds the red mask, and the crone holds the blue mask. The maiden also holds the red rose.

Most of the lines in this ritual are spoken by the poets. Prior to the start of the ritual, read through the script together and decide who will say what. You may have only one person do all the talking, or you may divide the lines up amongst all of the participants, depending on how actively people want to take part in the rite. Try to make sure that everyone who wants a speaking part gets one.

Performance

To begin the ritual, the poets join hands and one of them invokes the Goddess:

POET: Great Goddess of the poets, triple muse of inspiration, we invoke and invite you now. Join us and receive our adoration! We, your poets, do appear before you to humbly beseech your divine favor. Bestow upon us the silver tongue you gave to the ancient gleemen, that we may sing your praises to all who would know you!

The mother puts on her red mask and extends her hands toward the poets as the poets invoke the mother aspect of the Triple Goddess:

POET: The Goddess as the mother guards the mystery of birth. We praise you who give life and creation.

The crone puts on her blue mask and extends her hands toward the poets, mirroring the mother. The poets invoke the crone aspect of the Triple Goddess:

POET: The Goddess as the crone guards the mystery of death. We praise you who give wisdom and solace.

The maiden puts on her white mask and extends her hands toward the poets as well, so that all three Goddess figures have the same posture. The poets invoke the maiden:

POET: The Goddess as the maiden guards the mystery of beauty. We praise you who give delight and freedom.

The three aspects of the Goddess join hands with each other and the poets finish the invocation of the Triple Goddess:

POET: None greater than the Triple Goddess! She who is three in one and one in three, who keeps the mysteries of the waxing and waning moon, who watches over the cycles of human life. None greater than you, our muse!

The Goddess figures say in unison:

GODDESS: Three in one and one in three, none in the world as great as me.

The poets begin to dance in a circle around them. The Goddess figures release each other's hands and the maiden lifts the rose, plucking a petal from it. As she does so, the poets say:

POETS: For the maiden.

She then passes the rose to the mother, who plucks another petal as the poets say:

POETS: For the mother.

The mother then passes the rose to the crone, who plucks another petal as the poets say:

POETS: For the crone.

The Goddess figures continue in this way, passing the rose amongst themselves and plucking petals one at a time, while the poets dedicate the petals in turn to the maiden, mother, and crone. They do this until they reach the last petal of the rose. When the poets name an aspect of the Goddess on the final petal, they stop chanting. The figure corresponding to the named aspect of the Goddess lifts her arms, and the other two Goddess figures remove their masks and move to join the poets. Now, all the ritual participants stand in the presence of one aspect of the Triple Goddess.

The poets now recite the poems they have prepared for the ritual, naming this aspect of the Goddess and offering their poetry to her. When they have all read their poems, the Goddess says:

GODDESS: My beloved worshippers, I accept your offering of poetry in dedication to my guise as [the aspect of the Goddess being represented]. May the breath of inspiration flow through you, may your words be sweet and joyous, and may art enlighten your lives. None greater than the Triple Goddess!

The poets echo her in unison, marking the end of the ritual:

POETS: None greater than the Triple Goddess!

Immediately after finishing the ritual, the participants should do something creative to honor the Goddess: dance, paint, draw, write, or make art in some other way. What they do doesn't need to be of professional quality, and if they are shy about sharing their work it can be private and for their eyes only, but they should do something.

Solitary Variation

For this version of the ritual, you light three candles sacred to the aspects of the maiden, mother, and crone. You perform a small divination to determine which aspect of the Triple Goddess will receive your sacrifice, and then you will make an offering of poetic inspiration.

You Will Need

+ Three candles: one white, one red, and one blue
+ A piece of poetry you have prepared for the occasion
+ A red rose

Preparation

Choose a piece of poetry to read in this ritual. It can be something you have written yourself, specifically for the rite, or you can choose a poem by someone else that has deep significance for you. To set up for the ritual, line up the unlit candles with the white one on your left and the blue one on your right. Set your rose off to the side, along with the printed text of your poem.

Performance

To begin the ritual, lay a hand over your heart and say:

> Great Goddess of the poets, triple muse of inspiration, I invoke and
> invite you now. Join me and receive my adoration! I, your poet,
> do appear before you to humbly beseech your divine favor. Bestow
> upon me the silver tongue you gave to the ancient gleemen, that I
> may sing your praises to all who would know you!

Light the red candle and say:

> The Goddess as the mother guards the mystery of birth. I praise
> you who give life and creation.

Light the blue candle from the red candle. Once the blue candle is lit, extinguish the red one. Say:

> The Goddess as the crone guards the mystery of death. I praise you
> who give wisdom and solace.

Light the white candle from the blue candle. Once the white candle is lit, extinguish the blue one. Say:

> The Goddess as the maiden guards the mystery of beauty. I praise
> you who give delight and freedom.

Light the red candle from the white one, then the blue candle from the red one, so that all three candles are lit. Say:

> None greater than the Triple Goddess! She who is three in one and
> one in three, who keeps the mysteries of the waxing and waning
> moon, who watches over the cycles of human life. None greater than
> you, my muse!

Take the rose and hold it in both hands. Pass it briefly over the flames of all three candles, then pluck a petal from it, saying:

> For the maiden.

Pluck another petal, saying:

> *For the mother.*

Pluck a third petal, saying:

> *For the crone.*

Continue plucking petals from the rose, one at a time, dedicating them in turn to the maiden, the mother, and the crone. Do this until you reach the last petal of the rose. When you name an aspect of the Goddess on the final petal, lift up the colored candle corresponding to that aspect. Hold the candle for a moment and reflect on that face of the Goddess. Then, set the candle back down and extinguish the other two candles.

You may now read or recite the poem you have prepared for this ritual. Put emotion and inflection into it; you are reciting this poem as an offering to the Triple Goddess. When you have finished reading, say:

> *O Goddess, I humbly offer this poem in dedication to you in your guise as [the aspect named with your final rose petal]. May the breath of inspiration flow through me, may my words be sweet and joyous, and may art enlighten my life. None greater than the Triple Goddess!*

Extinguish the remaining candle. The ritual is now concluded.

Immediately after finishing the ritual, you should do something creative to honor the Goddess: dance, paint, draw, write, or make art in some other way. What you do doesn't need to be of professional quality, and if you are shy about sharing your work it can be private and for your eyes only, but you should do *something*.

8

THE WICA (1954)

THE NIGHT I WAS initiated into the Gardnerian tradition of Wicca, I ended up in a diner at two o'clock in the morning. I was starry-eyed and reeking of incense. It was long past my usual bedtime, but I was buzzing with energy, and the world looked different than it had before. The colors seemed brighter. The sounds—even the noise from the kitchen and the traffic outside—had a musical quality. I felt settled in place, like a compass needle that had been swinging in circles and had finally found north. The Goddess had welcomed me home.

Sitting in that red vinyl booth, the beauty and absurdity of the situation struck me. I had just had the most powerful, transformative experience of my life, and now I was doing one of the most mundane things imaginable: sitting in a diner wolfing down a cheeseburger and fries. My initiation had taken me on a journey to the otherworld, presented me to the Gods, and seen me reborn as a new person, but now I was in an ordinary place, surrounded by strangers who didn't know what I had been through. I had just had a life-changing mystical experience, and *no one knew*.

That is, of course, the point. Part of the function of initiation in Gardnerian Wicca is that it's private. My initiation was an intimate ritual that welcomed me into my coven and remade me as a priest of the Goddess. It wouldn't have been appropriate for that to be a public affair. What happened there was between me, my fellow witches, and the Gods, and for anyone else to have witnessed it would have profaned the experience.

As I slurped on my milkshake and eyed a group of drunk hedge fund managers on the other side of the diner, I considered what this meant. A new dimension had been added to my relationship with the Goddess. I felt closer to her now, and I knew her better, but I was also aware that I could never share this experience of her with most people. Only the other members of my tradition, who had undergone the same initiation, would be able to talk about it with me; even if I broke my oath of secrecy and tried to discuss this new experience with people outside the tradition, we simply would not have the common ground for me to be able to communicate it.

But I also realized that there were other traditions, other initiations, other people in the world who had similarly had transformative experiences with the Goddess and would never be able to share those experiences with me. My initiation had given me a new understanding of the Goddess, but the face she had showed me was not her only one. I still did not know all of her, and I never will. The Goddess as she was revealed to me in my initiation is the patroness of my particular tradition of Wicca, but there are countless other traditions dedicated to her honor. Each of them has its own rites sacred to her, names by which she is known, and myths and stories about her. None of them is better, more true, or more all-encompassing than any of the others; no tradition has the one perfect truth about the Goddess. Instead, each of them offers its own truths, showing different parts of the Goddess's nature like facets on a jewel.

I felt honored to have undergone my initiation and seen a new facet of that jewel—and at the same time, I felt so humbled and so small, overcome with the realization that I would never see the whole. My initiation was the most magical night of my life, not just because of what I now knew about the Goddess, but because of what I realized I would never know. She is a mystery beyond the limits of my comprehension, and I will spend the rest of my life seeking to understand her.

The Father of the Witch Cult

Until 1951, it was illegal to call oneself a witch in the United Kingdom. There was a law on the books called the Witchcraft Act, which had been passed in 1735 and which no one had ever bothered to repeal. Under this law, anyone who claimed to be a witch or to exercise supernatural powers was subject to imprisonment for up to a full year.[184] This was actually much gentler than the witchcraft law preceding it, the Act against Conjuration and Witchcraft from 1604, which

---

184. "1735: 9 George 2 c.5: The Witchcraft Act."

had made witchcraft a capital offense.[185] Nonetheless, declaring oneself a witch was a crime well into the twentieth century, and it wasn't until 1951 that doing so was permitted by British law.

By the 1950s, there was increasing pressure on parliament to repeal the Witchcraft Act and a related law called the Vagrancy Act, due in no small part to the rise of Spiritualism as a religious movement in the United Kingdom. Spiritualist churches focus, among other things, on mediumship and communion with the spirits of the dead, but these activities were illegal under the extant witchcraft laws. In 1951, the baron Hugh Dowding introduced a bill to repeal and replace the Witchcraft Act, noting the political pressure from Spiritualists to legalize the practice of their religion. He remarked that under the Witchcraft Act, "Though spiritualists now have the assurances of the Home Secretary...that fraud must be proved if a medium is to be held guilty of an offence, these assurances are in no way binding upon a court."[186] Spiritualists had been frequently prosecuted under British law since the 1870s, and were looking for greater legal protections.

Thus, Lord Dowding introduced the Fraudulent Mediums Act, which increased the penalty for fraud but also made it so that claiming to practice witchcraft and mediumship was not a crime in its own right. Rather, the crime was to defraud people of money or other valuable goods by claiming magical powers, and the law specified that "a person shall not be convicted...unless it is proved that he acted for reward."[187] By the letter of the law, it was no longer illegal to call oneself a witch, medium, or magician in the United Kingdom, so long as the witch did not charge money for magical services. Similar laws still exist today in the United Kingdom and the United States, making fraud a criminal offense without criminalizing specific claims to the practice of witchcraft.

At this point, a retired British civil servant named Gerald Gardner came forward with a shocking announcement: he was a witch.

Gardner purported to be an initiate of a surviving pre-Christian witchcraft cult, which had been the indigenous religion of the British Isles and had gone underground with the arrival of Christianity. If this narrative sounds familiar, it should; Gardner was a member of the Folk-Lore Society with Margaret Murray. He knew

---

185. "1604: 1 James 1 c.12: An Act against Witchcraft."
186. Dowding, "Fraudulent Mediums Bill."
187. "1951: 14 & 15 George 6 c.33: Fraudulent Mediums Act."

Murray personally, though not intimately, and he was strongly influenced by her ideas. She even wrote the introduction to his book *Witchcraft Today*, released in 1954.[188] Gardner described a witch cult highly similar to the one envisioned by Murray. He called the members of this cult "the Wica," after the Old English word *wicca* or *wicce*, meaning "witch."[189] Later on, the religion itself would come to be known as "Wicca."

It is now known that Gardner's claims to an ancient provenance were unfounded. There is no evidence to indicate that his witch cult was the genuine survival of an ancient pagan religion, and in fact there is a good deal of evidence to the contrary. Gardner's discussion of the witch cult was evidently influenced by published sources including *The Witch-Cult in Western Europe*, *The Gospel of the Witches*, and *The White Goddess*, as well as sources in ceremonial magic, including the works of Aleister Crowley. Gardner had even met Crowley personally in the year prior to Crowley's death, although they had no extended personal correspondence.[190] Even if there were an ancient pagan witch religion, it would not have closely resembled the witchcraft that Gardner introduced to the world, which drew on these sources and was decidedly modern in flavor.[191]

However, the best evidence suggests that Gardner was sincere in his claims. It is likely that he was initiated into *something*, and that he genuinely thought it was an ancient pagan survival. Popular historian Philip Heselton has plausibly identified potential members of the group that initiated Gardner, showing where Gardner's own accounts line up with membership records for Rosicrucian, Theosophical, and Co-Masonic esoteric organizations.[192] Based on the available evidence, it seems most likely that a group of people began practicing a novel form of witchcraft in the early twentieth century, inspired by published works like *The Witch-Cult in Western Europe* and borrowing from the structure of initiatory fraternal orders such as Freemasonry. These people initiated Gerald Gardner into their newly made tradition, and he—misled about the tradition's origins—elaborated on it and presented it to the world as "the old religion" of the British Isles.[193]

---

188. Gardner, *Witchcraft Today*, 15.

189. Gardner, *Witchcraft Today*, 102.

190. Hutton, *The Triumph of the Moon*, 214.

191. Hutton, *The Triumph of the Moon*, 247.

192. Heselton, *In Search of the New Forest Coven*, 42.

193. Gardner, *Witchcraft Today*, 34.

Whatever Gardner may have received from his initiators, there can be no doubt that he added a great deal to it. Gardner had a particular romanticized notion of what witchcraft and paganism would have been in the ancient world, and he drew from modern sources to create a religion that fit that vision. Doreen Valiente, one of Gardner's first High Priestesses, describes the early days of working with Gardner, when she noted the strong undercurrent of Freemasonry and various published materials in his witch rites: "He explained this to me by saying…that the rituals he had received from the old coven were very fragmentary and that in order to make them workable he had been compelled to supplement them with other material."[194] Gardner's witchcraft was something new and unique, strongly influenced by modern ideas even as he passed it off as ancient. Some are tempted to characterize Gardner as a charlatan and a con man; personally, I'm inclined to see him as sincere, engaged in the project of trying to salvage what he thought was an ancient religion on the verge of dying out. Regardless of how sincere he was or how old the witch cult was in reality, he certainly puffed himself up with bravado when marketing it as the ancient and true religion of Britain.

Moreover, the world was poised to receive such a claim. Authors like Frazer, Leland, and Murray had primed the popular imagination with a particular view of what ancient paganism had been like. In light of that view, it didn't seem all that outlandish for Gardner to claim that a pagan witch cult had survived up until the present day. Paganism took root and grew rapidly, and Gardner's witch cult quickly established itself as a religion for the twentieth century. It was the "old religion" in name only, but as a new religion it was an extraordinary success.

The Goddess of the Wica

The witch religion as Gardner presented it was an initiatory Mystery cult. This meant that people could only become witches if they were initiated by those who already belonged to the religion, and that upon initiation they took an oath of secrecy that there were certain things they wouldn't reveal to outsiders. Gardner wrote, "Their association could only be entered by initiation, and learning and practising their secret lore."[195] Within this cult, witches practiced magic, observed

---

194. Valiente, *The Rebirth of Witchcraft*, 57.
195. Valiente, *The Rebirth of Witchcraft*, 37.

the cycles of the seasons and the phases of the moon, and celebrated the promise of reincarnation. All of these features should be familiar by now. Gardner's witchcraft picked up on the defining traits of Paganism as it had been imagined by thinkers throughout the late nineteenth and early twentieth centuries. Naturally, this included the veneration of a Great Goddess.

According to Gardner, the Wica were a priesthood dedicated to the service of two deities: a lunar Mother Goddess and her consort, the Horned God of death and rebirth. In his book *The Meaning of Witchcraft*, he wrote:

> It must be understood clearly that witchcraft is a religion. Its patron god is the Horned God of hunting, death and magic, who, rather like Osiris of Egypt, rules over the After-World… [and] the Goddess, the Great Mother, who is also the Eternal Virgin and the Primordial Enchantress, who gives rebirth and transmutation, and love on this earth.[196]

He focused on the figure of the Goddess as the Great Mother. Following in the footsteps of Frazer and Graves, he assigned her a male consort, the God of death and resurrection to complement the Goddess of life. As Gardner remarks rather succinctly, the witch deities are "the Lady of Life, the Lord of Death and What Lies Beyond; and between them the web of magic has been spun."[197] Interestingly, the consort is identified with Osiris, and the Goddess is implicitly linked to Isis. This follows a tradition laid down by Frazer, Crowley, and Fortune, all of whom used Isis and Osiris as a foundation of their new myths of the Great Goddess. There are also three aspects given for the Goddess, tying her to Graves's Triple Goddess: the Great Mother, the Eternal Virgin, and the Primordial Enchantress.

Gardner further identified the Goddess with the moon, magic, and sacred sexuality, all of which are traits seen in earlier authors. He notes, "The goddess of the witch cult is obviously the Great Mother, the giver of life, incarnate love. She rules spring, pleasure, feasting, and all the delights…and has a special affinity with the moon."[198] Here are all the familiar points from previous discussions about the Goddess. In fact, the truly remarkable thing about Gardner's witch

---

196. Gardner, *The Meaning of Witchcraft*, 17.

197. Gardner, *The Meaning of Witchcraft*, 153.

198. Gardner, *Witchcraft Today*, 42.

cult is not that it added something new to Goddess worship, but that it synthesized everything that had come before. Dion Fortune and Aleister Crowley
were inspired by similar sources, but Fortune's Isis and Crowley's Nuit differ in
important ways; Robert Graves drew from Frazer and Murray, but his Triple
Goddess was untouched by the work of twentieth-century ceremonial magicians.
It is not until Gardner and the Wica that all of these influences come together to
create one unified, coherent myth of the Great Goddess.

The bibliography of Gardner's book *The Meaning of Witchcraft* cites all but
one of the authors I have discussed here: James Frazer, Charles Godfrey Leland,
Margaret Murray, Aleister Crowley, Dion Fortune, and Robert Graves.[199] Gardner had read all of these people, and their work had a direct influence on the for-
mation of his modern witch cult and the way he thought about the Goddess. The
only name missing from this list is Bachofen, and there's no evidence to suggest
that Gardner ever read Bachofen directly. However, Gardner certainly bought
into Bachofen's ideas and was influenced by the theory of ancient matriarchy, even
if he did not know where that theory originated. He hypothesized that the witch
cult "is a Stone Age cult of the matriarchal times, when woman was the chief."[200]

Gardner had a vision of witchcraft as an ancient and true pagan religion, one
that had survived to the present day—but was in danger of dying out. He wrote
that after centuries in hiding, the witches had lost many of their rites and their
religion had shrunk almost to the point of nonexistence, so that "we must say
goodbye to the witch. The cult is doomed, I am afraid."[201] In trying to salvage
this dying religion, Gardner reached for the sources available to him, the voices
that were considered authoritative about ancient paganism, magic, and Goddess
worship. He drew on a popular idea of the Goddess and her worshippers as given
by figures like Murray and Graves, and he supplemented that idea with details
from authoritative magical figures of his time—ceremonial magicians like Aleister Crowley and Dion Fortune. The result was decidedly modern, because it was
taken from modern ideas. Nonetheless, those ideas were, themselves, situated
with an eye to the ancient past. Gardner was reaching out to antiquity the best

---

199. Gardner, *The Meaning of Witchcraft*, 269–71.

200. Gardner, *Witchcraft Today*, 43.

201. Gardner, *Witchcraft Today*, 129.

way he knew how, and in trying to rekindle the fire of ancient paganism, he found himself cultivating a modern Goddess myth.

Gardner's witch cult did add one new and significant feature to that modern myth. He described the worship of the Goddess as an initiatory religion with closely guarded secrets, noting that "there are certain secrets of the witch cult that I cannot by reason of my pledged word reveal."[202] While anyone might know the Goddess in broad terms—worshipping her as the earth or moon, as the Great Mother, and so on—there were certain rites and mysteries that were not available to the broader public. With Gardner, Goddess worship became cloaked in mystery and secrecy, and no one outside of the witch cult was entitled to know what witches actually *did* to worship their Goddess.

One such secret was the name of the Goddess herself—and that of her consort. According to Gardner, the Mother Goddess and Horned God were known to witches by secret names, which were not disclosed to those outside the witch cult. He wrote, "For one reason or another they keep the names of their god and goddess a secret."[203] These were the true names of the Gods, and knowing the names afforded the priesthood of the Wica a privileged relationship with their deities. Other people might know the Goddess as the Great Mother or the God as the Lord of Death, or they might syncretically identify the Gods with deities from world mythology—but only the initiated priests and priestesses could call the Goddess by name.

Gardner's witch cult took the modern myth of the Great Goddess and added a new dimension to it. The universal myth of the Goddess and her dying-and-resurrecting consort was still there, but now it was accompanied by a secret, esoteric body of knowledge and ritual practice. There was the Goddess as she was known to everyone, and then there was the Goddess as she was known to her priesthood. By introducing secret rites, names, and lore for the cult of the Great Goddess, Gardner gave people the opportunity to know her deeply and intimately. He introduced the notion that some aspects of Goddess worship were private, made more sacred for not being open to the public, and that "witchcraft was, and is, not a cult for everybody."[204] With Gardner, the universal cult of the

202. Gardner, *The Meaning of Witchcraft*, 12.

203. Gardner, *Witchcraft Today*, 24.

204. Gardner, *Witchcraft Today*, 29.

Goddess had its public face, but its true face was kept to the shadows, hidden from the eyes of those who might profane it.

The Charge of the Goddess

Although Gardner was the person to introduce the religion that came to be known as Wicca, he was by no means the only influential figure in Wicca's development. Gardner was the beginning of a twentieth-century witchcraft revival, as more and more people claimed to have preserved, discovered, or revived the religion of the Great Goddess. Some of the most influential figures in Wicca are women whom Gardner initiated into his witch cult, and who then went on to become priestesses, authors, and public witches. The most famous of these is Doreen Valiente, who is sometimes affectionately called the mother of modern witchcraft.

Valiente noticed the amount that Gardner had drawn on published sources in fleshing out his witch cult. When she expressed distaste for this, he told her, "Well, if you think you can do any better, go ahead."[205] Subsequently, she reworked many of Gardner's rituals, putting her own fingerprint on Gardner's witchcraft and making it something more original and unique. Valiente was also a poet and an author in her own right, and she wrote a great deal of Pagan-inspired devotional poetry with themes revolving around the Goddess, the Horned God, and witchcraft. Valiente's poetry is still available in print, including in a small anthology called *The Charge of the Goddess*, and much of it is accessible online through the Doreen Valiente Foundation's website.

Her most famous piece of work is a short piece of prose poetry called "The Charge of the Goddess," written as a speech delivered by the Goddess herself. The Charge closely paraphrases the "Whenever ye have need of anything" speech from *The Gospel of the Witches* (see chapter 3), as well as material from Crowley's *Book of the Law*, but it synthesizes these sources and adds original material that is entirely Valiente's own. The full text of "The Charge of the Goddess" is as follows:

> Listen to the words of the Great Mother, who was of old also
> called Artemis; Astarte; Diana; Melusine; Aphrodite; Cerrid-
> wen; Dana; Arianrhod; Isis; Bride; and by many other names.

---

205. Valiente, *The Rebirth of Witchcraft*, 61.

Whenever ye have need of anything, once in a month, and better it be when the Moon be full, then ye shall assemble in some secret place and adore the spirit of me, who am Queen of all Witcheries.

There shall ye assemble, ye who are fain to learn all sorcery, yet have not yet won its deepest secrets: to these will I teach things that are yet unknown. And ye shall be free from slavery; and as a sign that ye are really free, ye shall be naked in your rites; and ye shall dance, sing, feast, make music and love, all in my praise. For mine is the ecstasy of the spirit and mine also is joy on earth; for my Law is Love unto all Beings.

Keep pure your highest ideal; strive ever toward it; let naught stop you or turn you aside. For mine is the secret door which opens upon the Land of Youth; and mine is the Cup of the Wine of Life, and the Cauldron of Cerridwen, which is the Holy Grail of Immortality.

I am the Gracious Goddess, who gives the gift of joy unto the heart. Upon earth, I give the knowledge of the spirit eternal; and beyond death, I give peace, and freedom, and reunion with those who have gone before. Nor do I demand sacrifice, for behold I am the Mother of All Living, and my love is poured out upon the earth.

Hear ye the words of the Star Goddess, she in the dust of whose feet are the hosts of heaven; whose body encircleth the Universe; I, who am the beauty of the green earth, and the white Moon among the stars, and the mystery of the waters, and the heart's desire, call unto thy soul. Arise and come unto me.

For I am the Soul of Nature, who giveth life to the universe; from me all things proceed, and unto me must all things return; and before my face, beloved of gods and mortals, thine inmost divine self shall be unfolded in the rapture of infinite joy.

Let my worship be within the heart that rejoiceth, for behold: all acts of love and pleasure are my rituals. And therefore let there be beauty and strength, power and compassion, honour and humility, mirth and reverence within you.

And thou who thinkest to seek for me, know thy seeking and yearning shall avail thee not, unless thou know this
mystery: that if that which thou seekest thou findest not within
thee, thou wilt never find it without thee.

For behold, I have been with thee from the beginning; and I
am that which is attained at the end of desire.[206]

The Charge identifies the Goddess with a number of goddesses from world mythology. Many of these names are already familiar: Astarte and Aphrodite are named by Frazer, Diana is the Goddess of the witches in Leland and Murray's accounts, and Isis is at the center of both *The Golden Bough* and *The Sea Priestess*. Dana is one of Graves's alternate names for Dôn, and Cerridwen and Arianrhod are both discussed at length in *The White Goddess* as aspects of the Triple Goddess.

Beyond the names given for the Goddess, the Charge identifies her with two principal aspects: the Great Mother and the Star Goddess. Here, Crowley is an influence; these two epithets are titles of Babalon and Nuit, respectively, and seeing them juxtaposed with each other invites at least a partially Thelemic view of the Goddess. The Goddess of the Charge has both faces: the immanence and embodiment of Babalon as well as the cosmic transcendence of Nuit. She is simultaneously of this world and beyond it. Valiente associated the Goddess with "the beauty of the green earth, and the white Moon among the stars," but also with a more mysterious, abstract force, "the rapture of infinite joy."[207] She connected the Goddess to the earth, the moon, and motherhood, but also to love, mirth, and the feeling of freedom and ecstatic release.

"The Charge of the Goddess" is a beautiful piece of liturgy, and its impact on the contemporary Goddess movement is immeasurable. It has been included in countless books, often without attribution to Valiente as the author; for many decades, it was passed around among Goddess worshippers without people knowing who had written it or when.[208] It has become a ubiquitous and defining document of modern Goddess worship. Only with the 1981 publication of Janet and Stewart Farrar's book *Eight Sabbats for Witches* did the broader Pagan and

---

206. Valiente, *The Charge of the Goddess*, 12–13. Reproduced with permission of the Doreen Valiente Foundation.

207. Valiente, *The Charge of the Goddess*, 13.

208. Starhawk, *The Spiral Dance*, 244.

Goddess-worshipping community come to recognize Valiente's authorship of the Charge.[209]

Valiente filled another important role in popularizing Wicca: she helped to reformulate it as something that should be accessible to everyone. Although she initially belonged to Gardner's initiatory witch cult, she parted ways with Gardner after only a few years, pursuing her own form of witchcraft and working with a number of other influential figures in the Pagan revival. She wrote a book called *Witchcraft for Tomorrow* in response to Gardner's own *Witchcraft Today*, stating that its purpose was to "put witchcraft within the reach of all."[210] Gardner had insisted on secrecy as a hallmark of his Old Religion; Valiente argued that in the twentieth century, with witch trials a thing of the dimly remembered past, there was no longer any persecution of Pagans and thus no need for secrecy. She suggested that anyone should be able to worship the Goddess and practice as a witch, and *Witchcraft for Tomorrow* laid out the basics of how a noninitiate might do such a thing. Valiente was not the first or only person to democratize witchcraft, but her work was essential in making Wicca accessible to all.

As Wicca spread throughout Britain—and subsequently, throughout the world—demand vastly exceeded supply. People were interested in the worship of the Goddess, drawn to this new witch religion that had been presented to them as something ancient. However, traditional witch covens on Gardner's model were small and slow to grow; they capped out at about a dozen people, and someone needed to belong to a coven for a period of several years before they were qualified to leave and start a group of their own.

As such, new witch traditions started to crop up, from people who were either inventing their own practices or claiming to have rediscovered another branch of the Old Religion. In many cases, people claimed to belong to ancient witch families, and to have been initiated by a grandmother or other relative.[211] Consequently, there was a proliferation of witchcraft traditions—particularly in the United States, where the sheer size of the country made Gardner's witch cult particularly inaccessible. If you go looking for Wicca today, you will find some people who belong to Gardner's original initiatory witch cult, some who belong to other

---

209. Farrar and Farrar, *A Witches' Bible*, 42.
210. Valiente, *Witchcraft for Tomorrow*, 21.
211. Hutton, *The Triumph of the Moon*, 337.

traditions of varying degrees of similarity, and yet others who practice entirely on their own without belonging to any definite tradition. Across the globe, there were people who wanted to worship the Goddess but who didn't have access to traditional covens, so they started doing their own thing and calling it Wicca. Contra Gardner, witchcraft and the religion of the Goddess were no longer the sole purview of the initiated.

——— **EXERCISE** ———
ELEMENTAL TOOLS

Because of the diversity of modern Wicca, there are few, if any, practices shared by all Wiccans. However, one commonality is that Wiccans generally use a set of ritual tools in their magical and religious operations. The specifics vary between traditions and practitioners, but most variations of Wicca will include four core tools: the athame, wand, cup, and pentacle. These, in turn, are often linked to the four classical elements of air, fire, water, and earth. In *Witchcraft for Tomorrow*, Valiente writes:

> When man became a maker and user of tools, he lifted himself up from the beasts. He made himself an edged tool to cut, a staff to walk with and to defend himself, a platter to eat from, a horn or cup for his drink, and a length of twine or rawhide to bind with. Today, witches use these elemental weapons or implements: the wand, the knife, the cup, and the disk or pentacle…They are called elemental weapons because they are attributed to the four elements of life: the wand for fire, the cup for water, the knife or dagger for air, and the disk or pentacle for earth.[212]

You can acquire all four of these tools easily and cheaply and incorporate them into your ritual work.

---

212. Valiente, *Witchcraft for Tomorrow*, 79–80.

Athame

Valiente writes, "The typical weapon of witchcraft is the athame, or ritual knife (pronounced a-*thay*-me)."[213] She describes the athame as a ritual dagger with a black hilt, and she associates it with the element of air, although some witches associate it with fire. Gerald Gardner suggests that the athame is typically given to the new witch upon initiation, and that "in a witch family there are often old tools to be had."[214] For those who don't have the luxury of an inherited athame, this tool is easy enough to acquire. You'll need a dagger or boot knife. Valiente recommends a black handle for the knife, but many contemporary witches have abandoned this convention, and you shouldn't feel restricted by it unless you belong to a tradition that requires it. Your athame doesn't need to be large, nor even sharp; if you're uncomfortable using a sharp knife in ritual, you can look for a prop dagger with a blunted edge.

In ritual, you can use your athame for any magical act involving severing, banishing, defending, or commanding, as well as anything relating to speech or intellect as attributes of elemental air. The athame is a purely symbolic weapon and is never used to cut or stab anything physical, nor to physically harm anyone.

Wand

Where the athame is a tool of magical defense, the wand is a tool of strengthening and empowerment. Valiente associates it with fire, although some witches connect it to air instead. According to Valiente, "The wand is the expression of the magician's will and is used for invocations."[215] As a magical tool, it directs energy in a gentler way than the athame; it requests rather than commands. For this reason, it's useful in invocations of deities, whom it would be inappropriate to command at knifepoint. Due to extensive folklore about fairies disliking iron, it would also be appropriate to use the wand instead of the athame for any work with the fair folk. More broadly, the wand can be used for magical or ritual purposes involving will, passion, and creativity, all of which are associated with elemental fire.

---

213. Valiente, *Witchcraft for Tomorrow*, 78.
214. Gardner, *Witchcraft Today*, 150.
215. Valiente, *Witchcraft for Tomorrow*, 80.

Different Wiccan traditions may have their own specifications for what the wand should look like, but at bottom, the wand is just a stick. Choose a stick of a wood with folkloric or magical associations that you like for your ritual work; if you're stuck for inspiration, look through Robert Graves's tree alphabet and see if any of the woods mentioned there seem appropriate. The stick should be roughly the same length as the distance between your elbow and the tip of your middle finger. You can use a stick that has fallen naturally from a tree, or if you like, you can cut a fresh stick; if you do the latter, take care to make a clean cut that doesn't damage the tree. Your wand can be as simple or as elaborate as you like. Some people prefer a plain stick with the bark still on it. Others will sand off the bark, carve or burn designs into it, wrap it in wire, and even add crystals or feathers to it.

Cup

The cup is the tool of elemental water and can be used for magic dealing with emotions, healing, and purification. Valiente also notes that the altar holds a cup of sacramental wine, which is blessed in the course of the ritual. Unlike the athame and the wand, which are projective, the cup is a receptacle; its nature is to shape and contain things, and Valiente identifies it as a "yonic or feminine" symbol corresponding to the womb.[216] Any cup can serve as a ritual tool. It can be a simple wineglass or a silver chalice, depending on your aesthetic sensibilities. The most important thing is that whatever cup you use should be set aside exclusively for ritual use; you should keep it apart from the other cups in your home, and never use it for ordinary drinking. It is a special magical tool, and it should be treated as such.

Pentacle

Finally, there is the pentacle, a flat disk with magical signs marked on it. Various magical traditions have different symbols used on their pentacles—the Hermetic Order of the Golden Dawn uses a pentacle painted with a hexagram, and a famous grimoire called *The Key of Solomon* lists dozens of different pentacle designs for specific magical purposes—but in Wicca, you'll most commonly see a

---

216. Valiente, *Witchcraft for Tomorrow*, 80.

plain circle inscribed with a five-pointed star. As the elemental tool of earth, the pentacle can be used magically for prosperity, security, and any practical ends.

You can buy a premade altar pentacle, or you can make your own. Valiente suggests that for the sake of discretion and secrecy, "the pentacle was made of wax or wood, which in an emergency could be quickly destroyed in the kitchen fire," but you can make your pentacle out of whatever materials are handy.[217] When I first started training with a Wiccan coven, our pentacle was a saucer that had a star drawn on it in Sharpie; if all else fails, you can cut a circle out of construction paper and draw a five-pointed star on that.

From the Goddess to Goddesses

As Wicca continued to develop in the twentieth century, a new trend emerged among some Wiccan practitioners: rather than seeing Wicca as the religion of *the* Goddess and *the* God, they saw it as the religion of *a* goddess and *a* god. Inspired in part by a Dion Fortune–like syncretism and the idea that all goddesses are ultimately faces of the same deity, these practitioners moved away from the view of the Great Goddess as a particular deity. Rather, they suggested, individual practitioners or covens should form relationships with a particular goddess of their choosing.

Thus, Janet and Stewart Farrar, in their book *A Witches' Bible*, wrote rituals to be filled in with "whatever God and Goddess names the coven uses."[218] Later, Scott Cunningham elaborated on this idea in his bestselling book *Wicca: A Guide for the Solitary Practitioner*, writing that "When envisioning the Goddess and God, many of the Wicca see them as well-known deities from ancient religions…Anyone with a special affinity with particular deities should feel free to adapt the rituals."[219] These authors presented Wicca largely as a ritual framework, the specifics of which could be filled in with the names of different deities according to the preference of an individual or group.

This was a radically different perspective on Goddess worship than what I have traced throughout this book; more accurately, it should be called goddess worship with a lowercase G. On this view, the central theology of Wicca was an emphasis on

---

217. Valiente, *Witchcraft for Tomorrow*, 165.

218. Farrar and Farrar, *A Witches' Bible*, 37.

219. Cunningham, *Wicca*, 10–11.

venerating deity as both male and female, rather than as exclusively male. It rejected the dominant Christian paradigm of God the father, and instead underscored the idea that women and men were reflected equally in the nature of the divine. The view of gender here is still quite binary and essential; you'll notice that "women" and "men" are the only two options given, and those categories were implicitly defined in terms of biological reproduction. A more nuanced understanding of sex and gender did not make its way into the mainstream of the Goddess-worshipping community until the twenty-first century. Still, for the time, this was an important and progressive theological stance. It signaled, however imperfectly, that everyone was divine, and everyone had direct access to deity.

However, beyond this core principle, the details of deity worship were largely left up to the practitioner's individual preference. There was no specific Goddess to worship—no Great Goddess with a particular, well-defined mythology and symbolism. Instead, many practitioners chose to honor a goddess and a god of their choosing, pairing extant deities from world mythology. These might be traditionally paired in myth as consorts or siblings—Hera and Zeus, Freyja and Freyr—but they might also be completely unrelated, and even come from different pantheons of world mythology.

In this more eclectic, individualistic approach to Wicca, a practitioner might choose to venerate the Cailleach and Loki as their goddess and god, or Sekhmet and Mithras. Often, the choice of deities would be based on some particular affinity to the individual practitioner: a poet might choose to worship a goddess and god of inspiration, a soldier might choose war deities, and so on. Specific deities might also be called in for an occasion—Aphrodite could be invoked for a love spell or Persephone could be honored at a harvest celebration. This new approach to Wicca was highly flexible, eclectic, and individualized.

That is not to say that the worship of the Great Goddess went away entirely in Wicca. Many traditions, as well as individual practitioners, persist to this day in the worship of "the" Goddess, rather than choosing particular goddesses to honor. Gardner's original tradition of witchcraft is still alive and thriving today, as are many similar traditions that were born out of it or inspired by it. In these traditional strands of Wicca, it is still common for people to view themselves as a priesthood of the Great Goddess and her consort. However, that attitude is no longer the only one found in Wicca. As Wicca continued to grow and diversify over the course of the twentieth century, new ritual practices and theological perspectives were introduced. There is no longer just one thing that calls itself Wicca. Rather, countless varieties of religious experience and practice share the label. Many of those are still dedicated to the Great Goddess—but in many others, a tradition, coven, or individual practitioner will eschew the Great Goddess in favor of particular patron gods from history and mythology.

Key Takeaways: Gardner and Valiente

- Introduction of a modern witch cult inspired by Murray
- Synthesis of ideas about the Goddess into a cohesive whole
- "The Charge of the Goddess" as liturgy for Goddess religion
- Witchcraft as an initiatory priesthood with secret rites and names for the Gods
- De-emphasis of "the" Goddess in some strands of Wicca

―――― RITUAL ――――
Naming the Goddess

Drawing inspiration from Gardner's secret witch cult, you can use this ritual to petition the Goddess to give you a secret name by which you may know her. This name may be for your personal use or for a group—and if you practice with a group, you may even want to do both, performing the ritual once all together and once more on your own so that you have shared *and* individual names by which you know the Goddess.

Group Variation

In this version of the ritual, you petition the Goddess for a coven-specific name, which can be used by all the members of your group whenever you do ritual together. Because this name will be used by all the members of your group, it's a good idea to make sure that everyone gets to participate, either by saying a line, drawing a tile, or using a magical tool.

You Will Need

- An altar
- An athame
- A wand
- A cup full of water
- A pentacle
- A six-sided die
- A set of Scrabble tiles
- Two cloth bags

Preparation

Arrange an altar in the center of your ritual space with your athame, wand, cup, and pentacle on top of it. Separate the Scrabble tiles into consonants and vowels, placing each group of tiles into one of your cloth bags. Put the bags of tiles on the altar along with the six-sided die.

Performance

At the start of the ritual, one member of the group picks up the wand. Lifting the wand above the center of the altar, they invoke the Goddess:

> *Mother of all living things, queen of witchcraft, eternal and ever-changing Goddess of the moon, hear us now! We invoke and beseech thee, Great Goddess who has been known to the world by so many names. Bestow unto us a secret name by which you shall be known to us and us alone. Let our lips utter thy sacred name with reverence and love, that we may know thy innermost face. Goddess, reveal thy mysteries to us! Be known to us and receive our worship!*

They replace the wand on the altar. Another member of the group steps forward. Dipping their fingers in the cup of water, they lightly sprinkle the die and the two bags of Scrabble tiles, saying as they do so:

> *Unnamed and holy Goddess, bless these instruments of fortune, that through them we may know thy name and thy will. So mote it be!*

They step back and another member of the group steps forward. This person rolls the six-sided die, saying:

> *Goddess, reveal thy name.*

The number they roll is the number of consonants in the name of the Goddess. The person who rolled the die takes the bag of consonant tiles, draws one, and places it on the pentacle. They then pass the bag to another member of the group, who draws another tile and puts it on the pentacle next to the first one. This person then passes the bag off to another, who draws another consonant, and so on until the correct number of tiles have been drawn.

As an example, if the number rolled on the die was a four, then four people would draw tiles from the bag and place them on the pentacle. Let's suppose the letters they drew were M, H, N, and T. These letters would then be arranged in order on the pentacle:

$$\text{M H N T}$$

These are the consonants that make up your group's name for the Goddess. Now, look at the letters and determine where you need to add vowels in order to make a name. This will depend on the specific letters you have drawn, and you'll have to discuss with each other and use your intuition and aesthetic sensibilities to determine what's best. You may want vowels in between each consonant, or there may be two consonants that look like they go together. Likewise, you may or may not want vowels at the very beginning or very end of the name. This choice is yours; do what feels right to you. (If one of the letters you have drawn is a Q, you should add an implicit U after it; you don't need to draw a tile in order to do so.)

One member of the group now takes the bag of vowel tiles and draws one, placing it in the first place you have determined you need a vowel. They then pass the bag off to another member of the group, who draws and places the next tile, and so on until all the vowels have been chosen.

In this example, let's say that you decide to add three vowels: one at the beginning of the name, one between the H and the N, and one between the N and the T. This gives you a three-syllable name:

*M H * N * T

Let's suppose the vowels you draw are an A, a second A, and an E. This gives you:

AMHANET

When you have finished, put together all the letters you have drawn, reading them out as a single name. In the example, your group's private name for the Goddess would be Amhanet. Say the name aloud in unison, repeating it to get a feel for it. As you do so, one member of the group takes the athame and traces the letters of the name in the air above the altar. Keep chanting the name until you reach a crescendo, then stop.

The person holding the athame replaces it on the altar and picks up the wand. Holding the wand high over the center of the altar, they say:

> Eternal and beloved Goddess [name], we thank thee for the gift of
> thy name. We shall guard it truly and keep it as our deepest secret,

for this is a mystery not fit for the ears of others. Blessed be thy
name [name], and now we part!

The ritual is ended. You may now use your secret name for the Goddess any time your group does ritual together. Do not share this name with anyone who is not a part of your group; it is yours alone, and no one else has the right to use it or to know it.

Solitary Variation

In this version of the ritual, you petition the Goddess for a personal name, which can be used in your solitary rituals and should never be shared with anyone else. This is the secret face that the Goddess shows only to you.

You Will Need
- An altar
- An athame
- A wand
- A cup full of water
- A pentacle
- A six-sided die
- A set of Scrabble tiles
- Two cloth bags

Preparation
Arrange an altar in the center of your ritual space with your athame, wand, cup, and pentacle on top of it. Separate the Scrabble tiles into consonants and vowels, placing each group of tiles into one of your cloth bags. Put the bags of tiles on the altar along with the six-sided die.

Performance
At the start of the ritual, pick up the wand. Lift the wand above the center of the altar and invoke the Goddess:

*Mother of all living things, queen of witchcraft, eternal and
ever-changing Goddess of the moon, hear me now! I invoke and
beseech thee, Great Goddess who has been known to the world by
so many names. Bestow unto me a secret name by which you shall
be known to me and me alone. Let my lips utter thy sacred name
with reverence and love, that I may know thy innermost face.
Goddess, reveal thy mysteries to me! Be known to me and receive
my worship!*

Replace the wand on the altar. Dipping your fingers in the cup of water, lightly sprinkle the die and the two bags of Scrabble tiles, saying as you do so:

*Unnamed and holy Goddess, bless these instruments of fortune, that
through them I may know thy name and thy will. So mote it be!*

Roll the six-sided die, saying:

Goddess, reveal thy name.

The number you roll is the number of consonants in the name of the Goddess. Take the bag of consonant tiles, draw one, and place it on the pentacle. Then draw another tile and put it on the pentacle next to the first one, and keep doing so until the correct number of tiles have been drawn.

As an example, if the number rolled on the die was a four, then you would draw four tiles from the bag and place them on the pentacle. Let's suppose the letters you drew were M, H, N, and T. These letters would then be arranged in order on the pentacle:

M H N T

These are the consonants that make up your personal name for the Goddess. Now, look at the letters and determine where you need to add vowels in order to make a name. This will depend on the specific letters you have drawn, and you'll have to use your intuition and aesthetic sensibilities to determine what's best. You may want vowels in between each consonant, or there may be two consonants that look like they go together. Likewise, you may or may not want vowels at the very beginning or very end of the name. This choice is yours; do what feels right to you. (If one of the letters you have drawn is a Q, you should add an implicit U after it; you don't need to draw a tile in order to do so.)

Now, take the bag of vowel tiles and draw one, placing it in the first place you have determined you need a vowel. Then draw and place another vowel in the next place you need one, and so on until all the vowels have been chosen.

In this example, let's say that you decide to add three vowels: one at the beginning of the name, one between the H and the N, and one between the N and the T. This gives you a three-syllable name:

* M H * N * T

Let's suppose the vowels you draw are an A, a second A, and an E. This gives you:

A M H A N E T

When you have finished, put together all the letters you have drawn, reading them out as a single name. In the example, your private name for the Goddess would be Amhanet. Say the name aloud in, repeating it to get a feel for it. As you do so, take the athame and trace the letters of the name in the air above the altar. Keep chanting the name until you reach a crescendo, then stop.

Replace the athame on the altar and pick up the wand. Holding the wand high over the center of the altar, say:

> *Eternal and beloved Goddess [name], I thank thee for the gift of thy name. I shall guard it truly and keep it as my deepest secret, for this is a mystery not fit for the ears of others. Blessed be thy name [name], and now we part!*

The ritual is ended. You may now use your secret name for the Goddess any time you pray to her, invoke her, or do ritual in her honor. Do not share this name with anyone else; it is yours alone, and no one else has the right to use it or to know it.

9

GODDESS FEMINISM (1971)

OCCASIONALLY, A MYSTICAL EXPERIENCE descends upon me out of nowhere. Sometimes, the Goddess arrives and wants to make herself known, and when that happens, I find myself quaking with religious rapture in the middle of the sidewalk, on the subway, or sitting in the library. On one such occasion, I had just gotten a haircut—hardly a religious experience in its own right. As I stepped out of the barbershop, I felt a strange chill pass through me, but I didn't think much of it. I exited the alley where the barbershop was located and stepped out onto the main street.

Then, the Goddess hit me across the face with a proverbial frying pan.

A pregnant woman pushed a stroller with a giggling toddler inside. She glanced up at me, and behind her sparkling blue eyes I saw not just her, but the Goddess. The experience of a thousand mothers, stretching back across millennia, stared back at me through the eyes of this stranger. I blinked, trying to clear my head, but there was no denying it. The Goddess was in her. As she met my gaze for the briefest instant, I felt a shocking, deep connection to her; my soul reached out to the soul of this woman and found the Goddess herself reaching back for me.

Uncomfortable with this sudden intimacy, I dropped my gaze to the toddler, and there again, I saw the Goddess looking back at me. Carefree, exuberant, full of life and the love for life, she smiled as she watched me. She raised a hand and waved, and I couldn't help waving back, grinning at the playful joy that spread across her face.

Further down the street, two college students were sitting on a bench and kissing. I glanced at them as I passed, and I saw the Goddess split in two, sharing love with herself in a tender embrace. The teenagers didn't look up at me; they were lost in each other. But even so, I could feel the passion of the Goddess, her infinite love expressing itself in the love of these two finite creatures, as I passed them and continued on my route.

An old man with a cane stood on the street corner, waiting for the light to change. I drew up next to him, and he glanced at me with the Goddess's quiet patience. The barista at the coffee shop further down the street handed me a cup of cocoa, and in that moment, it was more than a hot chocolate. It was the Holy Grail, the cup of life, the blessing of the Goddess. Everywhere I looked, I saw her. Everyone I met had the Goddess within them, burning like a hidden flame that had been invisible to me until now. She was everywhere. She was everyone.

It's often said that the Goddess lives within us, and that's a beautiful sentiment, but for many years, I thought it was just poetic language. That day, I saw things differently. I understood that the Goddess truly does exist inside all of us. She is everywhere, in everything. She is the life force that animates the universe and that binds us all together.

The magic began to fade as the sun went down that night, and the people around me went back to being just themselves. But I knew the Goddess was still there as the inherent divinity of every person, waiting to be seen. I just had to look for her.

Matriarchy Returns

When Gardner introduced his witch cult to the world, he presented it as a survival from the imagined past, a continuation of antiquity into the modern world. There were other people, however, who wanted their religion not to return them to the past, but to launch them into the future. Starting in the early 1970s, a growing movement of feminist thinkers and writers combined the language of Goddess worship with a political polemic that advocated for women's social and political equality. For these thinkers, the Goddess was a symbol of liberation. She promised that women could be powerful, sacred, and valued by society—that they could be free from the patriarchal structures that dominated all aspects of life. The myth of the Goddess, and the possibility of a Goddess-centric society, held with it the hope that a different world was possible. It allowed feminist thinkers to imagine and strive for a society with a wholly new set of values and social mores.

In 1971, Elizabeth Gould Davis published a book called *The First Sex*. In it, she made a familiar claim:

That in ancient times, indeed well into the historical era,
woman had played a dominant role…The further back one
traced man's history, the larger loomed the figure of woman. If
the gods and goddesses of today are but the heroes and hero-
ines of yesterday, then unquestionably the goddesses of historical times were but the reflected memory of the ruling hierarchy
of a former civilization.[220]

Davis revived the notion of prehistorical matriarchy, arguing that matriarchal societies were responsible for the original cultivation of agriculture, language, tex-
tile production, and all the other cornerstones of human civilization. Humans had lived peacefully and in egalitarian societies up until what Davis called the "patriarchal revolution"—the violent overthrow of matriarchal order by men, who introduced warfare, private property, and rigid social hierarchy, bringing about the collapse of the utopian society that had gone before.[221] Davis explicitly based her view of ancient matriarchy on Bachofen's *Mother Right*, writing that "Bachofen recognized the truth of our gynocratic origins."[222] In her narrative, of course, ancient matriarchy must have centered its religious life on the worship of the Great Goddess.

Davis was not merely interested in ancient matriarchy as an archaeological phenomenon. She saw it as a tool of women's liberation, which could be used in the modern day. At the time Davis was writing, a married woman could not open a bank account in her own name.[223] Spousal rape was not recognized as a crime.[224] Women made up less than a third of the work force in the United States.[225] They were, moreover, institutionally excluded from public life, and only eleven women held elected positions across both chambers of US Congress.[226] Abortion was not federally protected until 1973 (and lost its federal protection in

220. Davis, *The First Sex*, 15–16.

221. Davis, *The First Sex*, 139.

222. Davis, *The First Sex*, 77.

223. Equal Credit Opportunity Act, H.R.8163 (1973).

224. "Spousal Rape Laws."

225. "Women in the Labor Force, 1970–2009."

226. "History of Women in the US Congress."

2022).[227] In all areas of life, women were deprived of their autonomy—political, financial, bodily, and spiritual.

The promise of Goddess feminism was like water in the desert. It carried with it a message that *things didn't have to be like this*, and the value of that message must not be understated. According to Carol P. Christ, a pioneer of feminist spirituality, the heart of the movement was "an affirmation of the legitimacy and beneficence of female power," and such an affirmation was desperately needed in a world that too frequently denied or denigrated that power.[228] In a world where women were boxed in on all sides by culture and law alike, this reimagining of religion showed them a way out. The Goddess offered a new religion focused on liberation and justice—and with it, the possibility of a new world.

Starhawk, a leading figure in the movement, wrote in her landmark 1979 book *The Spiral Dance*, "True social change can only come about when the myths and symbols of our culture are themselves changed. The symbol of the Goddess conveys the spiritual power both to challenge systems of oppression and to create new, life-oriented cultures."[229] The goal of Goddess feminism was never merely to retell history with a different narrative, but instead has always been to use that narrative to imagine a better future for women's social, political, and religious lives. If matriarchy had existed once, it could exist again. If women had once held positions of authority, had been safe from violence and sexual abuse, had been respected for the work they did, then they could be all of those things once more. In short, if the past had been better than the present, the future might be better as well.

Witchcraft and Women's Power

Goddess feminism grew rapidly throughout the 1970s and 1980s. Books with titles like *When God Was a Woman* and *The Language of the Goddess* advanced the theory of ancient matriarchy, and of Goddess-centered prehistoric religion, as a foundation of modern feminism. At the core of the movement was the project of building a spirituality centered on women's power—as it actually existed, as it might have existed in the past, and as it could exist in the future. Feminist spiritu-

---

227. Jane Roe, et al. v. Henry Wade. 410 U.S. 113 (1973).

228. Christ, "Why Women Need the Goddess," 10.

229. Starhawk, *The Spiral Dance*, 35.

ality reached for symbols that would uplift, inspire, and empower women. Chief among those symbols was the image of the witch.

Witchcraft is inescapably gendered in the popular imagination. The word *witch* conjures a mental picture of a woman, whether she's a seductress or a hag. The witch is the woman in the woods who lives in a house made of candy, the evil stepmother holding a poisoned apple, or the pink-garbed mentor descending to Munchkinland in a bubble. Sometimes she is malicious and sometimes she is benevolent, but consistently, she is a woman and she is powerful. These two things together made the witch an ideal image for Goddess feminists. As scholar of feminist spirituality Cynthia Eller writes in her book *Living in the Lap of the Goddess*:

> The witch is the powerful outsider, the despised and excluded person that is threatening to the established order...By proudly acknowledging their exclusion, spiritual feminists demand their inclusion. For the outsider's power is threatening only to a narrow, oppressive oligarchy of men; it is evil only in the eyes of those who relegate it to the margins of society. In itself, it is good power, the best power: it is women's power.[230]

Powerful women are scornfully referred to as witches. Feminism in the twentieth century took this word and reclaimed it, reimagining it as a badge of honor. In 1968, a feminist group was founded in New York, calling itself the Women's International Terrorist Conspiracy from Hell: W.I.T.C.H.[231] Subsequently, similar groups across the United States emerged under this banner. The members of W.I.T.C.H. championed the role of the witch as a disruptive influence in society who could challenge and overturn oppressive structures. They participated in public displays of political resistance, often involving elaborate costumes and staging to highlight the witch theme of the organization. Although not itself a religious group, W.I.T.C.H. became inspiration for the generation of Goddess-worshipping feminists who would come after.

Witchcraft and feminist religion became inextricably linked. Drawing on Bachofen, Murray, and Gardner, Goddess feminists imagined the worship of the

---

230. Eller, *Living in the Lap of the Goddess*, 195.
231. Eller, *Living in the Lap of the Goddess*, 53.

Goddess as the original Stone Age religion of the human race, and they connected this worship with magic and witchcraft. Starhawk wrote, "Witchcraft is a religion, perhaps the oldest religion extant in the West."[232] As women started to carve out a special kind of spirituality for themselves, many chose to make that spirituality in the image of the witch. Traditions of feminist religious witchcraft began to emerge, focusing on the veneration of the Goddess and the inherent power of women.

The most famous of these is the Dianic tradition of Wicca, a women-only form of religious witchcraft founded by Hungarian refugee Zsuzsanna Budapest. In 1971, Budapest started the Susan B. Anthony Coven of witches, the flagship coven of the Dianic tradition.[233] Unlike Gardner's Wicca, which venerated a God as consort to the Goddess, Budapest's feminist version was monotheistic and depicted the Goddess as unique and encompassing the whole of the divine. In this vision of feminist spirituality, the Goddess is everything; she is the source of all creation, all transformation, and all power. The sacred universe is fundamentally female, and women have privileged access to the Goddess as their birthright. A witch, in this picture, is a woman who claims her power and leverages her divine nature in order to heal herself and the world from the harms done by patriarchal oppression.

Budapest's Dianic Wicca is by no means the only form of feminist witchcraft to emerge in the twentieth century. The connection between witches and feminism became a cornerstone of popular culture, appearing in television shows like *Charmed* and *Buffy the Vampire Slayer*. By the 1990s, the ideas of witchcraft, feminism, and the Goddess were drawn so closely together that it was difficult to find a book about one that didn't at least mention the others in passing. Many other forms of Wicca took on a feminist flair, and witchcraft was touted as an alternative to the oppressive patriarchal Christianity that dominated American culture. Here was a religion where, according to Starhawk, "there is no split between spirit and nature, no concept of sin, no covenant or commandments against which one can sin."[234] Witchcraft encouraged women to break free from the laws that men had set down for them, and to claim their own kind of power—women's power—instead.

---

232. Starhawk, *The Spiral Dance*, 26.
233. Adler, *Drawing Down the Moon*, 75.
234. Starhawk, *The Spiral Dance*, 35.

This women's power was not the kind of power that is used to dominate and subdue. Indeed, Dianic priestess Ruth Barrett claimed that domination was antithetical to the project of spiritual feminism, a vestige of the patriarchal religion that feminist witches sought to cast off; she said that Dianic witches "define patriarchy as the use of 'power-over' thinking and action to oppress others, both institutionally and within the personal sphere of our lives."[235] The feminist witch sought to reimagine what it meant to have power in the first place. Witches' power was not the power over others, but rather the power of collective freedom. It was a power unique to women, given to them by the Goddess whom they embodied, a blessing with which they could shape a better, safer, more egalitarian world.

The Web of Life

Presenting itself in contrast with the angry Father God of patriarchal religion, Goddess feminism emphasized the nature of the Goddess as loving and relational. Carol Christ wrote that the Goddess was "the intelligent embodied love that is the ground of all being."[236] According to her, the nature of the Goddess is divine love, which unites all people and puts them in relation with each other. Starhawk expressed a similar view, writing, "Love for life in all its forms is the basic ethic of Witchcraft."[237] The love of the Goddess was not constrained to romantic or sexual forms, although it certainly included them; rather, it was a deep, all-encompassing, universal divine love, the love that binds together all of creation. It was the love that stems from the awareness that you and I are equally holy, that we are sacred simply by virtue of existing, and that we partake together in the nature of the divine.

This view of the Goddess offers a deep understanding of the interconnectedness of all life. This interdependence, in turn, leads to a radical egalitarianism. We are all holy, and none of us are any more or less connected to the Goddess than anyone else. She lives in me, in you, in every atom and every galaxy—and therefore, to honor the Goddess, people must equally honor themselves, each other, and every facet of creation. The Goddess does not merely design the universe as a dispassionate architect; she is the universe itself, embodied in every living thing,

---

235. Adler, *Drawing Down the Moon*, 125.

236. Christ, *Rebirth of the Goddess*, 107.

237. Starhawk, *The Spiral Dance*, 36.

participating in the eternal act of creation. Starhawk notes, "The Goddess does not rule the world; She *is* the world. Manifest in each of us, She can be known internally by every individual, in all her magnificent diversity."[238] Carol Christ expresses a similar view in her book *She Who Changes: Re-imagining the Divine in the World*, writing:

> The whole universe is alive and changing, continually co-creating new possibilities of life. Every living individual is born, grows, and then dies. The world is a web of changing individuals interacting with, affecting, and changing each other…Goddess/God is fully involved in the changing lives of every individual in the universe and in the evolution of the whole. Creation is co-creation. The whole world or cosmos is the body of Goddess/God.[239]

The vision of Goddess feminism involved acknowledging every person and thing in the material world as the body of the Goddess, participating equally in her divine nature. The Goddess is not a creator who makes the world and then hands it off to humans to rule. Instead, she co-creates the world with us, existing equally as part of us and of all other things. Taken seriously, this theology—or rather, *thealogy*—requires a revolutionary reimagining not just of religion, but also of traditional power structures in society, government, education, industry, and more.

For one thing, it requires that people view their relationships to each other not as a hierarchy where one person dominates and the other is subdued, but as a partnership; all living things exist in the image of the Goddess, and therefore no one has the right to subjugate any other. Christ explains that "the power of Goddess/God can never be 'power over,' but always and everywhere is 'power with.' Power over is domination. Power with is cooperation, partnership, and mutuality."[240] Goddess feminists advocated that true power lay in partnership, in honoring each other as equals and working together rather than trying to exploit one another for individual benefit. They presented a view of the self as inextrica-

---

238. Starhawk, *The Spiral Dance*, 33.
239. Christ, *She Who Changes*, 45.
240. Christ, *She Who Changes*, 93.

bly interdependent with all other living things, part of a communal whole rather than being an isolated unit. For these advocates of feminist spirituality, there was no self without an acknowledgment of others.

This relational understanding of identity and power was presented as a stark contrast to the hierarchical power-over of patriarchal religion. Authors Monica Sjöö and Barbara Mor wrote in their book *The Great Cosmic Mother*, "Under patriarchy, there is a literal belief that all life is created for men to *use*. And what patriarchal men see as useable is also seen as contemptible."[241] Patriarchal society seemed to be founded on exploitation, denigration, and contempt, but the Goddess offered a radical new way that people could relate to each other, one based on communal identity, shared respect, and a mutual participation in the divine.

Understanding the Goddess in this way also had direct material consequences. For many of the people worshipping the Goddess prior to the 1970s, Goddess religion was relatively confined to the ritual sphere. The Goddess was addressed in temples or magic circles, invoked with passages of beautiful poetry, and called upon to aid in magic, but her religion didn't much expand to touch on people's politics or their everyday lives. Gardner's witch cult did not align itself with any particular political stance, although he did mention that his coven had once done a spell to prevent the Nazis from invading Britain.[242] Crowley and Graves similarly recoiled from what Crowley called "the prevalence of infantile cults like Communism, [and] Fascism," but neither *The Book of the Law* nor *The White Goddess* outline a clear social and political project.[243]

But for the feminist spirituality movement, worshipping the Goddess became linked with material political activism. This radical new view of the Goddess's presence in the world, and of the embodied interconnectedness at the heart of Goddess worship, demanded real action. The pioneers of Goddess feminism did rituals to honor the Goddess in the world and in themselves, but they also forcefully brought forth the notion that religion could not be confined to ritual alone. For them, worshipping the Goddess meant acting to help co-create a better world with her. The feminist spirituality movement blurred the lines between religion

---

241. Sjöö and Mor, *The Great Cosmic Mother*, 316.

242. Hutton, *The Triumph of the Moon*, 216.

243. Crowley, *Liber AL Vel Legis*, 17–18.

and politics, showing that the religion of the Goddess was necessarily a religion of liberation.

The Goddess became a symbol of women's rights, and campaigning for those rights was, itself, a way of worshipping her. Starhawk describes leading a ritual at a Take Back the Night rally in 1978, combining Goddess worship with direct political action in a protest against rape.[244] Cynthia Eller writes that "spiritual feminists feel a particular need to emphasize abortion rights...to ensure that women's ability to reproduce does not necessitate their actually doing so."[245] For these people and groups, worshipping the Goddess was inherently political: if the Goddess lives in everyone, then everyone must be endowed with the same rights. Fighting for these rights is fighting for the Goddess, and political activism becomes an act of worship in its own right.

Moreover, this activism was not confined to women's rights. Because all things are connected in the web of life, many Goddess feminists became fierce environmental activists. Wiccan priestess and journalist Margot Adler wrote that she "had entered the Craft in part because it was 'an ecological religion,'" and she was not alone in this.[246] Concern for environmentalism and ecology became hallmarks of Goddess religion in the late twentieth century, and they persist as such to this day. Eller lists environmentalism as a defining feature of Goddess feminism, arguing, "The key points of feminist spirituality's political agenda are environmentalism, feminism, nonviolence, and community."[247] The Goddess does not just connect people to each other, but to all life, and the duty of care that Goddess feminists feel toward partnership and egalitarianism extends to the earth itself— not just to other humans. In the religion of the Goddess, humans are not masters of the earth any more than they are masters of each other, and they have no right to pillage it for its natural resources. Respect for the environment and all forms of life is as essential as the respect for the dignity of other humans.

At the heart of feminist spirituality, whether in ritual, politics, or ecology, sits a view of each individual's place in the world as relational and interconnected. No person is an island. Instead, all of humanity breathes one breath, is sustained by

---

244. Starhawk, *The Spiral Dance*, 156.

245. Eller, *Living in the Lap of the Goddess*, 194.

246. Adler, *Drawing Down the Moon*, 395.

247. Eller, *Living in the Lap of the Goddess*, 191.

one heartbeat, walks on one earth. The Goddess permeates all life, and all life is sacred to her. Goddess feminism seeks to recognize and honor that innate divinity by overhauling how people treat each other and the world they inhabit.

——— EXERCISE ———
ACTIVISM

One of the great lessons of feminist spirituality is to worship the Goddess not just in ritual, but by going out in the world and participating in the sacred act of co-creation to shape a better future. Social activism is one of the best ways to connect to the mission of Goddess feminism. Volunteer your time or your resources to help protect and empower women and gender minorities. There are countless ways you could do this: serve as an escort at an abortion clinic, volunteer for a rape crisis hotline, donate clothes to a women's shelter, or even just give money to a charity or nonprofit organization that works on women's issues. For those living in the US, here is a short list of organizations you may be interested in:

+ **Covenant House.** (https://covenanthouse.org/) Provides shelters and programs to help homeless youths, with special care for underage mothers.

+ **Her Justice.** (https://herjustice.org/) Connects women with pro bono legal representation for issues including immigration, child support, and domestic abuse.

+ **Malala Fund.** (https://malala.org/) Dedicated to providing girls with access to education around the world.

+ **National Network of Abortion Funds.** (https://abortionfunds.org/) Helps fund the fight for reproductive rights across the country.

+ **Planned Parenthood.** (https://plannedparenthood.org/) Provides healthcare and family planning services, including cancer screenings, birth control, abortions, and STI testing.

+ **The Polaris Project.** (https://polarisproject.org/) Fighting to end human trafficking.

+ **Rape, Abuse, & Incest National Network.** (https://rainn.org/) Dedicated to combating sexual violence.

- **Sex Workers Project.** (https://swp.urbanjustice.org/) Offers social support and legal resources to combat human trafficking and protect sex workers.
- **Transgender Legal Defense & Education Fund.** (https://transgenderlegal .org/) Provides educational and legal resources to inform public policy and protect trans people from discrimination and violence.
- **The Trevor Project.** (https://thetrevorproject.org/) Offers crisis counseling and peer support to reduce the risk of suicide among LGBTQ+ youths.
- **UN Women.** (https://unwomen.org/) An organization under the heading of the United Nations, invested in the global advancement of women's rights.

There are countless other organizations fighting for gender equality on a variety of issues. Some of these organizations are national or international; others operate on a much smaller scale, within a particular county or city. All of them are doing important work. What's more, you can pursue activism without getting involved with a particular organization or charity, if you prefer to help people directly. For example, bringing money, food, and blankets to homeless women on the street is a wonderful way to make an impact.

The most important thing is to do *something*. Goddess feminism offers a reminder that religion and spirituality are closely intertwined with the real world and the people who inhabit it. The Goddess is a liberator who calls people to action in the name of justice and freedom. For Goddess feminists, worshipping the Goddess cannot be extricated from those ideals—and the ideals themselves are nothing if people do not act on them.

Finally, don't forget about electoral politics. Voting is no substitute for direct personal action, but it is an important and consequential way that you can have an effect on the laws that shape our society. Equality depends on much more than laws, but laws do matter, as do the people who make them. Get more engaged in electoral politics, either by cultivating yourself as an informed voter or by running for office yourself. As you evaluate candidates, parties, and policies, ask yourself whether they stand for the ideals of justice, equality, and empowerment at the heart of Goddess feminism.

Remember that the project of feminist spirituality is not just about cultivating a certain set of beliefs. It is about acting on those beliefs in order to co-create a better world.

Feminist Religion Today

Goddess feminism was at its most publicly visible in the 1980s and 1990s, but it has continued to evolve since then and remains a key component of Goddess worship today. It has grown with feminism more broadly, and the conversations being had in larger feminist discourse color the understanding of the Goddess in feminist spirituality. As scholarship has discredited Bachofen's theory of ancient matriarchy, feminist thought has moved away from the matriarchal myth, seeking to establish a better future without basing its legitimacy on an imagined utopian past. Beyond this historical claim, the focus and goals of Goddess feminism have evolved as well.

Some strands of feminist thought moved away from the collectivism of the 1970s and toward a notion of individual empowerment. The "Girl Power" movement of the 1990s focused not on overturning existing power structures, but on enabling women to advance within them—promoting the idea that women could be successful entrepreneurs and leaders in the same conventional settings where men had historically dominated. This movement has had a lasting effect on feminism in the popular imagination. As professor Sarah Banet-Weiser points out in her 2018 book *Empowered: Popular Feminism and Popular Misogyny*, "Contemporary popular feminism reimagines and redirects what 'empowerment' means for girls and women...popular feminism often restructures the politics of feminism to focus on the individual empowered woman."[248] Rather than underscoring human interconnectedness and collective partnership, this form of feminism prioritizes the ability of individual women to achieve and advance themselves in society.

With a different focus for feminism comes a different understanding of the Goddess. Feminist spirituality in this strain focuses on the ability of the Goddess to strengthen and empower women. It draws on myth, ritual, and meditation to provide a framework where individual women can see themselves as powerful and independent, without needing to rely on external aid. Thus, Heather Ash

---

248. Banet-Weiser, *Empowered*, 17.

Amara writes in her bestselling book *Warrior Goddess Training*, "This commitment to self shows us that there is no hidden treasure or savior outside of ourselves; we are the treasure we have been searching for...we are the one we have been waiting for. Your commitment to this idea is the activation of your Warrior Goddess power."[249] This version of feminist spirituality is less overtly political. Instead of large-scale social change, it prioritizes creating a spiritual environment that allows women to feel supported and enfranchised as they navigate the various challenges of their lives.

That's not to say that the politically mobilized Goddess feminism has disappeared—far from it. The twenty-first century has seen the emergence of the #MeToo and #TimesUp movements, as survivors of sexual violence spoke out, found solidarity in their shared experiences, and demanded accountability for the perpetrators of that violence. It has also seen the founding of the Women's March, a national movement for women's rights that began in response to the election of Donald Trump as the forty-fifth President of the United States. These movements have forced popular culture to reckon with how common sexual violence is and how often society lets predators get away with abuse. More than just raising awareness, they have shifted social norms and helped begin to build a culture of accountability.

None of these movements are explicitly religious, but they have all affected and been affected by feminist spirituality. In religious ritual, art, and commentary, feminists of the #MeToo era have turned to classical mythology, drawing on the stories of goddesses who survived sexual assault as a way of finding strength for their own movement. In an article titled "Reading Ovid in the Age of #MeToo," *New Yorker* staff writer Katy Waldman wrote about the myth of Philomela, who was raped and then mutilated so that she couldn't identify her attackers. Waldman argued:

> It is hard to read this ancient tale without running into a web
> of #MeToo-era tropes and preoccupations: how men silence
> the women they violate; how women are made to feel complicit
> in their own violations and those of their sisters; how female

---

249. Amara, *Warrior Goddess Training*, 2.

rage can overflow the banks of just retribution, sweeping patriarchal taboos aside.[250]

Both ancient goddesses and the modern Great Goddess have helped to
inspire and guide many people during the ongoing push for gender equality and
an end to sexual violence. This was true in 1978 when Starhawk performed her
Take Back the Night ritual, and it remains true today in the era of #MeToo. Goddess mythology is, for many, a source of healing and inspiration that carries them
forward in the quest for justice.

As the feminist conversation has moved into the twenty-first century, the voices
involved in that conversation have expanded and diversified. In particular, feminist
discourse has grown more attentive to who gets to speak and who is silenced. Many
of the major figures of Goddess feminism in its early days were college-educated
cis white women, and the voices of other women—working-class women, trans
women, and women of color—were less often heard. In the words of Lasara Firefox
Allen, the author of *Jailbreaking the Goddess*, "Awareness of complex relationships
between gender, sexuality, race, ethnicity, nationality, and class is the edge of the ris-
ing wave with which we—as feminists, as women, as those who worship the fem-
inal as a facet of the divine—must rise up."[251] Goddess spirituality in the twenty-
first century has worked to understand the intersection of these various identities
and to give voice to people who have previously been silenced.

As more perspectives are included in feminist religion, the understanding of
the Goddess herself diversifies as well. For example, Zsuzsanna Budapest's Dianic
Wicca defines the Goddess in terms of the power to give birth, and trans women
are excluded from the tradition on the basis that they do not have wombs—a
choice that was a matter of intense controversy and pushback even in the 1970s.[252]
In contrast, Allen wrote *Jailbreaking the Goddess* to dismantle biological assumptions about the Goddess, building a fivefold vision of the Goddess that seeks to
understand her beyond the mere capacity for biological reproduction and to create
a feminist spirituality more welcoming to trans and gender-nonconforming practitioners. Likewise, Goddess religion in recent decades has seen the inclusion of
underrepresented racial and ethnic groups, with attention being paid to goddesses

---

250. Waldman, "Reading Ovid in the Age of #MeToo."

251. Allen, *Jailbreaking the Goddess*, 4.

252. Adler, *Drawing Down the Moon*, 126.

204 — Chapter 9

in the indigenous religions of Africa, Asia, and North America. Along with ongoing conversations about cultural inclusivity, sensitivity, and appropriation, these diverse perspectives are helping to challenge assumptions about the nature of goddesses and the Goddess.

The landscape of feminism has changed a great deal since Elizabeth Gould Davis published *The First Sex* in 1971, and with it, so has the landscape of Goddess worship. Feminist spirituality is rich and diverse, and as it expands, new perspectives are constantly being introduced to the Goddess community. Just as women are not only one thing, neither is the Goddess; she is reflected in countless ways by the people who worship her. Whether in feminist witchcraft, the collectivist activism of the twentieth century, or the #MeToo movement and intersectional feminism of today, the Goddess is there. And as feminism continues to change over time, its relationship to the Goddess will change as well.

Key Takeaways: Davis and Goddess Feminism

+ Reviving Bachofen's theory of ancient matriarchy
+ Witchcraft as a reclamation of female power
+ Activism and ecology as key features of Goddess spirituality
+ Power-with as an alternative to power-over
+ Diversification of feminist perspectives on the Goddess in the twenty-first century

—— RITUAL ——
The Body of the Goddess

This ritual highlights the sacred nature of the body. The group variation is a celebration of trust, community, and interconnectedness. The solitary variation is about recognizing the nature of the divine within yourself. In both cases, this ritual helps to show that the Goddess is immediately present in the world, in yourself, and in the connections you share with other people and with all life.

Group Variation

In this version of the ritual, the members of your group will emphasize your interconnectedness and your connection to the divine power of the Goddess. You will bless each other's bodies as the bodies of the Goddess herself, showing each other the same love you feel for her.

You Will Need

- Bathing suits
- A bottle of baby oil
- Towels—this will get messy!
- A ewer full of fresh water. You may want extra water to refill the ewer, depending on how many people are in the ritual
- A space where you can safely make a mess and get the ground or floor wet

Preparation

Perform this ritual with people you trust intimately. The ritual involves a great deal of nonsexual physical touch, so it's important that you be comfortable with the other people in the room. Everyone should be wearing bathing suits for this ritual. If you have a group with which you already practice ritual nudity, that is also an option, but it is in no way necessary. This ritual is best performed outdoors or in a space where you can get the floor wet and easily clean up afterward. Keep a stack of towels nearby for the end of the ritual; if you are indoors, you may want to lay towels on the floor as well, in order to minimize the mess.

Performance

At the beginning of the ritual, all participants stand in a circle holding hands, with the ewer and the baby oil at the feet of one person. This person says:

> LEADER: We are here to celebrate the Goddess in the world and in ourselves. The Great Mother is with us, within us, and all around us. She is the force of love that unites us. She is the force of life that quickens us. Through her, we are all connected in the great web of life, and all things are one. I am you and you are me, and through the Mother we are made one.

> ALL: Through the Mother we are made one.

The participants stop holding hands. The ritual leader now turns to the person to their left. Taking the ewer, they pour some of the water over that person's head, saying:

> LEADER: [Name], feel the waters of the Goddess washing over you. She is in the widest ocean and the smallest drop of dew. She cleanses and renews. Let her renew you now.

The leader then sets down the ewer and picks up the bottle of baby oil. Squirting some of it into the palm of their hand, they anoint the other person's forehead, saying:

> LEADER: I bless your mind. It is the mind of the Goddess, who wakens all beings into consciousness.

They then anoint the person's throat, saying:

> LEADER: I bless your throat. It is the throat of the Goddess, who sings a song of comfort to all her children.

They then anoint the person's hands, saying:

> LEADER: I bless your hands. They are the hands of the Goddess, who weaves the fates of all living things.

The leader places a hand over the other person's heart and finishes by saying:

LEADER: I bless your heart. It is the heart of the Goddess, the source of infinite divine love. Your body is holy. It is the body of the Goddess.

ALL: The body of the Goddess!

The newly consecrated person then takes the ewer and the oil and turns to their left, consecrating the next person in the circle in exactly the same way. This proceeds around the circle until everyone has been consecrated. When the consecrations are complete, the leader proclaims:

LEADER: The Goddess charges us with divine love, to love each other and ourselves. Will we fulfill the charge?

ALL: We will.

Turning to the person to their left, the leader says:

LEADER: Where do you struggle most to love yourself?

This person indicates, verbally or by gesturing, some part of their body that they are most insecure about. The leader takes the baby oil and anoints that body part, saying:

LEADER: I bless your [body part]. It is the [body part] of the Goddess.
    I love it as I love her and you.

The two then embrace. The next person takes the oil and blesses the person to their left in the same manner, hugging afterward. When everyone has received their special blessing, all the members of the ritual join hands once more. The leader closes the ritual by saying:

LEADER: We are joined in the love of the Goddess! Our bodies are the bodies of the Goddess, in her infinite names and faces. We are holy. We are sacred. We are powerful.

ALL: We are holy. We are sacred. We are powerful.

The ritual is ended. Everyone will be wet and oily, so it is a good idea to towel off before changing back into ordinary clothes.

Solitary Variation

This version of the ritual allows you to bless your own body as the body of the Goddess, consecrating yourself as a sacred vessel for her divine power. This ritual is a powerful opportunity to explore the embodied aspects of the Goddess, and it is also a chance for you to ritually familiarize yourself with your own body, expressing love even for the parts of it that make you feel insecure.

You Will Need

- A bathing suit
- A bottle of baby oil
- Towels—this will get messy!
- A ewer full of fresh water
- A space where you can safely make a mess and get the ground or floor wet

Preparation

For this rite, you should either be nude or wearing a bathing suit. The ritual is best performed outdoors or in a space where you can get the floor wet and easily clean up afterward. Keep a stack of towels nearby for the end of the ritual; if you are indoors, you may want to lay down more towels on the floor, in order to minimize the mess.

Performance

Stand with the ewer and the bottle of baby oil at your feet. Take a moment to center yourself. Say:

> I am here to celebrate the Goddess in the world and in myself. The Great Mother is with me, within me, and all around me. She is the force of love that unites me with all others. She is the force of life that quickens me. Through her, I am connected to the great web of life, and all things are one. Through the Mother we are made one.

Pick up the ewer. Say:

I feel the waters of the Goddess washing over me. She is in the
widest ocean and the smallest drop of dew. She cleanses and renews.
Let her renew me now.

Gently pour the water from the ewer over the top of your head, feeling the cleansing power of the Goddess washing you clean. Set down the ewer and pick up the bottle of baby oil. Squirting some of it into your hand, anoint your forehead, saying:

I bless my mind. It is the mind of the Goddess, who wakens all
beings into consciousness.

Anoint your throat, saying:

I bless my throat. It is the throat of the Goddess, who sings a song
of comfort to all her children.

Anoint the backs of your hands, saying:

I bless my hands. They are the hands of the Goddess, who weaves
the fates of all living things.

Place your hand over your heart and finish by saying:

I bless my heart. It is the heart of the Goddess, the source of infinite
divine love. My body is holy. It is the body of the Goddess.

Set down the bottle of baby oil. Do something now to put yourself fully in your body. Stomp your feet, clap your hands, shout and jump up and down. Work yourself into a frenzy and move around until you are out of breath, your heart is pounding, and you feel embodied and powerful. When you come to a rest, wrap your arms around yourself in an embrace. Say:

The Goddess charges me with divine love, to love others and myself.
I will fulfill the charge!

Pick up the bottle of baby oil again. Think about the part of your body that you struggle the most to love, the part that makes you feel insecure and unsure of yourself. Squirt some oil into your hand and anoint that part of your body, saying as you do so:

> I bless my [body part]. It is the [body part] of the Goddess. I love it
> as I love her.

If there are other parts of your body that you struggle with, anoint those in the same manner. Keep going until you have addressed all of your insecurities and you feel like you have fully consecrated yourself as the embodiment of the Goddess. When you are done, say:

> I am made whole in the infinite love of the Goddess! My body is the
> body of the Goddess, in one of her infinite names and faces. I am
> holy. I am sacred. I am powerful.

The ritual is ended. You will be wet and oily, so it is a good idea to towel off before changing back into ordinary clothes.

CONCLUSION
A GODDESS FOR THE
TWENTY-FIRST CENTURY

I COME NOW TO the end of this book. Together, you and I have walked the path of the Goddess, from the first imaginings of ancient matriarchy in 1861 to the feminist revolution of the late twentieth century. We have seen her myth emerge into the world, shaped by poets, magicians, anthropologists, and self-proclaimed witches. Though the modern myth of the Goddess draws inspiration from the goddesses of pagan antiquity, it is new, unique, and special. Never before had the world known a Great Goddess quite like this one. She is:

+ The Great Mother and the earth that bears life
+ The universal Goddess of life and love, beloved of the dying-and-resurrecting God
+ The lunar Goddess of witchcraft and the liberator of the oppressed
+ The genderless, primordial deity of fertility, as much God as Goddess
+ The Star Goddess beyond the world and the Mother of Abominations painted scarlet with the blood of life
+ The syncretic Great Goddess who is known to the world by countless names and faces
+ The Triple Goddess who rules over the cycles of death and rebirth
+ The secret patroness of the Wica, whose inner nature is kept behind a veil of initiatory secrecy
+ The champion of feminist liberation, bearing the promise of a hopeful future rooted in the myth of a utopian past

The Goddess as she is known today is all of these things at once. Absent any one of these faces, an understanding of the modern Goddess would be incomplete. What's more, there are themes and commonalities that unite all these faces of the Goddess. These threads of continuity show that she is one Goddess, extended across history, growing and changing alongside human society. She is the Goddess of the earth, the moon, the sea, and all of nature. The human body is sacred to her, as is the cycle of death and rebirth. She rules over sexuality and physical ecstasy, but more broadly, she is a Goddess of love. The forms of love between romantic partners, between siblings, between parent and child, and even between close friends are all sacred to her. A patroness of poets and artists, she provides divine inspiration in all its forms. And finally, she is the Goddess of witchcraft and magic.

These are the features that make the Goddess who she is, and they are found again and again across the modern iterations of the Great Goddess myth. From J. J. Bachofen to Elizabeth Gould Davis, the Goddess makes herself known. She is a distinct, recognizable, specific figure, with her own definite mythology and symbolism, ready for the world to worship her. In tracing the historical development of her myth, I hope that you have come to know the Goddess herself more deeply and more intimately, looking at her from new perspectives and seeing how historical figures have shaped the deity the world knows today.

Moreover, this is the path all devotees walk in getting to know the Goddess, whether they're conscious of it or not. When you come into Goddess worship for the first time, the ideas you encounter and the stories that are told come from the thinkers and movements I have explored throughout this book. If a teacher or priestess gives you a reading list, it's likely to include these texts, from *The Gospel of the Witches* to the *White Goddess*—and if it doesn't include them, it's certain to include books that cite them or are directly influenced by them. My hope is that by reading this book, and seeing these authors placed in context alongside each other, you'll gain a broader perspective on the overall development of the Goddess movement and the core themes of modern-day Goddess worship.

Now, the question arises: where do you go from here?

Remember that the relationship with the past is a dynamic, ever-changing thing. History is not static and fixed; the narrative people tell, and the way they imagine and interpret the past, changes as they change. This is true not only of ancient history—the cult of Aphrodite and Adonis, the Mysteries of Isis, and so on—but also of more recent history. James Frazer with his unifying theory of world mythology, Dion Fortune with her Rite of Isis, and Gerald Gardner with his initiatory witch cult are all part of Paganism's history now. They are part of the Goddess's history. And as such, they stand in a complicated, reciprocal relationship to Goddess worshippers today. They shape who we are, but at the same time, who we are shapes our understanding of them.

As we continue to change over time, we will look back at these figures and see them in new ways, finding things we had never seen before. We will critique them for flaws we don't currently notice, and we will value them for contributions we now take for granted. New figures, thinkers, ideas, and texts will come to our attention, forcing us to reevaluate what we think we know about who the Goddess is and how she came into the modern world. There is so much for us to discover, so much to learn and relearn and unlearn.

Even just thirty years ago, the landscape of Goddess worship was largely ahistorical. The Pagan, New Age, and Goddess feminist communities were infamous for revisionist history. The party line was that the religion of the Goddess was ancient, eternal, and unchanged since the prehistorical matriarchy that had definitely existed. Where archaeological or historical evidence contradicted this narrative, that evidence was set aside. Now, the pendulum has swung in the other direction: Paganism and Goddess worship exhibit a broad concern with research, scholarship, and carefully supported claims. The cost of this is that historical accuracy can get conflated with religious legitimacy, and the more modern aspects of Goddess worship sometimes get thrown out or disregarded as unimportant because they are not ancient.

This is, if you'll permit some editorializing on my part, a bit of a shame. Robert Graves, for example, was a dreadful scholar, but he was inspired by something far larger than himself. He was seized by a vision of the Goddess, and the value of that vision can be disentangled from the ill-founded historical claims that went along with it. The figures who shaped modern Goddess worship do not have to have been flawless scholars in order to matter or be valuable. They helped create a new myth, a new history, a religion for the modern world. Mythology and religion are not just about historical accuracy; they are about a deep poetic truth, something timeless that extends beyond any one person and reaches into the eternal. In this book, I have discussed thinkers who—despite their foibles—helped bring that poetic truth into the world. If not for them, Pagans would not be able to know the Great Goddess as they do today.

No one can know what the worship of the Goddess will look like twenty, fifty, or a hundred years from now, but if the past 160 years are any indication, the movement will continue to grow and change rapidly. Goddess worshippers of the future will look back on today's religion with the same critical eye that I have turned to Bachofen, Frazer, and the rest. In addition to a turn toward historical rigor, the twenty-first century has seen a critical reassessment of the beliefs about sex and gender that underpinned much of nineteenth- and twentieth-century thought. This conversation will continue as society learns more about gender and questions its own assumptions—and just as nineteenth-century ideas are now out of date, current ideas eventually will be as well. As those ideas change, the language used to describe the Goddess will inevitably change too.

The past is not static, but neither is the future. Who we are today affects how we view the past, and it sets us on the course for the future. The past, present, and future are all bound together, part of the everlasting dance of history. And at the center of that dance, at the center of everything, is the Great Goddess, presiding over the eternal ebb and flow of time. Our past is her past. Our future is her future. The story of the Goddess will grow as we grow, because the Goddess is within us.

> I am all that has been, and is, and shall be, and my robe no mortal has yet uncovered.[253]

---

253. Plutarch, *Moralia, Volume V*, 25.

BIBLIOGRAPHY

"1604: 1 James 1 c.12: An Act against Witchcraft." The Statutes Project. Accessed September 22, 2022. https://statutes.org.uk/site/the-statutes /seventeenth-century/1604-1-james-1-c-12-an-act-against-witchcraft/.

"1735: 9 George 2 c.5: The Witchcraft Act." The Statutes Project. Accessed September 22, 2022. https://statutes.org.uk/site/the-statutes/eighteenth -century/1735-9-george-2-c-5-the-witchcraft-act/.

"1951: 14 & 15 George 6 c.33: Fraudulent Mediums Act." The Statutes Project. Accessed September 22, 2022. http://statutes.org.uk/site/the-statutes /twentieth-century/1951-14-15-george-6-c-33-fraudulent-mediums-act/.

Adler, Margot. *Drawing Down the Moon: Witches, Druids, Goddess-Worshippers, and Other Pagans in America*. Rev. ed. New York: Penguin Books, 2006.

Allen, Lasara Firefox. *Jailbreaking the Goddess: A Radical Revisioning of Feminist Spirituality*. Woodbury, MN: Llewellyn Publications, 2016.

Amara, Heather Ash. *Warrior Goddess Training: Become the Woman You Are Meant to Be*. San Antonio, TX: Hierophant Publishing, 2014.

Apollodorus. *The Library, Volume II: Book 3.10–End. Epitome*. Translated by James G. Frazer. Loeb Classical Library 122. Cambridge, MA: Harvard University Press, 1921.

Apuleius. *The Golden Ass: Or, A Book of Changes*. Translated by Joel C. Relihan. Indianapolis, IN: Hackett Publishing Company, 2007.

Bachofen, Johann Jakob. *Myth, Religion, and Mother Right: Selected Writings of J. J. Bachofen*. Translated by Ralph Manheim. Princeton, NJ: Princeton Univer- sity Press, 1967.

Banet-Weiser, Sarah. *Empowered: Popular Feminism and Popular Misogyny*. Durham, NC: Duke University Press, 2018.

Billock, Jennifer. "Visit the Site of the Biggest Witch Trial in History." *Smithso-nian Magazine*, September 14, 2016. https://www.smithsonianmag.com/travel/visit-site-biggest-witch-trial-history-180959946/.

Blanton, Crystal, Taylor Ellwood, and Brandy Williams, eds. *Bringing Race to the Table: Exploring Racism in the Pagan Community*. Stafford, UK: Megalithica Books, 2015.

Burr, George L. "Reviewed Work(s): The Witch-Cult in Western Europe: A Study in Anthropology by Margaret Alice Murray." *The American Historical Review* 27, no. 4 (July 1922): 780–83.

Carter, Mark. *Stalking the Goddess*. Winchester, UK: Moon Books, 2012.

Christ, Carol P. "Why Women Need the Goddess." *Heresies* 2, no. 1 (Spring 1978): 8–13.

———. *Rebirth of the Goddess: Finding Meaning in Feminist Spirituality*. Reading, MA: Addison-Wesley, 1997.

———. *She Who Changes: Re-imagining the Divine in the World*. New York: Palgrave MacMillan, 2003.

Crowley, Aleister. *The Book of Thoth: A Short Essay on the Tarot of the Egyptians*. York Beach, ME: Weiser Books, 1974.

———. *Liber AL Vel Legis: The Book of the Law*. Newburyport, MA: Weiser Books, 2004.

———. *Magick: Liber ABA, Book 4*. York Beach, ME: Weiser Books, 1994.

Cunningham, Scott. *Wicca: A Guide for the Solitary Practitioner*. Rev. ed. St. Paul, MN: Llewellyn Publications, 2004.

Darwin, Charles. "On the Origin of Species." In *The Works of Charles Darwin*, edited by Paul H. Barrett and R. B. Freeman. New York: New York University Press, 1988.

Davis, Elizabeth Gould. *The First Sex*. New York: Penguin Books, 1971.

Dowding, Hugh. "Fraudulent Mediums Bill." May 3, 1951. https://api.parliament.uk/historic-hansard/lords/1951/may/03/fraudulent-mediums-bill.

DuQuette, Lon Milo. *The Magick of Aleister Crowley: A Handbook of the Rituals of Thelema*. San Francisco: Weiser Books, 2003.

Eller, Cynthia. *Gentlemen and Amazons: The Myth of Matriarchal Prehistory, 1861–1900*. Berkeley: University of California Press, 2011.

———. *Living in the Lap of the Goddess: The Feminist Spirituality Movement in America*. Boston, MA: Beacon Press, 1995.

Farrar, Janet, and Stewart Farrar. *A Witches' Bible: The Complete Witches' Handbook*. Blaine, WA: Phoenix Publishing, 1984.

———. *The Witches' Goddess: The Feminine Principle of Divinity*. Blaine, WA: Phoenix Publishing, 1987.

Fortune, Dion. *The Mystical Qabalah*. San Francisco: Weiser Books, 2000.

———. *The Sea Priestess*. York Beach, ME: Weiser Books, 2003.

———. *Dion Fortune's Rites of Isis and of Pan*. Edited by Gareth Knight. Gloucestershire, UK: Skylight Press, 2013.

Frazer, James George. *The Golden Bough: A Study in Magic and Religion*. Oxford World's Classics ed. Edited by Robert Fraser. Oxford, UK: Oxford University Press, 1994.

Gardner, Gerald B. *Witchcraft Today*. New York: Citadel Press, 2004.

———. *The Meaning of Witchcraft*. York Beach, ME: Weiser Books, 2004.

Ginzburg, Carlo. *The Night Battles: Witchcraft and Agrarian Cults in the Sixteenth and Seventeenth Centuries*. Translated by John and Anne C. Tedeschi. Baltimore, MD: Johns Hopkins University Press, 1983.

Gimbutas, Marija. *The Language of the Goddess*. San Francisco: HarperCollins, 1989.

Gratian. "*Decretum Gratiani* (Kirchenrechtssammlung)." Münchener DigitalisierungsZentrum. Accessed September 6, 2022. https://geschichte.digitale-sammlungen.de//decretum-gratiani/kapitel/dc_chapter_3_3030.

Graves, Robert. *The White Goddess: A Historical Grammar of Poetic Myth*. New York: Farrar, Straus, and Giroux, 2013.

Heselton, Philip. *In Search of the New Forest Coven*. Nottingham, UK: Fenix Flames Publishing, 2020.

"History of Women in the US Congress." Center for American Women and Politics. Accessed September 6, 2022. https://cawp.rutgers.edu/facts/levels-office/congress/history-women-us-congress.

Hornblower, Simon, and Antony Spawforth, eds. *The Oxford Classical Dictionary*. 3rd ed. Oxford, UK: Oxford University Press, 2005.

Hutton, Ronald. *The Triumph of the Moon: A History of Modern Pagan Witchcraft*. Oxford, UK: Oxford University Press, 2019.

Kaczynski, Richard. *Perdurabo: The Life of Aleister Crowley*. Rev. ed. Berkeley, CA: North Atlantic Books, 2010.

Leland, Charles Godfrey. *Aradia: Gospel of the Witches*. Newport, RI: The Witches' Almanac, 2010.

Livy. "History of Rome 29." In *History of Rome, Volume VIII: Books 28–30*, translated by Frank Gardner Moore. Cambridge, MA: Harvard University Press, 1949.

Luebke, David M. "Traces of Non-Christian Religious Practices in Medieval Pentitentials" [*sic*]. Accessed September 6, 2022. https://pages.uoregon.edu/dluebke/Witches442/PaganTraces.html.

Michelet, Jules. *Satanism and Witchcraft: The Classic Study of Medieval Superstition*. Translated by A. R. Allinson. New York: Citadel Press, 1992.

Murray, Margaret Alice. *The Witch-Cult in Western Europe*. Rookhope, UK: Aziloth Books, 2019.

National Toxicology Program. "NTP Technical Report on the Toxicology and Carcinogenesis Studies of αβ-Thujone in F344/N Rats and B6C3F1 Mice." *National Toxicology Program Technical Report Series* 494 (Sept. 2005): 1–358. https://pubmed.ncbi.nlm.nih.gov/16362060/.

Nemiroff, Robert, and Jerry Bonnell. "Astronomy Picture of the Day Index - Solar System: Earth's Moon." NASA, November 13, 2005. https://apod.nasa.gov/apod/moon.html.

Ovid. *Fasti*. Translated by James G. Frazer. Cambridge, MA: Harvard University Press, 1931.

Pausanias. *Description of Greece, Volume III: Books 6–8.21 (Elias 2, Achaia, Arcadia)*. Translated by W. H. S. Jones. Cambridge, MA: Harvard University Press, 1933.

Plutarch. *Moralia, Volume V: Isis and Osiris. The E at Delphi. The Oracles at Delphi No Longer Given in Verse. The Obsolescence of Oracles*. Translated by Frank Cole Babbitt. Cambridge, MA: Harvard University Press, 1936.

Richardson, Alan. *Aleister Crowley and Dion Fortune: The Logos of the Aeon and the Shakti of the Age*. Woodbury, MN: Llewellyn Publications, 2009.

Sheppard, Kathleen L. *The Life of Margaret Alice Murray: A Woman's Work in Archaeology*. Lanham, MD: Lexington Books, 2013.

Sjöö, Monica, and Barbara Mor. *The Great Cosmic Mother: Rediscovering the Religion of the Earth*. 2nd ed. San Francisco: HarperOne, 1991.

Spencer, Craig. *Aradia: A Modern Guide to Charles Godfrey Leland's* Gospel of the Witches. Woodbury, MN: Llewellyn Publications, 2020.

Spencer, Herbert. *The Man Versus the State*. Caldwell, ID: Caxton Printers, 1940.

"Spousal Rape Laws: 20 Years Later." The National Center for Victims of Crime. Accessed September 6, 2022. http://www.ncdsv.org/images/NCVC_SpousalRapeLaws20YearsLater_2004.pdf.

Starhawk. *The Spiral Dance: A Rebirth of the Ancient Religion of the Great Goddess*. 20th anniversary ed. New York: HarperCollins, 1999.

Stone, Merlin. *When God Was a Woman*. Orlando, FL: Harcourt, 1976.

Valiente, Doreen. *The Charge of the Goddess: The Poetry of Doreen Valiente*. London: The Doreen Valiente Foundation, 2014.

———. *The Rebirth of Witchcraft*. Marlborough, UK: Robert Hale, 1989.

———. *Witchcraft for Tomorrow*. London: Robert Hale, 1978.

Waldman, Katy. "Reading Ovid in the Age of #MeToo." *The New Yorker*, February 12, 2018. https://www.newyorker.com/books/page-turner/reading-ovid-in-the-age-of-metoo.

Waxman, Olivia B. "How Christmas Trees Became a Holiday Tradition." *Time*. Updated December 21, 2020. https://time.com/5736523/history-of-christmas-trees/.

White, Manon Hedenborg. *The Eloquent Blood: The Goddess Babalon and the Construction of Femininities in Western Esotericism*. Oxford, UK: Oxford University Press, 2020.

Wilby, Emma. *The Visions of Isobel Gowdie: Magic, Witchcraft, and Dark Shamanism in Seventeenth-Century Scotland*. Chicago: Sussex Academic Press, 2010.

Wolkstein, Diane, and Samuel Noah Kramer. *Inanna: Queen of Heaven and Earth*. New York: Harper & Row, 1983.

"Women in the Labor Force, 1970–2009." January 5, 2011. US Bureau of Labor Statistics. https://www.bls.gov/opub/ted/2011/ted_20110105.htm.

Zimmer, Carl. "Evolution in Color: From Peppered Moths to Walking Sticks." *National Geographic*, October 9, 2013. https://www.nationalgeographic.com/science/article/evolution-in-color-from-peppered-moths-to-walking-sticks.